To: Helen
With eve
to you.

MY HIGH TOWER

ROSALIE E. F. ROSS

❖

Rosalie E. F. Ross.
December, 2016.

(Please forgive hand written
alterations and uneven
margins. This is the
original print)

ISBN - 13:978-1533473745
e-ISBN - 1533473749

Scripture quotations are taken from The Living Bible
Copyright © 1971.
Used by permission of Tyndale House Publishers, Inc.,
Carol Stream, Illinois 60188. All rights reserved.

What a Friend We Have in Jesus: Joseph M. Scriven.

Cover Design: Galesackss and Odeldesign on Fiverr.com

FOR RICHARD

AND

JONATHAN

WITH ALL MY LOVE TO YOU.

(50P!)

**With special thanks
to Jeannette Longworth
for all her help.**

Article Pinned on Noticeboard Outside the
Church Kingsley and Meredith Attend: 2015

*We extend a special welcome to those who are single, co-habiting,
married, divorced, straight or gay, filthy rich, dirt poor,
or don't speak English.
We extend a special welcome to the crying newborn, thin as a rail,
or could afford to lose a few pounds.
We welcome you if you can sing like Andrea Bocelli,
or like most of us, can't carry a note in a bucket!
You are welcome here if you are just browsing, just woke up,
or just got out of jail.
We don't care if you are more Catholic than the Pope, more
protestant than Billy Graham, or haven't been in a church
since Little Joey's christening.
We extend a special welcome to those who are over sixty, and are
not grown up yet, and to teenagers who are growing up too fast.
We welcome 'footie' mad mums, car crazy dads, starving artists,
tree-huggers, latte-sippers, vegetarians and junk food eaters.
We welcome those who are in recovery, or are still a bit sick.
We welcome you if you are having problems, or when you are
down in the dumps, or if you don't like organised religion:
we've been there too!
If you blew all your money at the betting shop, or the bingo,
you are welcome here.
We offer a special welcome to those who think the earth is flat,
work too hard, don't work, can't spell,
or are only here because, 'she/he made you!'
We welcome those who are tattooed, pierced - or both.
We offer a special welcome to those who could use a prayer
right now, who have had religion shoved down your throat as a kid,
or got lost in traffic and wound up here by mistake.
We welcome tourists, seekers and doubters, bleeding hearts -
and You! WELCOME!*

Extract from 'The Salvation Army Welcome.' (Anonymous).

CHAPTER 1

PLOVER BEACH HOLIDAY CAMP (1974)

Meredith did not hear the footsteps walking past her chalet. The three figures were silent, hardly daring to breath, never-mind talk. Stifled shuddering was all they could manage - and they felt as cold as the dawn wind blowing off the North Sea. And they were frightened. A gust caught them unawares; one of them screamed, just a small scream, but loud enough to penetrate Meredith's sleep. She was awake instantly and through her door, standing on the small veranda, hugging her arms close to her chest as she stood peering around. But she was too late. They had melted away, like vapour, into the grey light. She didn't know if she was more annoyed than alarmed. This was the third time in as many nights that she had been disturbed. Something was definitely going on, and she had an idea it was something to do with the kitchen staff. The voices seemed to be heading for the Tatty House, the old cottage at the edge of the camp. She turned and went back inside, resigned to the knowledge that now Tom would have to be told. That scream had made her mind up.

The bell pinged loudly on the reception counter. Meredith leaned back in her chair and looked out. As she had expected, it was Jacko. Breakfast was almost over and he had made his usual escape before being caught up in the mass exodus. 'Morning,' she called, 'be with you in a second.' She approached her colleague, 'Jacko's here.' Wendy was concentrating hard on the monthly booking register lying open before her. She grunted and inclined her head towards the side

1

of the cluttered desk. Meredith searched, but was unable to detect anything resembling the relevant list. 'Sorry, can't see it.'

Wendy reached across to uncover a slip of paper from a miscellany of others and handed it to her, knocking several rubber stamps out of their stand as she did so. 'Don't suppose he'd be interested, but the Sunnyside group want to come on the last week instead - chicken pox outbreak.'

Meredith handed Jacko the list, noticing the ketchup mark on the front of his canary yellow waistcoat. As usual, his denim cap, topped by a large, bright red pompom, was pushed back, revealing a mass of ginger frizz. 'Not many cancellations; just three families and a group of eight,' she said.

'Shame for them! This lot's driving me as batty as them already. One of them's just stopped me to ask how much a fourpenny stamp is!'

'Yes, we've had that too. Anyway, they're hoping to come later on,' she replied, feeling how useful sunglasses would be when having any dealings with the Entertainments Manager. She pointed at the red mark, 'You'd better wash that off before it stains, and are you going to the service?'

'Bloody hell, no! That bacon was hard enough to digest.'

'But don't you think you should? You know, show some support?'

He turned and headed for the ballroom, calling behind him, 'You go then. But tell him he's welcome to come and call the bingo any time he likes; they say he's got the voice for it.'

Disappointed, she stood looking after him, thinking that he was the one key figure that could have made a difference in drawing others in. Gregarious, and popular with staff and campers alike, it was well known that 'Uncle Jacko' was the main reason why the majority of campers returned every year. And, she supposed, that was what really mattered.

❖

Both women were dealing with the usual first morning queue in reception when Tom and Kingsley arrived.

'Morning all!' called Tom, his small, stocky frame almost hidden behind the large black guitar case he was carrying.

'Morning,' they replied in unison.

Kingsley followed, appearing to have no difficulty in maneuvering a sketch board and its stand through the main doors. He flashed a quick smile in their direction.

Meredith smiled back, deciding, not for the first time, how much like Bryan Ferry the new minister looked, although this man's eyes were bigger.

Tom clumsily pushed open one of the swing doors to the ballroom and the two men disappeared. He was still feeling unsure about all this, but Meredith had been very persuasive, and had eventually succeeded in getting him to agree to a one month's trial of the Gospel Service. He knew that some of the bigger camps had started having short services on Sunday mornings, and supposed it could do no harm. But right now, he had more important things on his mind.

Meredith noticed how drawn he looked when he approached the counter a few minutes later. 'Coffee? she asked. 'And did you ask Kingsley if he wanted one?'

'Only for me. Says he'll get one from the café afterwards.'

Wendy had already reached behind her to switch the kettle on. She looked up and studied his face. 'Bad night again?'

'Kid's kicking like crazy. We had to have three back-rubbing sessions.'

'Just got to be a boy,' she remarked. 'Well known for giving their poor mum's a load of gyp.'

Meredith made three coffees, making Tom's slightly stronger than usual. She knocked on his door and went straight in without waiting for a reply. He looked at her and attempted to smile. Was it her imagination, or did he have a few more grey hairs around his temple these days? And those bluey shadows under his eyes were definitely a shade darker than before. She placed the mug down on the corner of his desk and hesitated, debating with herself about whether she should tell him about the nights' goings-on after all.

'Ta.' He yawned, 'Your vicar's a live wire, isn't he?'

'Yes, but sincere.'

Despite his weariness, he had noticed her indecisive manner, and after taking a noisy sip, asked, 'Oh hell! I know that look. Come on, let's be having it. What's up?'

She made short work of telling him about the nocturnal disturbances. He listened, frowning heavily. 'And you say that was the third time? And you're sure they were kitchen staff?'

'Yes, and it must have been. Who else would be going that way and at that time of night - or morning? Their accommodation's the only thing down that way.'

He sighed heavily. 'Flame! Sounds like it's started already. Right, you'd better get Nick to start sending them over. Does Wendy know?'

'Thought I'd better tell you first.'

'Okay, I'll mention something to her. She'll have to make up some pay packets.'

Her alarm was obvious; all she had wanted to do was alert him that there might be a problem brewing, and hope that he would issue a warning. To her mind, to talk about sacking anyone at this stage was going in a bit heavy. 'Oh, but…'

'No Meri!' he interrupted, holding up a hand. 'Now don't you go all bleeding-heart on me. They were warned what would happen if they started mucking about. If they want to play silly buggers, then they can clear off and do it somewhere else!'

She turned to leave, knowing there would be no talking him around; Tom could be as stubborn as her mother when he chose to be, although, in this case, she didn't really blame him. There was always trouble of some sort or other with the young staff every season, and it was always Tom, as General Manager, who was left to sort it out. Without exception, the

4

owners and trustees were only too happy to leave all the day-to-day running of the camp to him - especially the hiring and firing.

'And get him to send them over in pairs when the rush is over,' he called after her.

She picked up the kitchen list and left reception. Kingsley's voice rang out from the ballroom, 'Some really great news for you today. One, two three testing. One two three testing. Jesus is alive and wants you to know that He loves you...testing...testing...'

She felt disappointed; she had been looking forward to today, and was hoping for an opportunity to go in and discover exactly how he was going to keep this particular group of campers, the vast majority of whom were *mentally handicapped**, sufficiently quiet and attentive for a whole thirty minutes. Now it looked as though she would have no chance of finding out.

❖

The atmosphere in the kitchen was noisy but well organised. Nick, the Chef, ran a tight ship, and woe betides anyone who threatened any slight deviation off course. She knew he wouldn't be happy about the unscheduled withdrawal of his staff throughout the day, and braced herself as she knocked and stepped through the open door of the small cubicle that seconded as his office.

'Hi Nick. How's tricks?'

'Satisfactory, apart from two tables that were late. You'd better put another tannoy out about it.'

'Will do. By the way, Tom wants to see the staff about something; two at a time. It can wait till the rush is over.'

*The term commonly used in the 1970's to describe any individual who had any form of learning difficulty.

He leaned back in his chair and gave her a penetrating look, pursing his lips together tightly as though forcing himself to keep whatever he wanted to say behind them.

'Oh yes, and why's that then?'

'Can't really say. But he's definite, and wants to see them all.'

'Don't tell me there's trouble already?'

'Might be.'

'Damnation! Here we go again. Well, you might as well make a start. You'll have a hell of a job rounding them up later.' Sighing heavily, he leant even further back in his chair and peered out and past her. '*Nigel, Pauline. Here - now!*'

A fresh faced youth, no more than seventeen years of age, stepped from behind one of the large sinks and approached the office gingerly. He was followed by a young woman of similar age, her dark hair bundled unceremoniously up into a white cap, a long strand hanging down the side of her face. Nick glared accusingly at them as though they had already been judged and found guilty, but as to what, he had no idea. 'Okay you two, the Boss wants to see everyone, and you two can start the ball rolling. You can finish off when you get back. And straight back mind, no skiving. Got it? Well, what are you waiting for? Go on, clear off!'

The whole of the kitchen staff were questioned throughout the day, with the result that two of them left on the nine o'clock bus the next morning. Despite various threats, Tom had been unable to persuade either of them to explain their nocturnal behaviour. However, it became obvious who had been involved when one young man became belligerent, and stated that, 'He could do what the hell he liked on his time off, and no bloody Hitler was going to tell him what to do with it!' Later, a young woman wept copiously into her grubby handkerchief, mumbling something about 'Scary things', and wanting to go home. Tom found this all very irritating, feeling sure that her appearance and listless demeanour fitted exactly with some involvement with drink or drugs - or both. He wasn't too concerned, there were always plenty more students around at this time of year who were just waiting for the chance to fill the temporary summer vacancies.

Meredith understood his reasoning, but wished he had been more patient with them. She felt that they deserved a second chance and wasn't at all convinced that it really was just a straightforward case of drink or drugs. She had definitely seen three figures last night, and knew that there was still one more person involved - one more unknown soul out there. And the thought made her feel uneasy.

CHAPTER 2

Meredith and her parents joined the queue slowly filing out of the church. Today's line was unusually long, mainly due to the fact that a considerable number of younger people had recently started to attend. News had soon spread around the town that the new Baptist minister was not only single, but 'gorgeous' with it. More than that, he did not pontificate, nor did he wear long frocks, and rumour had it that he was able to play the guitar like Eric Clapton. Curiosity was a powerful draw.

Reverend Kingsley Pryce did not disappoint. He was full of ideas, amongst them offering free guitar lessons in the church hall on Saturday mornings. After just a month, already two of his pupils were capable of playing some of the less demanding contemporary choruses he was introducing into the services. The drums and wind instruments would come later - but not much later.

Launchpad, the young people's group, was another of his initiatives, and was proving very popular. This was held in the manse's large lounge after the Sunday evening service. The ages ranged between eighteen to twenty-five, which meant that Meredith was still eligible - although only just; her twenty-sixth birthday was a few months away. Tea, coffee, soft drinks and chocolate biscuits were consumed as various topics and ideas were discussed, debated and prayed over. Christian, or Christian-like, films were due to start being shown on the last Sunday of each month, and outdoor activities were being planned for when the warmer weather finally arrived.

Meredith was particularly looking forward to tonight's meeting. Kingsley had left the camp before she had been able to ask him how the first Gospel Service in the ballroom had gone, although the few campers she had asked had made pleasant enough sounding remarks about the event. It appeared that she was not the only one keen to hear about it, as Fleur, one of the youngest members of the group, interrupted a conversation Kingsley was having with another member, to ask, 'Go on then, Rev, tell us how things went this morning.'

'Not bad, not bad at all,' he replied.

'How many turned up?'

'I counted seventeen, but it could have been more. There was a fair bit of movement going on.'

'Is that all?' she exclaimed, looking and sounding unimpressed.

'That was good, considering that most of them were unable to concentrate for long. The sketch board helped, and I think a few were able to grasp the fact that Jesus is still alive, and that He loves them. Anyway, it was useful to get a feel of the place. But I'll be telling you all about it later.' He excused himself and crossed the room to sit on the vacant chair next to Meredith. He had been wondering about this young woman. If he was right, and she did have a deep, personal faith, then she could be the answer to his current problem.

'Hello Meredith. Mind if I sit here?'

Meredith smiled up at him as she moved her bag off the seat and onto the floor. 'Please do.'

He sat, and put his mug carefully underneath the chair. 'I've been meaning to have a word with you about the service, especially if there's a way of getting it known about a bit more. I noticed there's an events board outside the ballroom. Do you think Tom would let me have a mention?'

'Can't see why not. I'll ask him if you like.'

'Would you? I'd be grateful. Time's short; just three weeks of the trial left.'

'You'll need a photo, but that can be easily arranged; the Shop Manageress is also the Camp Photographer.'

'Great! And maybe you could ring me and let me know? Do you have the manse's number?'

'We'll have it at home, I expect.'

'Let me give it to again, just in case. Got a pen?' He watched her closely as she reached down and produced a biro and small notebook from her bag. Her skin was clear and tanned. A very healthy looking girl this one. Very different from Deborah, she had been so fair. He wondered what other differences there were, and swallowed hard.

His number was engaged when she telephoned the next morning, but he finally answered on her fourth attempt.

'Hello, Kingsley Pryce here.'

'Hi, it's Meredith.'

'Hello Meredith. And how are things with you this bright but chilly day?'

'Good, thank you. And you?'

'Blessed, greatly blessed.'

'Oh, that's good! I'm just ringing to say that I've had a word with Tom about the events board, and he's fine about it.'

'Excellent!'

'Julia, that's the Camp Photographer, says she'll come and take your photo on Sunday, either before or after the service. I couldn't persuade her to take one during.'

'I appreciate that. Actually, I'm glad you've called. There's something I'd like to discuss with you. You'll have heard that Ruby's retiring as Church Secretary this summer?'

'I had heard something.'

'Well, Doreen's interested, and put her name forward. I can't see the rest of the diaconate having any objections. The only fly in the ointment is that she says she'll probably need to give up helping with Launchpad.'

'Oh, that's a shame. She's really good at it.'

'All the more reason to find someone equally gifted to take her place.'

She hesitated, surely he wasn't thinking of her?

'Which is where you come in,' he continued.

'Me!'

'Yes. Just an idea.'

'I...I see.'

'And possibly something you might like to think and pray about?'

'Er, well, alright. I could pray...'

'I've caught you on the hop, haven't I? But you aren't averse to the idea - in principle?'

'No, at least, I don't think so.'

'Fair enough. Would it help if we got together to talk about it? I'm planning on coming out your way later. I need to find a bit of beach suitable for open-airs, and I really could do with the help of a knowledgeable local. Don't suppose you're free at some time to show me around, are you?'

'I...suppose I could. But I'm not off again until tomorrow afternoon; it's my half-day.'

'That would suit me just fine. Where can I meet you, and at what time?'

'Er, here? Just outside the main building? Would after two be alright?'

'Excellent. There, at two thirty, it is then. And please don't think me rude, but you'll have to excuse me, I've got to rush off now.'

'Okay. Till tomorrow then.'

'I'll look forward to it. And thanks for getting back to me so quickly Meredith. Bye for now, and grace and peace to you.'

She replaced the receiver. The thought flashed across her mind that tomorrow's meeting could loosely be termed as some kind of date, but was immediately superseded by another, and one that she felt a keen sense of disappointment over. Stupid girl! Of course it wouldn't be. He had only been talking about church business. Like many of the other women around, she too liked this new minister - and not just for his dynamic faith; there was something different...something special about him. The phrase: **Deep calls to deep**, from **Psalms,** had crossed her mind on several occasions when they had spoken together. But spiritualising the obvious attraction she felt for him could prove awkward and embarrassing. She would have to watch herself carefully, just as she had been doing since day one of his arrival.

It happened again that night, although this time the footsteps and voices were louder. And there appeared to be more of them. Whatever they were up to, it was gaining in popularity. She had recognised the back view of one of the group: it was the girl who had arrived only that morning as a replacement for one of the sacked staff. With a sinking heart, she knew that, once again, she would have to report the incident to Tom, which was the last thing he needed to cope with right now; this baby business was really getting to him.

CHAPTER 3

The atmosphere in the kitchen was more tense than usual the next morning. The new girl had not shown up, and Nick the Cook was on the warpath. Ten minutes into the shift, he rang through to the office to complain and demand to be given an explanation. Tom hadn't arrived yet, and it was Meredith who took the call.

'Maybe she's overslept. I'll go and see,' she offered, knowing that reception would be quiet for a while, and hoping that this would be a good opportunity to ask some questions, and maybe even solve the mystery.

The front door of the Tatty House was never locked. She walked straight in, grimacing at the pervading smell of cigarettes and stale beer. There was no-one in the communal lounge or kitchen. She began negotiating the stairs, being careful to avoid the line of empty drink cans, stacked on the sides of each step.

She knocked on the first bedroom door; there was no reply. She tried the others - again no reply. She decided to retrace her steps and knock louder. If there was still no reply, she would risk taking a look inside any that weren't locked. The first two were extremely untidy: heaps of clothes were strewn haphazardly around, and empty packets of crisps, biscuits and sweet wrappings littered the surfaces. Plates and mugs, some still encrusted with half-eaten food and drink, were used as ashtrays, attracting the odd noisy bluebottle. The third, however, was altogether different; the drawers and small wardrobe were empty, and apart from the bed, which obviously been slept in, there was no other sign that anyone had ever been there. Meredith guessed that this had been the new girl's room.

❖

Tom arrived later, hot and already tired. The dentist had been running late and his mother-in-law had been on the telephone, issuing yet another list of demands. Meredith waited until an opportune moment, and then reluctantly reported the matter to him. Nick was quickly summoned as soon as breakfast was over, and the three held an impromptu meeting.

Meredith explained, 'Last night was the fourth time I've heard people walking back to the Tatty House in the early hours. I feel there's something queer going on. That scream the other night...the girl sounded genuinely scared. And now I'm wondering if the new girl was somehow frightened off, and maybe that's why she left in such a hurry.'

'For Pete's sake, what are you hiring?' asked the cook, his short, hot temper already beginning to boil as he stared accusingly at Tom. 'You'll have to give me better people than these yobbos. At least impose some sort of curfew. How'd you expect me to run the kitchen and dining room with a load of delinquents?'

'Can't do it,' replied Tom, 'much as I'd like to. We'd get no-one. And you know they get told that we don't put up with any horseplay when they get here.'

'We had none of this nonsense with National Service; that knocked some sense into them. Bloody softie government! Country's going to the dogs. It'll only get worse, mark my words. And then who'll...'

'Yes, well, that may be,' interjected Tom, keen to head off one of Nick's usual rants about the declining moral state of the nation. 'But that doesn't solve our problem here and now.'

His telephone rang: three rings, then stopped. All eyes focused on the instrument. It rang again: three rings, then stopped; the code his wife used when she needed to speak to him urgently. A look of obvious concern crossed his already furrowed brows. 'Anyway, I'll have to get going. You two keep your eyes open and ask around; someone's bound to know something.'

Nick harrumphed loudly as he stalked out. 'Bloody carry on! Behaving like a bunch of school kids. No discipline. I blame the parents, giving in to them; too damn soft.'

'But I don't think it's just high jinks this time, Nick. There's something weird going on, and I've got a…a kind of uneasy feeling about it,' said Meredith.

'Tosh! It'll be drink or the weed, you mark my words. And some of us have got work to do; that kitchen won't run itself,' and with that, he marched off.

She stood wondering what to do next. Things were slow again in reception; maybe she wouldn't be missed for a while. Tom had told them to ask around, so she might as well make a start. 'Won't be long Wendy. Just popping into the ballroom,' she said, leaving the office quickly, before her colleague had any opportunity to ask her why.

The café was situated at the back of the large room and looked quiet. Just a handful of elderly campers sat around, putting the world right over the morning newspapers. A bored looking young girl slouched behind the counter. Meredith approached her.

'Hello Kit. Not busy then?'

'Nah.'

'Where's Mandy?'

'Cash and Carry.'

'You share with Pauline don't you? A few chalet's down from me?'

'S'right.'

'I don't suppose you've heard anything…unusual going on have you? Especially at odd times of the night?'

Kit scrunched up her nose and looked at Meredith as though she had said something disgusting. 'You what?'

'It's just that I've heard people going past my chalet in the early hours of the morning, and I was just wondering…'

'Dunno. Nothing to do with me. Why you asking anyway?'

'Just curious. So you've heard nothing?'

'Told you, I dunno.'

'Okay. But it looks like that new girl from the kitchen has left already. Don't suppose you know anything about that either?'

At last Kit reacted; her eyes opening wide with surprise. 'Done a bunk has she?'

'Reckon so. She didn't turn up for work this morning, and her room's empty.'

'Oo-er!' she exclaimed, turning her back on Meredith, suddenly feeling the need to make a start on the pile of washing-up in the sink behind her.

'Thanks anyway,' said Meredith, 'but you'll let me know if anything happens that worries or upsets you, won't you?'

Kit shrugged. 'Might do.'

Undeterred, Meredith made her way back to the office, passing the bar as she did so. Then the thought occurred to her that if there was any place where people's tongues were loose, it would be around here. She heard some movement coming from behind the metal shutter and could just make out the sound of music. 'Hello. Is that you Marcus?' she called out. 'It's Meredith. Can I come in?'

The noises stopped and a deep baritone voice rang out. 'Stay cool.' A moment later the side door opened to reveal the Bar Manager's tall and colourful figure.

'Wazzup?'

'Sorry to bother you, but I was wondering if you'd heard anything about the new girl from the kitchen? She was meant to start this morning, but it looks like she's left without any warning. Don't suppose you know anything about it, do you?'

Marcus stood stock still, which was unusual for him because he was a man of motion - reggae being his thing. He was never far from its persistent beat, and his body seemed to have a constant sway, even when the air was silent around him,

16

which was hardly ever. He had an impressive Afro frizz, the result of regular perming on his naturally straight brown hair. This morning, he was dressed in his usual off-duty combination of clashing green, yellow and red tee-shirt and flared jeans.

She waited a few seconds, expecting him to resume his habitual swaying. 'Marcus?'

'Huh?'

'It's just that I'm a bit concerned. I think something, or someone, must have frightened her. Nick's lost some staff already, and it's not very nice to think that people can come here to work and something happens to scare them away.'

He remained uncharacteristically still and silent.

'You know something, don't you? You'll have to tell me, or you could be the next to lose staff.'

'Ah! Um, well.'

'Marcus, please! There's something odd going on, isn't there? I've seen staff creeping around in the early hours of the morning. And the other night one of them screamed. It's happened four times now, and whatever they're doing, I've got a feeling it's not right. Why would they be doing…whatever it is…so late? We need to find out so that we can, you know, maybe try and help them.'

He pressed his lips together, obviously undecided. So, Nick was losing staff. But kitchen help, like bar staff, were easy enough to replace; although it would be a real fag having to find and train up more when the season really kicked off. He liked Meredith, and would have fancied her if she hadn't have been so uncool. Her shoulder length brown hair had a nice kind of natural curl about it, and her hazel eyes reminded him a bit of his first girl. And he had to admit that she was making some kind of sense. There was also the fact that he had been getting strung out about the offhand attitude of one of his staff. He'd actually done some poking around himself and discovered that some of the younger ones were getting hooked on one of those kid's games. Maybe he should say something.

'Don't know about the kitchen lot, but I kinda think one of my new girls has got something going on.'

Meredith looked surprised; she had not expected to come up with a result so soon. 'What do you mean?'

'That kid's game, Ouija. Plays it a lot. Takes it kinda seriously.'

'Ouija? Are you sure? Who's playing it?'

He stopped to think. The girl would probably end up in trouble if he gave her name, but he hadn't liked the way she'd looked at him when he'd told her stop being so stuck up, and to be nicer to the punters. A right cold fish. And he was starting to get fed up about the way she swanned around; behaving as though she owned the place. What the hell - she'd be no loss. 'Katherine, Katherine Frith. You know: long hair, eyes blacked up like pandas; beads and bangles everywhere.'

'Oh yes, I know who you mean.'

'Got a seriously uncool attitude. Starting to get up my nose.'

'And you think she's playing that Ouija game?'

'Huh huh! Spooksville man.'

'Where? Where does she do it?'

'Hey man! Don't ask me. I don't dig that stuff. My god's Bob.'

Meredith had to think for a moment before remembering his obsession with Bob Marley. 'Maybe that's what's been going on then. I wonder who she's been doing it with?'

He held up his hands. He had a fair idea about a few of them, but no way was he going to spill the beans any more than he had already. 'Time out man! As long as they pull their weight behind here, they can chill anyway they like when they're off.'

'Okay, well thanks.' At least now she had something to go on, however wrong it might eventually turn out to be. 'I'd better let you get on. See you later.'

'Stay cool!' He watched her walk away, admiring her curves, and not for the first time wishing she was as free with her charms as some of the other girls.

She returned to the office and reported her findings to Tom. Katherine Frith was duly summoned and questioned. Although reluctant at first to admit to any involvement with the game, she did eventually confess, petulantly stating that, 'It was just a bit of fun', and only promising to stop playing it when threatened with the sack. Tom appeared to be satisfied - and Meredith hoped he was justified in being so. But she was not so sure; if only she could shake off her uneasy feeling. There was something about the young woman that made her feel slightly unsettled every time she saw her; it was as though she needed to be on her guard. But against what, she had no idea.

CHAPTER 4

Dressed in a corduroy jacket and slacks, Kingsley looked like any other holiday maker enjoying a casual stroll along the beach. He studied Meredith from behind his sunglasses, and decided, once again, that she was vastly different in appearance from Deborah. As for her temperament, well, only time would tell.

'Well, if it's shade you're after, there's only a few places along this stretch. It all depends on how far you want to go,' she said.

'Not too far. Near enough for people to be able to get to us without too much effort, but we don't want to be right on top of them.'

'How about over there?' She pointed to a copse of trees just over a hundred yards away. 'It's a nice spot; the Punch and Judy people use it.'

He laughed. 'I don't fancy competing with them. When are they here?'

'Friday mornings. But there's always some local dog walkers or joggers around, even in bad weather.'

They walked on. He stopped and looked around, examining and considering the merits of the area. 'You said there's a few other spots?'

'Yes, further up.'

'Let's take a look.'

They set off, their pace slower as they wove their way in between areas of sand and pebbles. She had been hoping that there might be an opportunity to tell him about the problem at the camp, and felt that now was as good a time as any. 'Kingsley, can I ask you something? It's to do with the camp, and a problem we've been having there.'

He bent down and picked up a shell. 'The camp? Huh, broken,' he discarded it. 'Okay. Fire away.'

'It's about that Ouija game. Do you know much about it?'

He turned to look at her, and replied, his tone one of unmistakable disapproval, 'Unfortunately, yes. Don't tell me you've been messing about with the thing?'

'Me? No! We've just found out that someone's been doing it, probably in one of the chalets.'

'One of the campers?'

'No. Staff. Seems they've been playing it late at night. In fact, one of the new girl's just up and left without a word, and I'm sure she was scared off somehow. Tom's had the main instigator in, and she's promised to stop doing it. But I've got a bad feeling about things.' She looked at him, and guessed that it was not the bright sun causing his brow to furrow so deeply. 'It's not good, is it?'

'No. Not good at all. It's one of the devil's little devices. Definitely occult. Unfortunately, I've seen this kind of thing before. The players can open the door to some pretty nasty forces and end up exposing themselves to more than they bargained for.'

'Crikey! I thought it was just a game! But why are they allowed to sell it, if it's so bad?'

'Huh, why indeed! The trouble is that it's not considered dangerous, and people actually still buy it for their children. There are moves to try to get it banned, and it can't happen fast enough as far as I'm concerned. It's been sold as a toy since the 1800's, then adults started to get interested in the thing and began using it as a parlour game. And you know how it works, don't you?'

'No, I've never done it. But it must be simple enough to play, especially if children do it?'

He nodded. 'And not helped by being sold as a so-called harmless board game.'

'I've seen them for sale in Smith's, but I've never actually seen one out of the box.'

'It's just a smallish board,' he opened his arms, 'usually about so big, with letters of the alphabet and numbers, and the words "Yes" and "No", and sometimes "Goodbye" printed on it. The players touch a small heart-shaped bit of wood, or plastic, called a planchette, and the thing moves around the board, pointing and spelling out words - messages - supposedly from "the other side."'

'It moves around? How? Do the players move it?'

'Sometimes, but not always, and therein lies the problem. In some circumstances the thing can move without any human agency being involved. There's been all sorts of tests done by various branches of the scientific community, and a few have issued warnings about how it can trigger serious personality disorders, especially in some vulnerable people. Others explain it away by saying that people are moving the planchette themselves on a subconscious level.' He nodded his head slowly, 'But I've seen too much of the thing to know that it's an evil, devilish practice.'

By now they had reached an area shaded by a high, concrete wall. Steps led up to a car park, with a block of public toilets and a café a bit further on. It was not as natural or attractive as the first spot they had examined. She pointed up and across towards the café. 'This bit's popular with the locals, and there's always groups of teenagers hanging around at weekends and in the evenings. There's a pub a bit further down and a fish and chip shop. We're near the tail end of the council estate.'

'That sounds promising. Let's go up and take a look.'

They climbed the steps. Once again, he took his time looking around, before announcing, 'Useful bit of parking. Yes, this might do very well, as long as the café owner and council don't raise any objections. You mentioned some other places?'

'They're a bit further on.'

'How far?'

'Ten minutes maybe.'

'Hmm, we might as well take a look now we're here.'

They set off once again, and then, to her surprise, he returned to the subject of the Ouija Board. 'I assume you're familiar with what the Bible has to say about people who try to contact the dead?'

'Yes, of course,' and then she added, more thoughtfully, 'but it's always puzzled me how mediums do it. If our spirits leave our bodies and go straight to Heaven or Hell when we die, how can anyone be contacted again?'

'Well now, Meredith, what you have to remember is that it's not just us humans and animals that live on earth, there's some nasty malevolent forces hanging around as well; familiar spirits amongst them.'

'Familiar spirits?'

'Devils, demons, deceiving and lying spirits - familiar with people and their lives. Very convincing for those who open themselves up to them.'

She looked as she felt, increasingly alarmed. 'It sounds horrible, but fascinating...in an awful sort of way.'

'Fascinating? I suppose so, for those who want to look anywhere but where they should be looking, in the Word of God. Unfortunately, since The Fall, us humans have a bias towards doing wrong. Our decision-making and moral mind-set have been warped. Or, to put it another way, we have an appetite for running after unhealthy things. There are plenty of spiritualist churches around; one just down the road from ours. I see them as the spiritually dead, feeding off rotten meat! The trouble is that too many people don't understand - or choose to ignore the fact - that we're spiritual beings as well as physical. The Church should be doing her bit and giving some clear teaching. I suppose it wouldn't be a bad idea for Launchpad to have a session or two on the dangers of the occult. Talking of the group, have you had any thoughts about what I said yesterday?'

'What, about taking over from Doreen?'

'Yes, and there's no rush. Don't feel any pressure. Take all the time you need to make a decision.'

Relieved that the unpleasant subject of the Ouija game had been dropped, she replied, 'Alright. I'll let you know soon. Actually, I'll be twenty six soon, and was going to have to stop going then anyway.'

'Is that right? That would have been a shame. From what I've seen of it you make a valuable contribution. And that's another grey area I'd like to do something about in the fellowship, the older singles, especially those who live alone. It can be hard on them, always being surrounded by couples and families.'

'Yes, I've often thought that.'

They walked on for several hundred yards. He slowed down, 'I think that's far enough. Don't know about you, but I've worked up quite a thirst. How about heading back to that café? I'd like to take another look around there.'

She readily agreed and they turned back.

'On the subject of singles, I haven't noticed you with anyone in particular, just your parents. Isn't there a boyfriend on the scene anywhere?'

Taken aback that he should ask such a thing, she replied, 'Boyfriend! No. Well, not really.'

'Not really?'

She paused, then said, 'There is someone I write to. I suppose you'd call him more of an occasional, absentee boyfriend.'

'Absentee? Lives away then?'

'He's in the R.A.F., in Germany.'

'Christian?'

'No.'

By now, they had reached the steps. He asked, 'So things are, what, just casual between you?'

'Yes, I suppose you could say that.' Why the interest? she thought. Or was he only wearing his minister's hat again?

'Just as well. You know that there could be a problem if things were to become more serious?'

'Oh, I don't think there's much chance of that,' she replied.

He tried to study her face as he opened the door for her; there seemed to be no sign of regret in her expression. And he was rather pleased about that.

CHAPTER 5

That night Meredith attended one of the midweek house-groups. These were another of Kingsley's initiatives. So far, four had been formed, each one made up of between six to eight of the regular churchgoers. After half an hour's social chat, helped by tea or coffee, there would be a time of Bible study, followed by some discussion and prayer. Another drink would complete the evening, after which everyone would disperse.

Kingsley himself was not committed to any of the groups, but attended each one in turn. He would recommend the theme for each six week session, usually on a book of the Bible, and provide accompanying study guides for the leaders to use as they saw fit. He was no strict, authoritarian taskmaster, and encouraged the use of individual gifts and strengths whenever they were evident. His whole aim was to serve and disciple his flock, as guided by the Holy Spirit; the very Living, indwelling Presence of God Himself. He wanted to help them to become spiritually mature, and, therefore, more capable of loving and glorifying Him in every area of their lives.

The theme for the past six weeks had been *Walking on the Water,* which had proved to be a stimulating study on faith. Everyone agreed that they had been particularly inspired and challenged by the passage in **Matthew 14.**

Meredith shared how moved she had been to realise that Jesus had not floundered around helplessly in the stormy depths, nor had He sank below the waves.

'He walked confidently *on* the water because He's The Lord of Creation. I find it comforting to know that He knows exactly whatever I might be going through, and that He's actually on top of the situation, no matter how I may be feeling. I know He's got the power to help me through, and makes sure that I don't get overwhelmed and start sinking, even if I sometimes feel I'm going to. But that's usually when I've ignored Him and let go of His hand.'

Some of the others agreed, and one after another they described how they too had been prevented from being overwhelmed by the storms of life.

Kingsley was attending the group that week, and found himself impressed by Meredith's willingness to open up and share her faith in this way. He had heard her before, in fact, each time he attended the group she had contributed something worthwhile. He made a point of going over to speak to her during coffee. 'Thanks for what you said, Meredith. I'm sure it blessed the others as much as it did me. It certainly encouraged them to speak up about their own experiences anyway.'

'And thank you for your help this afternoon,' she replied.

'My pleasure. By the way, I've been thinking, do tell Tom that I'd be happy to meet anybody who's been involved with the thing, and feels the need to talk to someone about it. That's what I'm here for, after all.'

'Thanks, will do,' she replied, feeling sure that no-one would admit to having such a need, especially Katherine Frith.

'And I thought you'd be interested to know that I've already written to the council about using that bit of beach for open airs.'

'Already!'

'No time like the present. We need to be making the most of the summer months.'

'Well, apparently we're in for a good one.'

'Is that right?'

'Yes, at least according to Wendy.'

'Wendy?'

'You've seen her; we work together in the office and reception. She's a great one for horoscopes, and they've been predicting that we're in for a really hot one this year.'

He looked askance at her. 'Horoscopes! You don't take any notice of them things do you?'

Obviously she had said something wrong. She hesitated, before replying. 'Well, er, no, not really. But it can be kind of interesting to know what they're saying.'

He sighed heavily. 'Thin edge of the wedge I'm afraid.'

'Really?'

'Really. Think of them as a mild, but insidious, type of infection. And I'm at a loss to see how giant balls of rock or gas, millions of miles away from the Earth, can have any effect on our lives down here!'

This was an unexpected turn in the conversation and she was not quite sure how to reply. She certainly wasn't going to tell him that it was always the first thing Wendy would look for in her newspaper each morning. A few seconds passed before she said, 'But what about the moon? We know that has some sort of pull on the tides, and women - you know. And we always feel better when the sun's out.'

'Granted. I've got no argument with astronomy. Now *astrology's* a different kettle of fish altogether.'

'Yes, I know. But it's really just a bit of harmless fun.'

'Okay, for argument's sake, do you know anyone who was born under the same sign of the zodiac as you and has similar character traits, or whose life seems to mirror yours?'

She immediately thought of Jacko. Like her, he was a Leo, although, in her opinion, they were as different in temperament as chalk and cheese. They might work in the same place, but there any similarity ended. 'Actually, I do know someone with the same sign.'

'And?'

She smiled. Something in her was not prepared to give into him quite so easily. 'We couldn't be more different. But maybe that's just coincidence. I've met other Leo's, and there are some similarities.'

28

'No doubt. But I'm sure we can all find ways we're like each other if we look hard enough. I bet you and I share quite a few characteristics, and I'm not a Leo. So, I take it then, that you read yours?'

She nodded. 'Sometimes.'

'You know that you could read half a dozen different magazines, and get half a dozen different so-called predictions, don't you? Although the law of averages means they can get some things right sometimes. Let's say...I could predict that your finances will have a boost tomorrow. Then how about if I warned you against making a rash purchase this weekend? I don't have to possess special powers to know that a lot of people get paid on the last Friday of the month. And the TV's been forecasting a warm front on the way, so how about if I throw in an unexpected invitation - possibly outdoors? I'm sure I could find a dozen different ways of describing how three or four different scenarios could play out.'

She saw his point. 'I see what you mean. But aren't there some astrologers who have a genuine gift, or ability? And what about mediums? Some of them really do seem to know some very personal things about people.'

'Well, yes. But whether they know it or not, and despite popular opinion, their powers aren't God-given. And they wouldn't be happy to hear the truth, which is that they've opened themselves up to the devil and his minions. We're back to those familiar spirits again. It's all occult, bad stuff, like every other form of fortune telling: the Ouija board, tarot cards, crystal balls, palmistry, tea leaves, candles, and any other kind of paraphernalia people use to try to titillate, comfort, or guide themselves and others. It's like I said before, us humans have a knack of putting our faith in everything except where we should be putting it: in a loving God and His written word. And you, Meredith, as a mature Christian, should already know that as long as you put Him first, then all your physical, emotional and spiritual needs can only be met in and through Christ alone.'

She looked down at her feet. The evening, in fact the whole day, had been a particularly good one. She had enjoyed his company that afternoon, but now she just wanted to escape, although she recognised that he had only spoken the truth, uncomfortable though it had been to hear. Obviously feeling deflated, quietly she agreed. 'Alright. I know now.'

She looked crushed, and he knew he had gone too far. Why was he being so hard on her? He recalled how he had always put up with and excused Deborah's 'little idiosyncrasies', as he had fondly dismissed them. And he had never resorted to lecturing her.

'I'm sorry, Meredith. Came on a bit heavy, didn't I?'

'It's okay. I hadn't really thought about it before, but I suppose none of us have any idea of how insidious these things really are.'

He agreed, nodding, 'Just goes to show that if someone like you can get hoodwinked, then how much we need to warn and educate those less mature in the faith.' He had her full attention now, and saw how clear her eyes were, and a pleasant shade of hazel; strange that he hadn't noticed that about her before.

She lowered her head, and said quietly, 'I feel really bad now, like I've insulted the Lord, you know?'

'Hmm, well don't let it get to you and become a big issue. You just have to talk to Him about it and confess your involvement, then say you're sorry.'

She nodded, but she still looked concerned.

'I can help if you like.'

'Help?'

'Yes, just a short time of prayer, nothing heavy. Very calm and orderly, none of that head-twisting and frothing at the mouth kind of stuff. I'm afraid Hollywood's got a lot to answer for. Anyway, think about it and let me know. And remember,

I'm here if you find yourself getting worried about that other matter - on the camp.'

'I'll remember.'

CHAPTER 6

There was always an air of resigned stoicism amongst the adults on Saturday mornings. The long awaited holiday was over and there was still the last minute packing to be done. Children of the more organised parents were allowed to go down to the beach one last time. Others were threatened that they would be given 'something to cry about,' if they couldn't behave themselves, which came particularly hard after all the noisy freedom they had enjoyed all week. The chalets had to be vacated by ten o'clock, allowing a small army of chalet maids to swoop in and get them cleaned before the next intake began arriving, any time after noon.

However, on this particular Saturday, heavy rain fell, dampening the departing campers' spirits even more, and resulting in rivulets of tears to fall down many young, suntanned cheeks.

Meredith had awoken with a headache, which, despite regular doses of aspirin, stubbornly persisted throughout the busy day. And it was with some relief that she began to tidy up her desk at five o'clock.

'Sure you won't change your mind?' Wendy asked, 'There's still loads of ham left on that shank I boiled yesterday, and Neville's promised to bring back one of those gorgeous pavlovas.'

Meredith put her hand on her aching forehead. 'Sorry Wendy. Sounds lovely, but I'd only be a damp squid.'

She made her farewells, and having no appetite for the usual Saturday fry-up and the noisy, excited hubbub of the newly arrived campers, returned to the relative peace and quiet of her chalet.

She decided to take a nap. Waking up some time later, she peered blearily at her clock. Half past nine! She had slept for almost four hours, and now she felt hungry and thirsty, but at least her head felt slightly better. Attempting to rally, she made a drink and ate some biscuits, then decided to start a letter to Conrad. Afterwards, she would go for a good long soak, knowing that the staff bathrooms would be empty at that time of night.

Just under an hour later, she gathered up her towels and toiletries and headed for the staff corridor in the main building. For some reason Nick had asked if he could come and live in this season. The general consensus was that he was having some marital problems, and she had volunteered to give up her usual room in the staff corridor for him, and go into a chalet instead. She didn't mind, there were advantages to both types of accommodation; at least the chalet allowed her to escape from all the late night noise coming from the ballroom, situated directly below.

It had gone eleven o'clock by the time she had finished. She heard raucous laughter coming from Jacko's room as she walked past, and guessed that he was still in performing mode and entertaining some of the other staff. Dressed in a long bathrobe and a towel wrapped around her head, she descended the back stairs and let herself out of one of the fire exits towards the back of the building. It had finally stopped raining, although the sea air was cold and damp. She hurried along, intent on getting back to her chalet to dry her hair before she could put her small, one bar electric fire back on. That was the one thing she missed about the staff rooms, at least they could plug in several electrical items at the same time without blowing the system.

She assumed that Marcus was doing some late night bar restocking when she noticed a sliver of light showing under the blind of the storeroom's window. She hurried past, but then stopped suddenly in her tracks when she heard what sounded

33

like a female voice calling out. *'Oh no! Don't tell me that! Please...'*

'Sssh! Be quiet! Sssh!' exclaimed another.

'I can't...I hate her...but I couldn't do that...'

'Shut up!' called another female voice, 'They'll hear us, and I'm in enough trouble already.'

Meredith recognised Catherine Frith's voice. Her heart sank as she realised why that blind had been drawn - and what must be going on behind it.

'It's really scaring me! Make it stop, *please!'* pleaded the first voice, its owner obviously becoming even more alarmed.

This was awful! Meredith knew that somebody had to put a stop to it, and decided to go into action. But the thought of confronting the group alone was not appealing; it would be much better if there was someone else with her: another witness. But who? Marcus? It didn't sound as though he was in there, and he already knew about the situation, so she wouldn't have to go into lengthy explanations with anyone else. And she really couldn't believe that he had sanctioned the late night use of his storeroom for any type of nocturnal activity. Yes, it would have to be him. She turned around and hurried back up the stairs to the staff corridor, almost colliding with someone coming out of Jacko's room.

The Shop Manageress looked Meredith up and down, taking in the wet curls that had worked their way free from the confines of the towel. 'Hey! Whe-e-re you off'n such 'urry?'

Meredith pointed at Jacko's door. 'Marcus, is he in there? It's urgent.'

Julia stepped forward, giggling and wiggling her forefinger in front of Meredith's nose, her breath full of brandy fumes. 'Yur too late, hun. He's g'n off with s'm tart 'ready. Serve 'im right if gets dose a'crabs. N'er mind, Medith. No cryin' over 'im now, 'member I'm 'ere for you.'

Meredith had no time to think about what had just been said as her mind raced on. Obviously, there was no point in knocking on Marcus's door now. For a split second she contemplated asking Jacko, then realised that he would probably have been doing some serious drinking too - and she needed someone stone cold sober. Tom, it would have to be him. She turned and ran down the stairs, hoping that there would be time to telephone him from the office and get him over before the clandestine group disbanded.

Two minutes later, Tom arrived, red faced and already annoyed, having driven the short five minute walk from his bungalow.

'What'll you do?' she asked, eager to know his tactics as they entered the deserted ballroom, the smell of alcohol and tobacco still clinging heavily to the air.

'Try and hear what they're up to, then sort this bloody lot out once and for all.'

He unlocked the side door to the bar. They stepped in quietly, using only the overnight security light from the ballroom. At first, there was no sound coming from the back, but a sliver of light showed from under the door. Trying to breathe quietly, they stood and waited, and were soon rewarded when Katherine's voice asked, 'Hello again Friend. Can you tell us a bit more?'

Some scraping noises followed. Meredith remembered what Kingsley had told her, and began to imagine a plastic planchette moving swiftly across a board.

Katherine's voice sounded again as she called out a series of letters:-

'B...A...B...Y...B...O...R...N...D...E...A...D.'

Obviously very frightened now, and sounding close to tears, the second voice exclaimed, *'B...A...B...Baby born dead! Bloody hell!* What baby? I'm not pregnant. Who's is it? Who's pregnant?'

'Not me,' said a third woman's voice, 'I'm on the pill...'

'Well it's not me!' exclaimed Katherine. 'I can't have kids.'

Meredith's blood began to run cold. The only pregnant woman she knew of around here was Sue, Tom's wife. His breathing was coming out forced and ragged now, and she stared at his dark profile in horror, expecting him to put an end to it all there and then. But he remained motionless.

Katherine went on to ask, 'Whose baby?'

A heavy silence followed, broken only by the same scraping sound. Once again, it was Catherine who called out the letters. 'A...H.'

Tony inhaled sharply.

'A.H!' one of the participants of the evil game exclaimed, 'Who's that? I'm A.D.'

'And I'm B.L.,' said another. 'It must've got it wrong.'

'Na-a-a! It never makes mistakes,' Katherine stated.

'It must have. Ask it again?'

'Wait a minute! What about that new Nannie, you know, you see her boobs coming before her?'

'Her name's Brenda...something.'

'Are you sure?'

'Course I'm sure! That's my sister's name.'

'Then - it must be your sister!'

'Flaming miracle then! She been sterilised.'

Catherine's voice rang out again. 'Oh I don't know! It's got to be related to one of us here. Here, let me have a go. Hello again friend. Who's this A.H. related to?'

More scraping. More letters spelled out.

'A..H..B..A..B..Y..S..T..I..L..L..B..O..R..N.'

Meredith had heard enough. Although part of her was fascinated, and curious to know who the identity of this mysterious A.H. was, she knew that someone had to do something to put an end to the unholy scene. Why had Tom let it go on so long? For an awful moment she wondered if he had fallen under the thing's evil spell too. She tapped his arm, but he seemed to have been frozen to the spot. She nudged him, harder now, and whispered, 'Tom, come on! Let's go in. Open the door!'

'I…I…it's me,' came his anguished reply.

'What? But you're T.H!'

'No, no, no!' he whispered forcefully. 'Remember, I'm Anthony…*Anthony!*'

❖

By now, Tom's shock had turned to rage. Cursing, he fumbled awkwardly with the key before throwing open the door. The occupants: Katherine Frith, Kit from the café, and one of the new barmaids, looked with horror at the unexpected and unwelcome sight of their shocked and enraged employer, standing in the doorway. All three were sitting low on boxes of spirits, which Meredith thought of as being incongruous, given the circumstances. The game was lying on an upturned beer crate between them.

'Give me that bloody thing!' Tom shouted, lunging forward and grabbing the board. He tore the thick cardboard in half, threw the iron-shaped planchette onto the floor, then proceeded to stamp fast and hard on it, breaking the brittle plastic into small, sharp pieces. Breathless and perspiring with the effort, he was forced to take several deep breaths before beginning to fire off a barrage of questions at the three girls.

It was not long before the barmaid tearfully confessed to having taken the spare bar keys from Marcus' desk earlier that night. Meanwhile, Kit who had obviously quickly recovered from the shock of being discovered, gave defiant, monosyllabic answers. Knowing the game was well and truly up, Katherine remained stubbornly silent and refused to say anything in her defence, which was almost a relief for Meredith, who now knew that anything she said could not be believed anyway.

Realising that he had gained all the information he was likely to at this stage, Tom began to calm down. He pointed at the open doorway and ordered the group to get out of his sight, adding, 'And be in my office at nine. Packed!' The girls looked at each other, then stood and edged warily past his rigid frame. He stared hard at the broken pieces of plastic on the floor.

'Go after them, Meredith. I'll stay and clear this lot up.'

Meredith followed the girls, receiving plenty of sarcastic comments from Kit and spiteful looks from Katherine en route, and it was with some relief that she was able to lock the main doors behind them. She returned to the office to wait for Tom. It was obvious that he had taken the incident seriously, and he still looked to be badly shaken when he appeared several minutes later. All she wanted to do now was to somehow get him to believe, as she did, that the thing 'speaking' through the board had been nothing but a malevolent, lying spirit. But he could not, or would not, listen. The damage had been done. He opened the cupboard and began pulling out the camp bed and bedding which was kept for emergency sleep-overs. With a voice full of anguish, he said, 'I can't go home and face Sue yet. I'll crack and blurt it out. And the last thing she needs right now is to be told something like *that!*'

'But it's nothing but lies!' exclaimed Meredith. 'It was a lie, a nasty, cruel lie. Please Tom, you mustn't believe anything it said. And won't she just worry if you don't go back?'

Struggling to open the bed's stiff metal leg sections, he replied, 'I'll phone…tell her the problem's been dealt with, but I've decided to stay on in case it starts up again. She's good at picking up on my moods, and it'll only make her blood pressure go up again if she thinks I'm out of sorts.' Both leg sections now opened, he positioned the narrow bed between the desk and wall.

'But you said that everything was fine at her last check up?'

'It was, but anything can make it go up. We're having to be really careful. And it's no good Meri, my mind's made up. I'm staying. I don't trust that Katherine. Who knows what other pranks she might try and pull? I'd better be here - just in case. I'll have to do some rounds. And I'll get their cards ready. The sooner we're shot of them, the better.'

'Are you going to sack them all, even the new barmaid?'

'Too right! We can't afford to keep any rotten apples.'

He threw the quilt over the green canvas and plumped up the pillows fiercely. 'Now, if you want to be of some use, put the kettle on and get the petty cash box out. They're bloody lucky to be getting anything.'

Upset at seeing him in such a state, and feeling next to useless, she did as she had been asked.

She returned to her chalet. Her hair hung in damp curls and her head felt cold, and now the headache had returned. Knowing that there was nothing else she could do, she knelt by her bed and prayed silently. At least she could do that.

There was no sign of the three young women by the time she reported for duty the next day. All Tom would mention about the affair was that he had personally escorted them off the premises. She took one look at his pale, drawn face, and guessed at what kind of a night he had had. Wendy had been told the briefest of details about the incident, but suspecting that something was seriously amiss, attempted to lighten the atmosphere by cracking a few jokes, only to be met with stoic silences or nondescript grunts from him each time.

Meredith found it an effort to smile and remain polite as she answered the usual barrage of questions from the new intake of campers. Kingsley was expected soon, and remembering what he had said about being willing to talk to anyone involved with the game, she decided to ask him to have a word with Tom before he left. She felt sure that he would agree, even though Tom wasn't a churchgoer.

'Morning Meredith,' he called, hurrying past the counter a few minutes later. 'Any news on the photographer?'

'Morning. You'll have to go and knock on the shop shutters. Her name's Julia. Actually Kingsley, I know you've got to dash off afterwards, but I'd appreciate a moment of your time before you go. There's been an…unfortunate incident…relating to what we discussed the other day, about that game. And I think we need to take you up on your offer, you know, you said you'd be willing to have a word with anyone involved?'

'Unfortunate incident?' He looked keenly at her, noticing that her usual open, carefree expression had been replaced by one of anxiety.

'Afraid so. It happened again last night, and Tom's really upset about what it said.'

'Tom! Don't tell me he's been doing it?'

'What! No. But he…overheard something. I told him it was all lies, but he's really taken it to heart and believes it. He's really in a bad way, Kingsley.'

'Alright. Tell him I'll come after the service,' then added, 'Don't worry Meredith, remember, the battle's already been won; we're on the winning side. See you in half an hour.'

CHAPTER 7

Wendy knew that Meredith had been hoping to attend the Gospel Service, and magnanimously offered to 'hold the fort' once things calmed down a bit outside.

Kingsley was dressed casually and sitting on a high stool, singing a solo and playing his guitar, when she entered the ballroom fifteen minutes later. He acknowledged her with a nod. Curious, she counted twenty three campers in all, the majority of whom were elderly, although there were a few children present. A dozen or so people sat at the tables behind them, waiting for the café to open. To the right she noticed that one of the shop shutters was half open, and wondered how Julia was feeling after the previous night's heavy drinking session.

Kingsley laid down his guitar as the song came to an end. He appeared to be completely at ease as he picked up his Bible and held it open in front of him. 'Now, can anyone tell me what that song was all about?'

Someone from the front called out, 'Joy.' Someone else called, 'Peace,' another called, 'Love.'

'That's right. And as we've already discovered from God's Word here,' he held the Bible up, 'that's something He's very much into. When we open our hearts to Jesus, He gives us His joy, His peace, His love. In fact, all the things we try so hard to find and keep hold of ourselves in this world. And I'm guessing that's what some of you are doing here this week, trying to have some fun and laughter - some joy. And there's nothing wrong with that. We all need times when we can get away from our normal, humdrum lives; times to get away and be refreshed. Or maybe there are those of you who are already content with your life, thank you very much, and are only here this week because you've been persuaded to come along to join the family break. You grandma's and pa's are the perfect baby-sitters after all!'

Assenting sounds were made as some of the grey and blue-tinted heads nodded.

He stood and walked over to the sketch board. 'And now a picture. Who can tell me what this is?' He began drawing quickly. Within seconds a long-legged bird with a thin neck emerged, its head buried deep in the ground. He drew a light bulb with the words *20 watts* next to one of its eyes. All could see that the bird was craning its neck to stare at the dim bulb.

'An ostrich,' an elderly man called out.

'An emu,' called another.

'Both correct, take your pick.' He continued drawing, 'No doubt you'll have lots of fun and laughter this week, but I don't need to tell you that it's of the fleeting kind: temporary, and soon forgotten. It'll be the sort that soon fades as it's buried under all the humdrumness of life. But the type of contentment and happiness I'm talking about goes deeper than that; it's of a type that the world can't give you, nor even understand.'

Now he drew a large sun, high above the bird's stooped body. Producing a yellow marker, he coloured in the circle and drew a series of flares around it. 'It's the type that stays when things aren't so rosy; the type that gives you peace and comfort, even when everything around you turns dark and gloomy, or starts to spin out of control...'

'You've got me spinning out of control!' heckled a woman's voice from somewhere behind them.

Meredith turned to look for the culprit. A group of young women sat at one of the café tables, one of them was flapping her hand furiously in front of her face in a mock effort to cool herself down. Meredith reminded herself that they were not in the safe and rarefied setting of a church sanctuary, but in the vastly different worldly environment of a holiday camp ballroom.

Kingsley did not miss a beat, as he looked over his shoulder and called over in the heckler's direction, 'And that's another thing trusting in Jesus can do, spin your world around, but in the right direction.'

He turned to face his audience again. 'Here's a few questions for you. We're surrounded by talk, much of it meaningless, empty chatter; why not spend a bit of time listening to those who gossip the Gospel instead? Why do we spend our lives…' he pointed at the bird, 'all that time and energy, craning our necks and forcing ourselves to be satisfied with things that can only dim and fade in time? Why don't we look up instead?' Now he pointed at the sun, 'And lift our heads and hearts to focus on the *real* Light of the World: the Light of Christ? The Son. That's S-o-n. Ah, but you might ask, how does that help? After all, isn't religion a private matter, and doesn't it cause more problems than it solves? And I could answer "yes" to both questions. Yes, in a way it is private and personal. Personal because each one of us should be allowed to make up our own minds about what we believe. Our governments, our cultures, employers, schools or families, can't, and shouldn't, do it for us. This is one decision we must all make for ourselves, and we should be free to make it without any fear or pressure. And yes, religion can indeed cause a lot of problems, especially when practiced by someone who hasn't had a *real* experience of the Living Christ, and whose heart is still shut to Him. As William Booth, the founder of the Salvation Army said:-

The chief danger that confronts the coming century will be religion without the Holy Spirit, Christianity without Christ, forgiveness without repentance, salvation without regeneration, politics without God, heaven without hell.

'But I'm not talking about a religion. I'm talking about a *relationship*. A relationship with the Living God - through a belief in Christ.'

'And thank God for that! I like me relationships,' came the female voice again, followed by some high-pitched giggling from her companions.

Undaunted, Kingsley took up the challenge. 'Then you'll be as pleased as I am that God's not into religion with its restrictive set of manmade rules and traditions. No doubt, many of you will be able to quote some: "Don't do this, don't do that, but you must do this and then you must do that..."'

'I can think of a few things we must do!' came the same voice.

If the young woman thought she would get away with that, then she was to be quickly proved wrong, for now Kingsley decided to take authority over the situation.

'Please, do come and join us! The Lord needs people like you who aren't afraid to speak their minds. Maybe you'd like to tell us a bit about yourself, and what makes you tick? I'm sure we'd all like to hear what's making you so happy this morning? Or maybe you'd prefer to wait until you meet Him? Then you can tell Him yourself, face to face.'

The young woman stared back. Obviously nonplussed, and not knowing how to react or respond to such a challenge, began to emit a series of high-pitched giggles.

'As you wish,' remarked Kingsley, turning his whole attention back to his audience. 'It's a lovely sunny day today, but let's imagine that it was overcast out there. We trust, and hope, that the sky is still blue, and that the sun is still shining above the cloud barrier. Now close your eyes - that's it, everyone - dark, isn't it? Keep them closed. Here we are, in a light-filled room, but we're in the darkness. Just because we can't see, feel, hear, taste, touch or recognise the light, it doesn't mean that it's not there! Okay, open your eyes again.'

A few people commented quietly to their neighbours.

'Now I want to tell you about that relationship.'

Kingsley turned over a fresh sheet on the sketch board. He began drawing a chrysalis with a large, colourful butterfly beside it.

'And this is one that sets you free to be the person you were created to be, like a butterfly emerging from the confines of a chrysalis. Do you know that all of God's "do's" are only for our wellbeing and blessing? And all His "don'ts" are only for our good and protection? A study of them reveals how full of common sense they are. So, whatever your circumstances are today, I've got some good news for you: God's free offer of the kind of contentment, happiness and peace that the world cannot give, and it's of the lasting, eternal kind. And it's free, completely free. But like all gifts, it needs to be accepted.'

He turned over another fresh sheet. 'And here's some even more good news for you. Did you know that you can have all your wrongdoings, or, as the Bible puts them, your "sins" - paid for? Or, to put it another way, cancelled out? Scripture tells us that we're all sinners; all have fallen short of God's holy standard.' He began drawing a large, wrapped parcel.

'It'll do us no good to neglect His gift, or refuse to open it by keeping our eyes tightly shut, and ignoring Him. We have to be sincere about wanting His gift.' He wrote the words *A New Life From God To You* inside the parcel. 'We have to be willing to open our minds, and then our hearts to Him.' He pointed at the parcel. 'Only then are we able to accept the new life He offers. And how do we do that? It's easy, and it won't cost you anything. Remember, it's completely free. You don't need your purses or wallets to complete this transaction.'

He drew a cross above the parcel, then a large red bow diagonally across the cross. He continued, 'Jesus willingly gave up His life for each one of us. God is Just, and He created us to be like Him, and so we too require - even demand - justice. And that's one of the reasons why His Son, The Lord Jesus Christ, came to Earth and took our place on the Cross.

He is the bridge back to God - our way back. His was the final sacrifice. His death - His blood - was shed to pay the price for all our sins. Our forgiveness is waiting, for *all* of us. For *all* our sins. For *all* time. Once we have accepted His free gift of a new life, then the saying, "God looks at Jesus - and pardons me" can be true for you too.'

The swing door opened. Meredith felt a tap on her shoulder a second later. 'Wendy's needing you,' whispered Ann, one of the children's nannies.

Once again, Kingsley pointed at the unwrapped parcel. 'He is *The Gift;* The Gift that is offered to us all, The Gift of Life, real Life, eternal Life. And it starts the moment you acknowledge that you're a sinner in need of a Saviour, and believe in His death for you.'

Reluctantly, she stood and began to leave.

'Only then you will know real Life, and that's Life with a capital "L". And one of the gifts He gives us is a quiet, deep sense of security, of a type of happiness we can't experience or manufacture for ourselves, no matter what happens to us in this life, no matter how many holidays we have...'

Kingsley came a few minutes later, guitar case and sketch board in tow. She signalled him to join her at the far end of the counter.

'Thanks for coming. I know you've got to rush off. But just before you go in to see Tom, you did know, didn't you, that his wife's due to have a baby in a few weeks' time?'

'I had heard.'

'She hasn't been too well with blood pressure problems. And he believes that the...message...he overheard last night was about her, and the baby.' She paused, reluctant to repeat the awful message, but knowing she had to. 'It said that the baby would be born dead, stillborn. It was awful Kingsley! He went mad!'

Kingsley frowned. 'What did he do?'

46

'He confronted them and smashed the game up, then sacked them all this morning.'

His eyebrows raised. 'Did he indeed? And where are they now?'

'They've gone already. But the thing is, he refused to go home afterwards. He said he couldn't face Susan; he was frightened she'd pick up that something was wrong and that it would upset her blood pressure again. Honestly, Kingsley, I've tried to tell him that it was nothing but a load of lies. He's really down and he's looking awful. I think, maybe, he'll listen to you if you can go and have a word with him.'

He nodded, his eyes moving past her to look in the direction of Tom's office.

'I'll go and tell him you're here, shall I?' she asked, hopefully.

'Okay. I'll see what I can do.'

'Oh, thank you! Stay here, I won't be long.'

She knocked on Tom's door and went straight in. She had decided not to forewarn him about Kingsley, feeling sure that he would have refused to see him; and she was determined that he would.

He was standing by the window, his hands deep in his pockets, his mind obviously deeper in thought.

'Kingsley's here,' she announced. 'Don't be mad with me Tom, but I told him what happened last night, and he'd like to have a word with you.'

He turned slowly and looked at her, 'Oh, he does, does he?'

'Yes, and I think you should see him. He's used to dealing with...things like that. Won't you see him, for both your sakes? You don't want this hanging over your head now, do you? You want to be able to enjoy things.'

It was several seconds before he replied, and when he spoke, it was as though he was in a trance. 'Enjoy...things?'

'Yes, you know, the baby. Shall I tell him he can come in? He hasn't got long; he's got to get back to church to do the morning service.'

He remained motionless, unresponsive.

'Tom?'

'Alright, but only for Susan...the baby...you know. Go on then, get him in. And Meri, more coffee.'

She had to disturb them when she took the drinks in a few minutes later. Tom's voice sounded again as soon as she shut the door. Kingsley emerged soon after. Knowing he was already running late, she did her best not to hold him up, only asking, 'Everything okay?'

He gave her a quick nod of acknowledgement. 'Got to get going Meredith. See you tonight?'

'Yes, I'll be there,' she called after him.

Full of curiosity, she went to knock on Tom's door, this time waiting to be called in. He was standing by the window again, watching the constant stream of passing campers. He turned, and she was relieved to see that his face looked less strained.

'He's a good man,' he said, his tone noticeably lighter.

'No argument there,' she replied.

'Wants to see me again, another chat...you know.'

'And will you?'

'I think so.'

She smiled. Tom was no saint, and his language could be blasphemous, but he was a good boss, and a decent person for all that.

'Might even get him to christen the sprog,' he added.

'Really! But isn't Sue a Catholic?'

'Yeah. But I do get my own way sometimes, you know!'

CHAPTER 8

Instead of the manse lounge, Launchpad met in the church hall after the evening service that night. Posters had been distributed throughout the town, and over thirty non-churchgoers, mostly teenagers, turned up to watch the film: *The Cross and the Switchblade,* a powerful, true story about how the members of some New York street gangs were challenged and reached for Christ by a lone pastor.

Meredith was helping to make the drinks before the film started and managed to have a few words with Kingsley when he came to the kitchen hatch. 'Thanks for staying on to talk to Tom. I hope it didn't make you late?'

'No problem. How's he been?'

'Much better. He even went home for an early lunch, and seemed fine when he came back.'

'Excellent. We can't let the Devil have it all his own way now, can we? And how are you about it all anyway?'

She was prevented from answering when they were interrupted by Fleur. This was something the young woman was beginning to do on a regular basis, and Meredith watched as Kingsley handled her with kindness, but firmness. She couldn't help comparing how differently he spoke to her, almost as though she was - what? What exactly was she to him? Just another helpful member of his flock? Another sister in The Lord? Or maybe something more? A friend maybe? It could be no more than that. But a friend? Even that would be far more than she could have hoped for, or expected.

Everyone sat attentively throughout the film. Afterwards, Kingsley went out to the front and gave a short Gospel presentation, to which five young men responded: five more hearts and lives opened to receive The Lord Jesus; five more souls saved from eternal separation from God - and all that that would mean. The group were split into two, and he and Dave, Doreen's husband, took the newly born children of God into the side rooms to be counselled and prayed for.

Many of the campers were out and about the next morning. Wendy and Meredith valued these quiet times when they were able to catch up with the correspondence and filing. Most of the children had been taken down to the beach to explore rock pools and go on short beachcombing expeditions. Some of the more energetic campers had joined Murphy, one of the pool's two life guards, on a Mystery Bike Ride. By now, various sports teams had been formed, and several practice sessions were already under way.

One of the week's great money-spinners took place later that afternoon when the Donkey Derby was held on the playing field. Six donkeys, each with a small stuffed jockey doll strapped onto its back, would be encouraged to race along a short track. Meredith always felt sorry for the animals, although even she had to admit that they always looked well cared for, and they never appeared to be bothered by the loud and almost hysterical shouting of the surrounding crowd.

Auditions for the Children's Talent Show were held after the evening meal, followed by the first part of the night's entertainment, the Ho Down. Along with any other available member of staff, Meredith was required to help bring some order into the chaos that was caused by three hundred and fifty adults and children trying to perform a variety of popular folk dances. At nine o'clock, the second part of the evening's entertainment began when a Country and Western band took the stage. Tonight's act was new to the circuit, and Meredith stayed on to hear their first set. Hot and thirsty now, she went to join the long queue at the bar.

Julia came to stand beside her, an empty glass in her hand. She pointed at the camera hanging around her neck, and said,

'On duty,' to the few people who glared at her, or accused her of queue jumping. Meredith thought how severe she looked in her black tailored suit, her hair scraped tightly back, and with no make up on her face.

'Here again?' Julia asked her. 'Don't tell me you've got the hots for Marcus?'

'Why would you think that?' Meredith replied, puzzled.

'Why not? You were after him the other night, weren't you?'

'Don't be daft!'

'Daft? Huh! Could've fooled me. I might have been out of my skull, but I remember how flat you looked when you found out that he'd hooked up with someone else.'

'Oh that! That was only because I thought I'd heard noises coming from behind the bar, and didn't want to get Tom out.'

The queue was moving fast. Julia screwed her eyes up and studied her. She smiled, a strange, secretive smile. 'Well, I'm kinda pleased to hear that.'

Meredith began to feel uneasy; although she knew that Julia always mixed easily enough with men and women, she had had her suspicions about the Shop Manageress's/Camp Photographer's sexual orientation for some time. Slightly older than her, Julia was an extremely attractive woman. She had a neat, petite figure, and was always well groomed, either in a variety of very short miniskirts and dresses, or, like tonight, in her masculine looking outfit. There were rumours about what she got up to on her days off, but Meredith had always felt that that was no one's business but her own.

Now what should she do? It would look odd if she suddenly made her excuses and dashed off. And she could be wrong anyway. Hoping that she was, she replied, 'I'm only stopping for bit. I've not heard the band before.'

'They're okay, been around for a while. The girl's got a fab voice, but not my kind, if you know what I mean.' Again, she gave the same, secretive smile.

51

'Okay ladies, what'll I have you for?' interrupted Marcus's voice.

Julia replied, jerking her head in Meredith's direction, 'What's her usual tipple?'

'Ginger beer, on the rocks.'

'That'll do, but spice it up with some vodka, would you? She needs livening up.'

'Whoa, hang on!' exclaimed Meredith, looking pointedly at Marcus. 'Don't you dare! Ginger beer, *just* ginger beer please.'

'Sure thing, honey,' responded the barman, used to such scenarios.

Julia pushed her glass towards him and slammed a five pound note down on the bar. 'Chicken! Well, I'll have another of these, and they're on me.'

Meredith found herself speculating how the other woman could afford to splash money around so freely on her modest wages.

The drinks obtained, Julia took her by the arm and pulled her, almost forcefully, towards an empty table near the back. 'This'll do. Nice and private.'

Reluctantly, Meredith sat down. There was a large pillar directly in front of them and she needed to pull her chair to the side to obtain a better view of the stage. 'I'm not staying long, Julia. All that charging about's worn me out.'

'Yea, silly girl, I was watching you.'

'You never join in, do you?'

'Nah! Not my scene, hun. I'm more into the slow stuff. I like to feel the affect I'm having on my partner.'

Something in Meredith began to sound a warning. She looked at the camera, now lying on the table in front of them. 'Have you developed those pictures you took of the Sunday morning service yet?'

'Not yet, but I will. He's a good-looking guy.'

'Er, yes, and a good minister. He's getting more people into the church anyway.'

'Your type then? Like 'em tall, dark and handsome, do you?'

Nonplussed, Meredith just smiled, and look away.

'That's a shame,' said Julia. 'I was hoping you'd fancy something a bit more…compact.'

'What do you mean?' asked Meredith, then immediately regretted asking the question, knowing that she didn't really want to know the answer.

Julia sipped her drink, all the while looking intently at Meredith over the rim of her glass. 'You know what I mean. Something with a few more curves, softer around the edges.'

That was all Meredith needed. Now there could be no mistaking the woman's intentions, and she felt she had the right to speak plainly - if only she knew exactly how to! In the end, all she could manage was a faint, 'I see.'

'Do you? I hope so. I've always been kinda sweet on you, Meri. But I've been…preoccupied somewhere else lately. But, hey, I'm here now! I know you're straight, but I'm kinda hoping you'd like to do a bit of…experimenting, and join the rest of us who swing both ways? You know, enjoy the best of both worlds?'

Horrified, Meredith could only stare back.

Julia laughed, 'Hey, what's up? Don't look so shocked! You're a big girl now. And haven't I always been extra nice to you?' She drained her glass and stood. 'I know what you need. Just you stay there.' She stooped and put her face very near to Meredith's. 'No running out on me now, you naughty, naughty girl! You've given me quite a…thirst.' She straightened herself and winked, then turned for the bar.

Meredith froze. She could hardly believe what had just happened. She was beyond horrified. Why was Julia, who she had known for four years, and with whom she had always had a good, working relationship, suddenly making this embarrassing and *very* unwelcome move on her? Had she been giving off the wrong signals? She tried to rally and force herself to think straight. Then a flash of anger swept over her, and giving her the energy and nerve to do what she knew she had to, she went to join Julia at the bar. Now was not the time to be sensitive and polite; some straight talking was needed. With a firm edge to her voice, she said, 'I've changed my mind. I'm off. And just so you know, I'm not in the least bit interested in doing any kind of experimenting!'

Julia sighed heavily. 'Aw! That's a shame. We could'a made sweet music, hun.'

'No, we could not!'

'You'll never know…'

'And I don't think I want to, thank you very much!' And with that, and feeling quite shaken, Meredith marched out.

Two figures sat at a table on the other side of the ballroom: Tom and his guest. Tom was enjoying the band, while his guest had been preoccupied studying the body language of the two women sitting opposite. It did not take a genius to guess at what had just happened.

'Glad you could come,' said Tom, gesturing at the stage, 'they're good, don't you think?'

'Yes, very professional,' replied his guest, watching Meredith's retreating figure, and realising just how very much God's love was needed in this place.

CHAPTER 9

The bus stop was situated just across the road from the camp's main entrance. Unusually, Meredith was waiting alone. She was relieved; she had a lot on her mind and was not in the mood to make polite small talk. From her vantage point, she watched the children's nannies attempting to keep control and load over a hundred excited children onto the double-decker bus, hired to take them to the circus. She smiled, imagining Wendy hurrying to close reception and make her escape before their return. Poor Tom, no doubt he would stay on to take the usual telephone call that would come later, asking him to come and collect the odd one or two strays that had carelessly been left behind.

She had thought long and hard about the horoscope issue, and had eventually decided to accept Kingsley's offer to pray about it with her. Now she was on her way. The bus came. The conductor took her fare, and she settled back and tried to sort out her feelings. The awkward scene in the ballroom had been upsetting, although Julia had been her usual friendly self when she came to collect the shop float the following morning. But the incident had left a bad taste in Meredith's mouth, and now she was beginning to experience feelings of guilt about the way she had handled the situation. Then there was Kingsley - and another puzzle. She was aware that she was keen to see him again, even if it was just for some prayer. Yes, she was keen; why else would she have taken such extra care over her appearance?

Doreen was already there when she arrived, and the two women chatted easily as Kingsley went off to take a phone call. In a way she was relieved that another person would be present; Reverend Thomas, the previous minister, always had his wife on hand whenever he needed to counsel a female member of the church. And she knew that Doreen would be discreet.

The counselling session that followed was as short as it was unremarkable. They began by looking up several Scriptures passages, and Meredith came to realise just where she had gone wrong. One in particular challenged her:-

> **When you arrive in the Promised Land you must be very careful not to be corrupted by the horrible customs of the nations now living there. For example, any Israeli who presents his child to be burned to death as a sacrifice to heathen gods, must be killed. No Israeli may practice black magic, or call on the evil spirits for aid, or be a fortune teller, or be a serpent charmer, medium, or wizard, or call upon the spirits of the dead. Anyone doing these things is an object of horror and disgust to the Lord, and it is because the nations do these things that the Lord your God will displace them. You must walk blamelessly before the Lord your God. The nations you replace all do these evil things, but the Lord your God will not permit you to do such things. (Deuteronomy 18:9-12).**

After a brief, but sincere, time of confession, she renounced her curiosity about the practice, and asked God to forgive her. Then she asked that He would be so gracious as to fill her again with His Holy Spirit. Finally, she thanked Him for His love and care.

Kingsley offered them both a lift when the session was over. Meredith refused, but changed her mind when Doreen, who lived just a few streets away from her parents' home, accepted. They were waving goodbye to her when he surprised her by asking if she was in a hurry. 'If you've not got any plans, how about joining me for another stroll along the beach? It's too nice to be shut in, and I could do with a bit of company.'

She agreed, trying not to sound too eager.

Ten minutes later, they parked the car and set off along the same stretch of beach they had walked along before. A handful of sunbathers lay dotted around, and a few children squealed excitedly as they ran in and out of the incoming tide.

'Should have thought there'd be more people about,' he remarked.

She looked at her watch. 'Most of the children are at the circus. The cricket knock-out will keep some of the men busy for a while, and a lot of the older folk will be at the tea dance, or the whist drive.'

'Spoilt for choice! Think I'd go for the cricket. So what else is happening today?'

'Well, let me see. There's always some sort of sports practice going on, especially in the pool, for the Gala, and later on there'll be the auditions for Friday's Farewell Concert.'

'And what happens tonight?'

'Children's film club, Adults' Fancy Dress, and then Jacko's Cabaret. He's very proud of his hair and likes to show it off every chance he gets, so he likes to squeeze in the Best Head of Hair Competition. He reckons he'd win every time if he wasn't staff.'

'He does have quite a mop. Seems to be a bit of a character too. Is he always so jolly?'

'Around the campers, yes, but he can be quite serious when they're not around; almost dour really.'

'I suppose a lot of your regular staff aren't the usual run-of-the-mill types? Can't be for everyone, spending half the year working on a holiday camp, then trying to keep themselves gainfully employed the other half.'

'Suppose not. Jacko used to work the winters on cruise ships, but now he finds what he can, mostly panto around

Christmas and New Year. The others end up doing hotel or bar work.'

'Hmm, a strange, nomadic way of life. That kind of existence must have some sort of effect on them. What about Tom, and that woman you work with in the office, Wendy, isn't it?'

'Tom's permanent, and Wendy and I only come in on the odd day to make up the booking registers and do any correspondence he may have.'

Two gulls screeched noisily overhead, excited and agitated by the sight of some tempting looking litter nearby.

'What do you do the rest of the time? It must be pretty dead around here when the camps are shut.'

'I go temping with that staff agency on the High Street, Man Power - you know the one, it's above Purdy's restaurant.'

A small black dog ran out of the water. It stopped close by them to shake its coat, spraying them liberally in the process.

'Thanks for that, Fido!' Kingsley laughed, brushing himself down. 'But I've already been baptised.' Then, returning to the subject, went on to ask, 'You must get to know the ones that come back every year quite well. Any special friendships amongst them?'

'No, not really. Although I get on okay with most of them, but they, you know, there's a fair bit of drinking...and other things that go on.'

'A lot of sleeping around?'

'Well, yes.'

'And, how does that make you feel? Being a Christian; living and working in that kind of environment?'

'It doesn't really affect me, especially now that I'm out of the staff corridor and in my own chalet.'

They skirted around the remains of a once impressive sand castle. He stooped to pick up a large fan-shaped shell that had been used to decorate the top of one of the crumbling towers, then offered it to her. 'But there must be times when you find yourself feeling concerned, or even uncomfortable?'

She accepted it and began wiping off the sand. 'Sometimes. Thanks.'

'I'll be honest with you Meredith, Tom invited me over the other night. I was there and saw what happened between you and Julia. We were sitting across from you. It looked like she was coming on to you a bit strong. I don't think anyone else noticed, certainly not Tom. You were well hidden behind that pillar.'

She took a step back, and for the second time in just a few days, found herself becoming horribly embarrassed as she blushed bright red, and stuttered, 'Oh, really? I…er…'

He smiled reassuringly. 'You know, I'm more than happy to listen, if you feel you'd like to talk about it.'

'Er, well…' she paused; maybe it wouldn't do any harm if she did confide in him. 'Actually, now you mention it, I think that she's…I have every reason to believe that she's a…a lesbian!' The word did not fall easily off her lips, unused as she was to saying it. 'And I think she was trying to, you know…'

'Chat you up?' he offered, helpfully.

'Yes. It was so…unexpected. Out of the blue! She's never done anything like that before. I often wondered…you know, she does dress differently sometimes. But she's always been okay with me, and never given me any reason to feel uncomfortable around her. I can't think why she should suddenly think that I'd be…interested. I'm afraid I was very abrupt. Well, I was shocked! Maybe I should have been a bit more sensitive about the way I handled it. And, to tell you the truth, I've been feeling a bit guilty about it ever since.'

He bent down again, this time picking up one of the pebbles that had been used to form part of a wall around the structure. He hurled it into the sea. 'Don't!'

'Don't what?'

'Feel guilty. Probably false guilt anyway. And it sounds like you were put on the spot. If anyone should feel guilty, it should be her. But let's think about this for a bit. You know, it could be that The Lord's at work here.'

'Really? How?'

'Well, we could see this as an opportunity for her to be reached for Him. There could be things going on with her if she's behaving out of character towards you; maybe she's had a recent upset. And remember, that none of us are beyond His love and care, no matter how confused we are about things, including our sexuality. He loves her just as much as He loves you and me.'

'You're saying that I should start talking to her about The Lord?' There was no mistaking the reluctance in her voice.

He nodded.

'But...where would I start? I can't just...I mean...'

'Don't worry too much about that. He'll guide you if it's His will. You just have to look out for any opportunity He gives you.'

By now they had reached the steps leading up to the café. She gave a small laugh, imagining what Julia's reaction would be at hearing the Gospel. 'Well, that'll do it! She'll probably steer clear of me forever!'

'Maybe, maybe not. You won't know unless you try.'

Reaching the top step, she confessed, 'But, Kingsley, I'm sorry, I really don't think I want to.'

'Are you sure? What did you just say, something about feeling guilty about the way you handled the situation?'

'Yes, but I've got no experience of this kind of thing, especially to...someone like her!'

'Perfect opportunity to get some then. After all, The Lord knew it was going to happen, and I wouldn't be surprised if He really does want to use you in the situation.' He held the café door open for her. 'And I may have a few pointers for you. Come on, let's see what we can come up with.'

60

CHAPTER 10

Customers chatted as the juke box played an old pop song. They bought tea and cake and went to sit by the window.

'You know, I'm quite liking this,' he commented.

She looked at him quizzically.

'Getting away from the phone,' he explained.

She nodded knowingly, 'I'm the same. I hear bells and tannoys in my sleep.'

'Hmm, must be difficult, you're surrounded by them, aren't you? By the way, I keep meaning to ask, have you thought any more about helping with the group?'

'Yes, I've done quite a bit of praying about it, and think I'd like to give it a go. That is, if you still think I'd be suitable.'

'Why wouldn't I?'

'You know, after the horoscope thing?'

'Oh, that!' Don't even think about it. Look upon it as a valuable lesson you've learned, and chalk it down to experience.'

His reassurance was all she needed. 'Well, if you're sure, then okay.'

'Hallelujah!' he exclaimed, tinkling his spoon against the side of his cup, and causing the nearby customers to glance their way. 'That's great. And I think it would be a good idea for you have a get-together with Doreen and Dave; I know they'll be relieved. Anyway, let's get back to your situation with Julia, and how to approach her. The thing to remember is that we have to be constantly on our guard against condemning, or condoning, such behaviour.'

'Condemning? You think I'm condemning her?'

'I don't know. Are you?'

'No! At least, I hope I'm not! Although, I must admit that I think that...that way of life must be very...unnatural.'

'More so than straight people who don't wait until marriage before having a sexual relationship?'

'Well, yes. That seems more...natural somehow.'

He surprised her by asking, 'Why?'

She wondered why he should even be asking her such a thing, and replied, feeling her face growing hot, 'You know, a man and a woman?'

'Unmarried, heterosexual sex is more excusable then? And less sinful than homosexual?'

She took a bite of her cake, then added, thoughtfully, 'Er, I suppose so. Although, I do remember how shocked I used to be about the way some people carried on when I first started at the camp.'

'And now you're unshockable when it comes to a man and a woman?'

She sensed some sort of trick question coming, and replied cautiously, 'Well, y-e-s.'

'And why doesn't it shock you now?'

'Well, I suppose I've just kind of...got used to it.'

'Hmm, that's often the way. But getting back to Julia, didn't you ever suspect that she was different?'

Relieved that his focus had shifted away from her, she replied, 'Maybe. There's always been some talk. And it's such a shame that this has happened; we've always got on so well.'

'And there's no reason you still shouldn't. Remember that she's just like you and me, just another sinner; only now you know that one of her particular sins is of a sexual nature.'

She was gaining in courage now, and asked, 'Why are you calling it a sin? She can't help it if she was born that way!'

He considered before replying. 'Sorry, I don't subscribe to that theory. We all have a tendency, or capacity, to give in to some things that can be...let's call them unnatural, or harmful. And for some it can be a lifelong battle.'

This was something of a surprise to Meredith, who, like those around her, had come to accept the usual excuses people gave about not being able to help themselves when they wanted to do things which were considered 'outside the norm.'

'Read **Genesis** again, Meredith,' he said. 'God created men and women to fit together with the express purpose of being fruitful - to have children. How can two people of the same sex achieve that goal without making use of a third party?'

Still unconvinced, she replied, 'I know that's what the Bible says, but things are different now; the world's moved on.'

'But isn't Jesus the same? Or don't you believe that His words stand forever? Does He need to "move on" too?'

'No, of course not!' she retorted, defensively.

'And His written Word, The Bible, does that need re-writing, modernising, with today's ethics? What about next year, or ten years' time, when things are different again? Another re-write? Then another ten years after that? Seems to be me that, the way things are going these days, if God wants to stick around, then He'll have to fit into our puny little box, and comply with our ever-changing standards.'

She sat and stared at him. Is that how she thought of God - as an ever-changing Being - Who needed to fit in with society's "ever-changing standards"? This would need some thinking about. Finding her voice again, she brought the conversation back to Julia. 'But I can't just go up to Julia and tell her she's a sinner!'

'Why? What's so special about her? Don't we all need telling at times, but in a timely and sensitive way? Isn't that how we came to realise how much we needed a Saviour? Remember what Paul says in Romans:-

Yes, all have sinned; all fall short of God's glorious ideal; yet now God declares us "not guilty" of offending him if we trust in Jesus

Christ, who in his kindness freely takes away our sins. *(Romans 3:23,24).*

Or do you think that some sins are more excusable than others?'

She needed a moment to think about that.

He pulled a small notebook out of his pocket and quickly wrote down some Bible references. 'Here, take a look at these when you get the chance.' He tore the page out and handed it to her. 'Sin's sin, Meredith. Jesus died and paid the price just as much for the smallest so-called misdemeanour as he did for the most heinous crime. And heterosexuals can be just as guilty of sexual sin as homosexuals. Monogamous, heterosexual sex between a male husband and a female wife is the only sexual relationship that God allows. Those with homosexual tendencies are called to live by the same set of rules as us singles: to remain celibate. Depending upon our nature, we're all tempted, some more than others, but that's no excuse to give in.'

He noticed now how serious, even browbeaten, she was looking, and immediately regretted his outburst. 'Darn it! I'm sorry, Meredith. Slipped into preaching mode, haven't I? You'll have to stop me when I do it. Just tell me to shut up!'

He was relieved when she gave him a winsome smile. 'Okay. If you insist. But I can't think why I haven't thought it all through before.'

'Don't feel bad. But I don't think there'd be any harm in letting Julia know you're still her friend, and only want the best for her, although you'll probably have to be patient; this may be unchartered territory for her. The last thing she needs is to feel rejected. I'm not suggesting that you give her any special treatment. We need to treat all people with care and sensitivity; we need to respect all people, whatever their sexual appetite and orientation.'

'Yes, I suppose that's fair enough.'

'And gently does it. In time, you might even be able to ask her along to church, or, if she chokes at that, then maybe along to one of the film nights.'

She shook her head, and remarked, 'I can't see her wanting to come anywhere near a church!'

'Maybe. But who's to say how she'll feel further down the line? Maybe she'll look back and remember how you were with her: a Christian who didn't judge, but held out the hand of friendship; someone who was prepared to listen to her. It's a shame the same couldn't have been done for those youngsters who were sacked over doing the Ouija board. I'd like to have tried to help them. They need Him just as much as Julia does.'

'Yes, I thought Tom was a bit quick there.'

'Has a tendency to shoot from the hip then, does he?'

'Sometimes. But he's got a lot on his plate now that the season's started, and I know he's not been sleeping too well. And when he heard that thing say…what it did…about a baby, and what with his wife being due any day, I suppose he just overreacted, and blew his top!'

'Understandable. I find it challenging enough just caring for the fellowship.'

She laughed. 'Well, it's a good job you're not responsible for entertaining and feeding us all twenty four hours a day as well then!'

'Huh! Try telling tell the manse phone that! Anyway, what do you say? Going to give it a go with Julia? Remember, I'm here if you need any backup.'

She studied his face. His words had not only challenged, but touched her. She knew he was right - absolutely right - but what he was suggesting, or rather asking of her, was not going to be easy, and well outside her experience. Still, if he was going to be there for her, 'Okay. I'll give it a try.'

'Good for you! And try not to force things. Just be natural, be yourself. And remember, she's just another soul Jesus died for, and loves very much. Be prepared to be rejected, although it won't really be you she'll be rejecting, but Him. And now I think a change of subject is needed. Tell me more about life on the camp, and what your parents think of having a daughter working there? From what I've seen of them, they're kind of conservative.'

And so the rest of their time passed quickly and pleasantly enough, all thoughts of people's sexual appetites and tendencies pushed to the back of her mind as she graphically described some of the more dramatic and amusing experiences she had had over the past ten years.

He thanked her as they strolled back to the car, then made her heart skip a beat when he added, 'Thanks for this, Meredith, I've enjoyed myself. We should do it again sometime.'

Had she heard right? Had he really asked her out on a date? 'Yes, I'd like that,' she replied, feeling that that might well turn out to be the understatement of the century.

Later, alone in her room, she took out the note he gave her, and opened her Bible:-

Don't you know that those doing such things have no share in the Kingdom of God? Don't fool yourselves. Those who live immoral lives – who are idol worshippers, adulterers or homosexuals – will have no share in his kingdom. Neither will thieves, or greedy people, drunkards, slanderers, or robbers. There was a time when some of you were just like that, but now your sins are washed away, and you are set apart for God, and He has accepted you because of what the Lord Jesus Christ and the Spirit of our God have done for you.
(1 Corinthians 6:9-11).

For all these worldly things, these evil desires—the craze for sex, the ambition to buy everything that

appeals to you, and the pride that comes from wealth and importance—these are not from God. They are from this evil world itself. *(1 John 2:16)*.

For God wants you to be holy and pure, and to keep clear of all sexual sin so that each of you will marry in holiness and honour...
(1 Thessalonians 4:3-4).

'Oh Julia!' she thought, kneeling to pray. And then she found she needed to pray for someone else just as much - herself.

CHAPTER 11

By eight o'clock it was already 74°F, and it seemed that everyone wanted to get wet, either in the pool or in the sea. Keen to make the most of the gift of such a warm morning, many of the campers turned up for breakfast already wearing swimwear beneath their cardigans and jackets. Uncle Jacko announced that the children's nannies would be supervising games down on the beach as soon as breakfast was over, whilst he would be organising games around the shaded area by the pool.

Tom left the relative calm of his office to come and join Meredith and Wendy for mid-morning coffee. As usual, Wendy opened her magazine and went straight to the horoscopes.

'Look at this! *Aries could have a surprise visitor this week.* She looked over at Tom and grinned, 'Could be the baby!'

He gave a low moan, 'More likely to be the mother-in-law; she's threatening to come any day now.'

Wendy looked aghast; she was still trying to get over Hilda Rodden's last visit. 'She won't be coming in here again, will she?'

'Who knows?' he replied. 'She'll need something else to have a go at me about. Anyway, what's it say about you two?'

'Oh, haven't you heard? Meri's not interested in it anymore. According to her, it's nothing but a load of superstitious nonsense! Says the people who write them are listening to the wrong power or something, or just taking educated guesses - law of averages - something like that anyway. It's that Kingsley, he's warned her off.'

'Is that right?' he asked, turning to Meredith.

She gave him a knowing look, willing him to recognise the unspoken meaning of what she was just about to say. Neither had discussed the Ouija board problem in any detail with Wendy, and she was reluctant to go anywhere near the subject again.

'Well, go on then! Tell him what he said,' persisted Wendy.

Meredith spoke up. 'It seems that some people are able to hear…forces that aren't particularly friendly, no matter how innocent or benevolent they appear to be.'

Tom frowned, a look of understanding crossing his face, and asked, 'And he reckons that people who write these horoscopes are listening to…those forces, and that's where they get their…information from?'

'Afraid so. There's evidence that some easily led and vulnerable people have been drawn into trying other forms of the occult after being taken in by putting too much store in their horoscopes.'

'Occult, my foot!' exclaimed Wendy. 'He's a real spoil sport. Everyone knows they're just bit of fun.'

Tom scowled as Catherine Frith's dark, diminutive form and pale features crossed his mind. Where had her unhealthy obsession with the occult started? Could it really have been with something as innocuous as reading her horoscope? Had she thought of it as 'just a bit of fun' too? He remembered his Granny, a harmless old soul, who regularly did regular tea leaf and tarot readings in her front parlour for family and friends - and had no doubt that she would have progressed to the Ouija Board if one had come her way. He sighed, nodding, his mind made up. 'Well, I reckon Kingsley knows what he's about, and I suppose it's better to be safe than sorry.'

Wendy was aghast. 'What…you mean…you don't want to hear yours any more either?'

'Reckon I can live without it,' he replied.

'Well, honestly!' she exclaimed, looking from one to the other, 'You're both mad!' Then, as a thought struck her, went on to ask, 'Hey, you don't honestly think I take it seriously, do you?'

'I hope you don't Wendy,' said Meredith, 'but it probably wouldn't do you any harm to do a sort of check on yourself every so often, you know, just to make sure.'

'Check! How?'

Meredith shrugged, 'Well, I suppose you could find yourself doing something, or maybe even avoiding something, just because of what it says.'

Wendy harrumphed loudly, remembering when she had once seriously thought about cancelling a weekend away because her horoscope had hinted that 'she could experience a disappointing end to the week'. She had to almost force herself to go, and everything had worked out just fine. So, that proved that she wasn't taking the thing seriously, didn't it? She smiled slyly at Meredith, 'You know, I think you've got a thing for that minister. Go on, admit it! Mind you, I wouldn't blame you if you had; he is a bit of alright.'

'Careful now!' said Tom. 'Don't let your Neville hear you talking like that.'

'I don't know what you mean! He's a great minister, and I'm not the only one who thinks so,' replied Meredith, sounding just a bit too defensive.

Wendy wasn't going to let her get away with that, and remarked, 'Come off it, Meri! Someone as good-looking as that. I've seen you out there, gazing at his photo on the board. I reckon you'd jump in the lake if he told you to.'

The reception bell pinged at the same time as Wendy's phone rang. Meredith stood, and leaving the office, gave Wendy a look of mock innocence. 'Good-looking? Do you think so? I'll have to take a good look next time I see him.' Then, she added quietly, 'And what would be so wrong with

taking a quick dip in the lake, especially if it was a hot day?'
But it was only Tom who heard her.

CHAPTER 12

She chose her long cotton dress that night; the light cream and green leaf pattern always looked cool and fresh, and it washed well. The ballroom was full when she walked in at twenty-five minutes past seven: five minutes before the prize giving was due to start. She knew that Jacko's team would be busy arranging an assortment of children's games, puzzles, boxes of chocolates, and bottles of wine and spirits, on one of the long trestle tables behind the stage. Loud cheers and applause broke out as he emerged. He cracked a few jokes, all of which she had heard many times before, then he began the rollcall of prize winners. A succession of children climbed the steps at the side of the stage. They responded with painfully shy whispers, or clear, confident voices, to his comments and questions. As usual, Meredith began to feel uncomfortable at a few of his remarks, some of which contained barely concealed sexual innuendoes. However, tonight, as on every other night, the campers appeared not to share her misgivings as they laughed and clapped with their usual gusto. She knew that there would be no point in mentioning anything about it to Tom; he would only tell her to 'lighten up' again.

The interval followed, and the younger children were taken off to their beds. Then the Campers' Farewell Concert started. This was one of the week's highlights, and Meredith had come to the conclusion that the opportunity to shine in the spotlight for a few minutes was the only reason why some campers came. The programme contained the usual mixture of talented - and some not so talented - home-grown novelty acts, singers, dancers, musicians and magicians. Drag acts had started to appear in recent years, and were usually of the comical, pantomime dame variety. However, tonight's performance turned out to be something altogether different. A young male camper had decided to surprise his unsuspecting fiancée, and appear as the incongruously named 'Luscious Lulu'.

The act started. An elegantly gloved hand, followed by a long, fishnet stockinged leg, complete with suspenders, began to writhe seductively from behind the side curtain to the strains of Shirley Bassey's *Big Spender*. The noise of cheers, cat calls and wolf whistles coming from the audience was almost deafening. Satisfied that he had won the crowd's full attention, the young man slinked into full view, miming, and resplendent in a long, dark wig; his face heavily made up, his tall, slim body wrapped in a black kimono, adorned with a dramatic, gold coloured Chinese dragon across the back. Balancing expertly on a pair of extremely high and dangerous looking stiletto heels, he appeared to be very comfortable as he strutted from table to table, pouting, posing, and stroking some of the men's faces as he perched and wriggled tauntingly on their laps.

Well into the act, he slowly opened the kimono to reveal a mini black, see-through negligee, under which he wore a black, lacy bra, copiously stuffed with wads of tissues, and a pair of almost indecent skimpy knickers. Those who knew who his fiancée was, and where she was sitting, forced themselves to look away from the scene and look over in her direction, expecting her to be enjoying the spectacle as much as they were. However, it soon became obvious that she was not being 'a good sport', and that, in fact, she was feeling nothing but acute shock and deep embarrassment. But it was not until she saw the negligee and underwear - *her* negligee and underwear that she had spent a whole week's wages on, for this, their first holiday away together - that her shock quickly turned into anger. Either her fiancé had not noticed her reaction, or had chosen not to - so engrossed was he in his own world - when, with tears of bitter disappointment and mortification streaming down her face, she ran sobbing from the ballroom.

Meredith hoped that someone would follow and try to calm and comfort her, and would have gone herself, had it not been for the fact that she was expected to be on the stage for the grand finalé, due to start at any minute.

❖

She was talking to Julia in reception the next morning, when the young man, now soberly dressed, and seemingly untroubled, came to hand in the chalet key.

'He'd have done better to open that kimono earlier in the act; he'd probably have won then.' Julia commented, watching his departing figure. 'There's no justice in the world. Someone told me they saw his girlfriend drive off in a taxi after the show. Silly woman!'

'Hmm,' replied Meredith, putting the shop float on the counter, and unwilling to enter into any discussion about the unhappy incident.

'I told him he's got flair and should try and get a few gigs in some of the clubs.' Noticing Meredith's closed expression, she went on to ask, 'I suppose you didn't approve?'

'Actually, I felt sorry for his fiancée. She looked mortified.'

'Oh, go on! You can't tell me she wasn't in on it!'

'It didn't look like that from where I was sitting.'

Julia took a step back and covered her mouth with her hands, a look of mock horror in her eyes. 'Oh no! He couldn't be one of those freaky cross-dressers? A tranny! A bi-sexual! To think that such people exist and are walking around among us. It's too awful! They're not fit to be around decent people. Take 'em out and lynch 'em all, I say!'

'What's going on out there?' Wendy's voice rang out. 'Is that you, Julia, causing trouble again?'

Julia called back, 'What, little old me? God forbid!'

'It's alright, Wendy,' said Meredith. 'She's just being daft.'

'Well, tell her to go and be daft somewhere else! I've got those spasms back, and we're out of aspirin.'

'I've got some in the shop,' Julia called, picking up the float tin. 'I'll leave you in peace, Meri. After all, you don't want to be contaminated by someone as unnatural as me, do you? You might catch something!'

Meredith watched her go, dismayed. Like a rubber ball, it seemed that her problem with Julia had bounced right back. Kingsley's advice about being prepared to understand and listen to her began to ring in her head. He was right, but the doing of it wasn't going to be easy, and she had been putting it off for weeks now. Was this the opportunity he told her to look out for? If so, how much she needed The Lord's guidance and wisdom, because she really felt she had none of her own.

Julia reappeared a few minutes later and placed a packet of aspirin on the counter. 'Don't suppose you've got a spare handbell back there, have you?' she asked.

'No. Why?'

'I need to ring it to warn people to stand clear. Unclean...unclean!'

That settled it. Meredith spoke up, 'Actually, Julia, I've been doing some thinking, and there's something I'd like to...say to you. Maybe at break - in the cafe? You have yours at half past ten, don't you?'

Julia was obviously taken aback. Then she gave one of her slow smiles. 'Mystery woman, eh? I like that. Sure thing, hun. Half ten it is. I'll look forward to it.'

Just over two hours later, and with some trepidation, Meredith entered the café. Despite all the busyness of the morning, she had found time to send up a few quick prayers, and now she felt as ready as she would ever be. She bought her coffee and went to sit at one of the tables. She looked over in the direction of the shop and watched Julia waiting patiently for a toddler to make up his mind over what colour water wings he wanted. Yellow was decided upon and the purchase made.

Only seven minutes of Meredith's break remained by the time Julia was able to hand over to the barmaid who came to relieve her. She arrived carrying a can of Coca-Cola. Today she was dressed in one of her extra-short mini-dresses, mustard coloured, which effectively set off the brown tones of her fashionably bouffant styled hair. A waft of Yves Saint Laurent perfume reached Meredith, and her mouth became suddenly dry, making her opening statement sound forced, even to her own ears.

'Thanks for coming Julia. I've been thinking about things, and feel I need to say how sorry I am about the way I reacted to you in the ballroom the other night. Don't get me wrong, I haven't changed my mind about things; it's just that you took me by surprise, and I feel that I could have handled things a bit better.'

Julia's pencilled-in eyebrows arched high. 'Hey, hun! What's all this? Saying sorry? You'll have to do better than that!'

Meredith was momentarily nonplussed. 'Better than that? How, what do you mean?'

Julia stared unblinking at her. 'You should know that I don't think much of sorry's; they're just a cop-out. You know the old saying, "Actions speak louder than words." You're going to have to prove yourself, hun, and show me that you really mean it.'

'"That I really mean it!" Of course I do. I *really am* sorry!'

'Are you?'

'Yes, I am!'

'Okay then, prove it. Come to Norwich with me on your next day off.'

'What?'

'You heard me.'

'But why? What's in Norwich?'

Julia leaned towards her, and with a low and husky voice, replied, 'Oh, you'd be surprised!'

Meredith began to feel very uncomfortable, and said quickly, 'Er, no. I don't think so.'

'Chicken! Too scared to even try?'

'Look, Julia, you'll have to believe me, I'm just not interested in…anything like that.'

Julia sat back abruptly. 'Oh come off it! What the hell do you take me for? If you weren't *interested* you wouldn't be here now. You know what I think? I think you are interested, but you're too bloody stubborn to admit it. Come on, stop wasting my time. Take it from me, little girl, it feels good. Now why don't you be a brave little bunny, and give it a try? And you're lucky, I can teach you everything you need to know, *and* introduce you to some very cool people.'

Things were definitely not going the way Meredith had hoped. Instead of accepting her apology, and allowing her to introduce something of her own world and 'cool people', Julia was actively trying, once again, to involve her in her own mixed up, clandestine way of life. Still, she persevered. 'Julia! Will you please stop it, and get it into your head that I'm definitely not interested in any of your…activities.'

'Is that so?'

'Yes, that is so!'

'Oh yeah?'

'Yes. All I wanted to do was apologise, and tell you about something…about Someone else.'

'"Someone else?" What "Someone else?"'

'Someone who *really* loves you. But with a pure, wholesome kind of love.'

Julia finished her drink. She stared hard at Meredith, as, with one hand, she slowly crushed the empty can. The act felt threatening. 'Now, why've I got a feeling this has got something to do with that religion of yours? Am I right?'

'Well, yes.' Meredith's confidence dipped even lower.

Julia threw her head back and laughed. A loud, coarse laugh, but one which somehow did not contain any humour.

'Aw Gawd! Here we go! The Bloody God squad's after me at last! Good grief, hun! I know you're a religious crank, but come off it! You can't go around talking like that; they'll lock you up in the loony bin.' She laughed again, then winked broadly, 'But don't worry, I'd come and visit you.'

Meredith rallied. 'You're not being fair Julia. If you were serious, and wanted to explain about your…way of life to me, I'm sure you'd expect me to listen without mocking or insulting you. All I'm asking is that you do the same for me.'

Julia needed a few seconds to think about that. Then she replied, 'Suppose you've got a point, hun. But don't you know how crazy you sound? You really can't go around the place spouting all that religious crap.'

'Crazy? What's so crazy about me wanting to tell you about God, and how much He loves you?'

'Nothing, except that I'd find a church if I wanted to hear crap like that.'

'But I'm trying to help you Julia! Can't you understand? I'm only trying to tell you about another way, another type of life. And one that's good and wholesome.'

'And what I'm asking you to try isn't?'

This was a direct challenge. Meredith knew she must not back down now, but before she could reply, Julia continued, 'And who said that the way I choose to live isn't "good and wholesome"? Your God's supposed to be all for love, isn't He? I'd have thought He'd be only too happy that some of us enjoy spreading it around!'

'No, not your kind of…love. What you're involved with is wrong, it's…unnatural.'

'Oh yeah! And who says so? Some old farts at that church of yours? Well hun, let me tell you, some of them probably did a bit of *loving* of their own when they still had a bit of life left in 'em!'

'That's not very kind of you. And it's *you* we're talking about now, not anyone else.'

Quick as a flash, Julia took hold of Meredith's hand and held it firmly in her own. 'I'm not going to get anywhere with you, am I? You're determined. A lost cause then?'

Relieved, although forcing herself to keep her hand trapped, Meredith nodded. 'That's right. We can all look for affection in some strange places; anywhere but where we should.' She tried not to wince as she felt her hand being almost crushed.

'Sorry, but you won't shift me, hun. Affection's in short supply these days, and I'll grab it anyhow and anywhere I can.' At last, she let go of her hand. Meredith flexed and curled her fingers as she glanced at the overhead clock. 'You'd better run off now, hun. You don't want to be late and break any rules now, do you? Or it's hellfire and damnation for you too!' She gave another, mirthless laugh.

'Is that what you think? Is that where you think you're going to end up?'

'Who knows? Who cares?'

'But that's what I've been trying to tell you, there *is* Someone.'

'No, not for me, hun. You're wasting your time, and mine. Now, go on. Off with you! I've heard enough claptrap for one day. I'm needing some peace now.'

Sighing heavily and deeply disappointed, Meredith stood and walked away, knowing that not only had she failed, but she had failed miserably.

The Gospel Service was well attended the next morning. This time Meredith was unable to get away and discover what all the clapping and cheering was about, but made a mental note to ask Kingsley about it later. Obviously in high spirits, Julia's laugh could be heard above the chatter of campers as they filed out of the ballroom and into the lobby afterwards.

Kingsley emerged a few minutes later. Seeing the long queue beginning to form at reception, he changed his mind about having a few words with Meredith, and headed for the main doors instead. 'Will we be seeing you tonight?' he called over to her.

'Yes, I'll be there,' she called back.

He waved and hurried away, and was just about to drive off when someone tapped on his rear window. It was Julia. 'Hello, have I left something behind?' he asked, winding his window down.

'No, but I'm glad I've caught you. It...it's just that I was in the shop and heard bits of what you were saying, and I...er...I feel I need to talk to someone. You know, you said we could come and talk to you? Only I've got a bit of a ...problem. I know I don't go to your church, but I don't suppose you'd have some spare time you could give me?'

He did some quick thinking as he studied her face, which he found extremely attractive, in fact, if it wasn't for the slightly lopsided angle of her mouth, she could almost have been described as being beautiful. And there were shades of Deborah about her colouring. She sounded sincere enough, and if this was a genuine cry for help, then he must do what he could for her. Obviously she wasn't too keen on talking to Meredith; understandable, but a pity.

'Yes, alright. Will you let me get back to you - to arrange something? I don't have my diary on me just now.'

He went to sit beside Meredith in the manse lounge before the group got under way that evening.

'Just thought you'd like to know that Julia's asked if she can come and have a chat with me.'

'Really? I am surprised! Especially after the way she was with me yesterday.'

'What do you mean?'

'Well, I had a few words with her, you know, like we spoke about, and she didn't sound at all interested; in fact, quite the opposite.'

'Kingsley, can you come and tell Michael that he's being a real dope, and that we're all going to help with the open-airs?' Once again, it was Fleur who had found it necessary to interrupt them.

'In a minute, Fleur. I'm busy,' said Kingsley.

The young woman pouted and dropped her shoulders dramatically. 'Yeah, but...'

'We'll be discussing it later.'

'When, before the prayer time? You know he always clears off before that,' she persisted.

Kingsley sighed, 'Yes, before then. And Fleur, you know, you really must stop interrupting me like this when I'm talking to someone.'

She glanced at Meredith. 'But you're always talking to someone.'

'Yes, and it's often to you, young lady!' he replied, a firm note in his voice.

She smiled coquettishly, then began wriggling and twisting her foot a little too close to his. 'Yeah, well, I need a lot of talking to.'

He nodded his head slowly at her, 'You're going to have to get used to being talked to as much as everybody else - and no more. Now, off you go!'

Knowing she was beaten, she flounced off, but not before tossing her head in Meredith's direction, and exclaiming, 'You spoke to *her* last week!'

'Yes, and I'll be speaking to her again next week too, and you, but only if you remember your manners.'

He turned his attention back to Meredith. 'You were saying - about Julia?'

Meredith watched Fleur go up to Dave and interrupt the conversation he was having with Jennifer. 'Well, I tried to apologise for the way I overreacted the other night, then I said I wanted to tell her about another type of love, but she

81

wouldn't listen. She just fobbed me off and called me a religious crank, and said I was sounding crazy.'

He did not respond immediately. Several seconds passed, before he asked, 'Do you think you went in a bit heavy?'

'Heavy? Maybe. I certainly feel that I failed, and miserably.'

He recalled Julia's concerned expression when she had stopped him after the Gospel Service. 'Not necessarily. She could have felt challenged.'

'Well, that didn't stop her from trying it on with me again!'

'What! You mean she made another pass at you?' he asked, surprised now.

'Afraid so. And that's why I felt justified in saying that she was looking for affection in all the wrong places, and that she could experience a more wholesome kind of love with God.'

He smiled.

'But I did add that she would want me to listen to her if she tried to explain about her way of life, and that I was only asking the same of her.'

'Did you indeed? And what did she have to say to that?'

They were interrupted again when Dave called, 'We're ready, Kingsley.'

'One second,' he replied, standing. 'We'd better get started. And take heart, Meredith. It sounds like you may have made some impact after all. By the way, Dave's suggested you meet up with him and Doreen sometime this week to see what's involved with planning for the group.'

'Okay, I'll arrange something with them afterwards.'

'Excellent. And well done for trying with Julia, I know it couldn't have been easy.'

CHAPTER 13

Tom received the long awaited call from a panicking Sue, informing him that her waters had broken and that she was starting to bleed. All he wanted to do now was get her to the hospital; he was well used to all the back roads, and would be able to get her there faster than any ambulance. Jacko, his official Number Two, was calling the bingo, and due to an exceptionally high number of children on camp that week, all four children's nannies had been required down on the beach Still, he must go. Grabbing his keys, he instructed Wendy and Meredith to inform Jacko about the situation, and left.

Wendy became agitated. She began to fidget unnecessarily with the already tidy stationery cupboard and anything else that she felt needed tidying up.

'What's the matter?' Meredith asked her restless colleague.

'Oh Meri! I…I don't know if I should tell you. It's awful!'

'What is?'

'I…no! I can't tell you.'

'For goodness sake, what is it? You're worrying me. Tell me Wendy, please!'

'Well, alright. But you've got to promise you won't go off the deep end at me? It's alright for you, but…you know me, I like to look at it. And it said something bad was going to happen to Tom this week. I didn't tell him, I couldn't. Not something like that!'

'Are you talking his horoscope?'

Wendy nodded. Her expression grim, as she opened her desk drawer and took out the magazine. Folding it at the appropriate place, she passed it over to Meredith. 'Look at Cancer.'

Meredith pushed it away. She had promised The Lord that she would never again look at another horoscope. 'I'd rather not Wendy.'

Exasperated, Wendy grabbed the magazine back. 'Oh, for goodness sake! Listen, just listen to this.' She began to read:-

Try not to let your emotions get the better of you this week, especially towards the end, even though something out of the ordinary and out of your control could happen. Someone close to you may need your support. The week could end badly. You must be brave and do your best to stay focused.

'And you think it's about Sue, and the baby?'

'What else could it be? Oh Meri, what if, you know, things go wrong? She's bleeding! It says he'll need to support her and be brave...'

'Stop it Wendy!' Meredith had heard enough. Then, trying to sound reassuring, added quickly, 'It's probably written by one of those people who get their information from a bad source anyway.'

'But even *you've* got to admit that it's a coincidence! Why *this* week? And she's not due for another four days. Anything could go wrong!'

Grateful now that Wendy had not been told any of the finer details of the incident with the Ouija board, Meredith persisted. 'It's probably just one of those things. And I was a month prem, and I came out okay. I'm sorry, Wendy, but you can't convince me that there's anything in it.'

Sighing, Wendy threw herself back down on her chair. 'Well, I hope you're right. I wouldn't mind it being proven wrong this time.'

'Look, the best thing we can do for Tom now is to make sure things keep running smoothly here. The bingo's nearly over. Why don't you go and tell Jacko?'

Wendy shook her head and shuddered dramatically. 'No, you do it, Meri. I can't face him; he'll just start cracking some of those stupid old jokes of his.'

It was to be another fifteen minutes before the crowd of bingo players emerged from the ballroom. Meredith went off in search of Jacko and found him downing his first pint of the day by the bar.

'Poor old Tom!' he exclaimed at hearing the news, 'Nothing but bottles, belching and stinky brown blobs for him from now on. He'll be the knife and troll of the party. And I'll keel over if I don't get another smoke. Do us a favour, and do the round. I'll call into the office after the quiz.'

Somehow Meredith wasn't too surprised; she knew this was how things were going to be.

A serious looking game was being played on the tennis court. She walked over to the cliff edge and looked down. At least a dozen children's heads were bobbing up and down as they bounced energetically on a cluster of trampolines. Another group were enacting some sort of pirate game nearby, and relay races were being supervised further along the beach. Then she noticed a toddler, paddling alone in the sea. She called out to the nearest nanny, who ran over and pulled the child safely back from the incoming tide. Relieved and thanking The Lord, she carried on with the round. The crazy golf pitch was deserted. There were some empty benches nearby, and she decided that a few more minutes in the fresh air wouldn't hurt. She sat and began to pray earnestly for Sue, the baby, and for Tom.

The quiz was going on in the ballroom when she returned to the main building, but it wasn't Jacko's voice calling out the questions, but Murphy's. She found Jacko perched on the edge of her desk when she went back into the office.

Wendy was talking, '...he'll need more time than that if things go wrong.'

'Yeah, but then she'll have to stay in. He might as well come back. It'll take his mind off things.'

'Why?' asked Meredith, 'What's so important that you can't cover for him? He hardly ever takes a day off in the season, and you know he'll come back the minute he can.'

Jacko held his always too-long nails up for inspection, then said nonchalantly, 'Got a chance of a winter season in Blackpool. Have to be there for talks over the weekend, and he already knows about it.'

'Tricky! Who'll cover for you then?' asked Wendy.

'I've had my eye on our Murphy for a while now. The girls like the look of him, and he's got a way with the old biddies. I've sounded him out, and he's up for it.' Then, knowing that the two women would have much to ask him about this, as well as plenty of other things he didn't want to discuss, he stood, and added, 'Anyway, can't hang around here all day, chewing the cud with you two. You know where I'll be, Donkey Derbying all afternoon. Find me - if you dare!' And with that, he exited the office, calling a loud, nonsensical greeting to a group of campers passing reception.

The two women looked at each other and sighed in unison. 'Looks like I shan't be taking my day off this week, nor my half-day,' said Meredith.

'I'll skip my half-day as well,' added Wendy. 'But I'll have to check with Neville about my day off, I know he's got plans.'

❖

Tom telephoned later that afternoon.

Wendy took the call. 'Tom! How are things? Is Sue okay?' she asked, a note of real concern in her voice. 'And what about the baby?'

'Grand, grand! She's a real trouper!'

'And the baby?' She stood and signalled to Meredith to come back into the office as soon as she had finished in reception.

'A girl! A beautiful, bouncing baby girl. Ten toes, ten fingers. All there. She's beautiful, *so* beautiful. Perfect!'

'Oh Tom, how wonderful! Oh, I'm so relieved. And Sue managed okay then?'

Meredith came hurrying in. Wendy whispered the news to her.

Tom's exultant voice could be heard clearly through the receiver. 'She had it a bit rough. They had to do a caesarean; something to do with the heartbeat. But she's fine. Just groggy.'

Obviously in need of more reassurance, Wendy went on to ask, 'And everything really is fine - mother and baby?'

'Grand, grand! She came out bright red, but they said that's nothing to worry about; it should calm down soon. And they reckon that Sue'll be up and about in a few days. Everything's marvellous, wonderful, *fantastic!* I can't believe I'm a daddy now, even if it is to a Red Indian.'

Wendy laughed. 'A-a-ah! You'll grow into it.'

'Anyway, how are things there?' he asked.

Wendy told him about Jacko and his proposal about Murphy.

'To be fair, he did tell me about the trip to Blackpool. It just went out of my head. I'll have a chat with him when I call in tomorrow. I'll need to sign some cheques. And can you ask Meri to make up the wages in the morning?'

'Will do.'

'Thanks Wendy. Better get going. Got a daughter to check up on! See you tomorrow.'

She replaced the receiver and sat back heavily in her chair. 'Well, thank God! All that panic had me worried, I can tell you.'

Meredith could have said so much; instead she patted her colleague's hand, and went through into Tom's office to deal with the rest of the post. But first she wanted to thank Jesus for answered prayer, and for the miracle of another baby - safely delivered into the world.

CHAPTER 14

Kingsley was standing at the bar with Julia when she walked into the ballroom a few evenings later. Meredith looked as surprised as she felt when she walked over to say hello.

'Meredith, good. I was hoping to bump into you,' he said. 'We didn't see you at church this Sunday?'

'I'm having to do a few extra nights here,' she explained. 'Tom's off: his wife's had the baby. He comes in during the day, but likes to visit her in the evenings.'

'Yes, Julia tells me they're doing well. That's good news.'

'Very good news. He's hoping to bring them home in a few days. Anyway, you'll have to excuse me. I'm doing the rounds and only popped in for a second.'

'Will we be seeing you later?'

'Maybe. Enjoy the competition. Oh, and it's just as well you aren't wearing your dog collar.'

'Why's that?'

'You might have found yourself in the line-up. Not everyone knows you're a local vicar.'

Julia laughed, then flashed Kingsley a brilliant smile. 'Shame, you could have won! I think the first prize is a cheap bottle of plonk.'

'Darn it! Wish I'd have known. Missed out again,' he said.

Meredith returned to the ballroom fifteen minutes later and noticed the pair sitting together at a table. Obviously something had amused them, they were laughing almost uncontrollably. Julia wasn't dressed in her black trouser suit, nor was her hair scraped back severely; tonight she was in her softer, feminine persona. Meredith told herself not to think too much about it as she took more change over to the bar. After all, Kingsley was only her minister, and a free agent, and Julia was - exactly what *was* Julia? Someone who, how had she put it - liked to 'experiment, swing both ways, and enjoy the best of both worlds'? Still, it was with a growing sense of disappointment, even some unease, that she left a minute later - without looking in their direction again.

❖

'The Eiffel Tower should have won; a lot more work obviously went into it, and it was definitely more technically accurate than the Stonehenge entry,' he commented, sounding almost disappointed.

She had joined Kingsley at his table some time later. Julia was busily snapping away across the room. 'I'm afraid they do tend to be patriotic.'

'Some of them must have spent a lot of time and effort on their costumes.'

'Yes, and there's always a few who take the whole thing very seriously, which is a shame, considering the prizes they get: just a bottle of wine, or a box of chocolates.'

'Hmm, all that human effort for very little earthly reward. Anyway, Meredith, you must be wondering what I'm doing here?'

'Er, well actually I was a bit surprised to see you, and with Julia.'

'She cornered me as soon as I walked in.'

'Yes, she seemed pleased to see you. Have you been able to meet up with her yet?'

'This morning. I think it went okay. Couldn't have been too bad because she's agreed to come again.'

By now Julia had worked her way across to them, and came to stand in front of their table; one hand on her hip and a camera hanging from a long strap around her neck. 'Phew! I'm bushed,' she exclaimed, pulling up a chair. 'And I've got a thirst that would shame a camel.'

'Well I'm ready for another. What can I get you both?' Kingsley asked, standing.

'You're an angel. Bacardi and Coke on the rocks, and hurry back, I'm dying on my feet.'

'Nothing for me thanks, I got to go in a minute,' replied Meredith.

The two women watched him walk over to the bar.

'He's a nice guy. A real looker too.'

'Yes,' agreed Meredith, 'and busy.'

'Good of him to agree to spend some of his precious time trying to sort little old me out then. Has he told you I went to see him today?'

'He did mention it. How did it go?'

'Well, okay.' She shrugged, not sounding too impressed. 'But I can't see how anything in that Bible of his will persuade me to change my ways. It's all he could talk about. Think I'll tell him to save his breath, and find another tack.'

'You won't get anywhere. It's where he gets his main inspiration from.'

'That's silly of him!'

'Why?'

'Well, correct me if I'm wrong, but wasn't it written by *mere* men anyway?'

'Yes. Why? Do you have a problem with that?'

'Too right I do! Talk about it being a man's world.'

'What have you got against men anyway?'

'Nothing. Except that every sensible woman knows that there's only two things wrong with them: everything they say, and everything they do! And, let's face it, they are the weaker sex.'

'Do you really think so?'

She shrugged again, 'Been my experience.'

Meredith thought about her father. Then she thought of Kingsley, and Dave, and many others she had known throughout the years. Wise, Godly men. 'But the men who wrote the Bible, they were all inspired by God.'

Julia frowned, 'Oh yeah! Forgot about Him. Another *male*.' She sneered the word. 'Why couldn't He have used women? Aren't they capable of being *inspired*? Or does He have it in for them as well?'

'You're forgetting the culture of the day; women didn't write books then, not like now. And there's loads of Christian books out there written by women.'

'Where?'

'Around, in Christian bookshops.'

Julia rolled her eyes, 'Oh yeah! Like I'd be seen dead in one of them!'

Meredith did not feel like responding; she remained silent, deep in thought. Both sat quietly until Kingsley returned.

'Quick service here,' he remarked, placing Julia's glass in front of her. 'Four ice cubes. The barman said that's how you like it.'

'Thanks, handsome!' quipped Julia, crossing her legs to reveal a large section of thigh below the high hemline of her tight miniskirt.

Meredith stood. 'Better get going; see you later.' She walked away. She was feeling out of sorts now, not only with herself, but with Julia, and now, sadly, even Kingsley.

❖

She was just setting off on another chalet round a few minutes later when she heard Kingsley's voice behind her. 'There you are. I've been looking for you. Want some company?'

'If you don't mind missing the entertainment,' she replied, only just managing to stop herself from adding, 'And Julia.'

'Think I can live without it for a bit. I'm needing some fresh air anyway, and it's you I came to see, after all.'

He had come to see her! Not to spend time with Julia. What a fool she was, and how quick to judge. Something in her felt released.

'Does Uncle Jacko always monopolise the stage?' he asked. 'He's not got a bad voice, but he should drop Sinatra and the rest of the Rat Pack from his repertoire, especially with that hair!'

'Don't let him hear you say that! And you'll miss his grand finale when he upstages the winner of the Best Head of Hair Competition. It's the highlight of his week.'

He laughed. 'Shameful! He should be made to wear a wig.'

'I'll have to suggest it. Come on then, best foot forward. There's a child crying over there.'

They soon found the chalet, from inside which the sound of a distressed baby could be heard. A red scarf had been tied around the door handle, signalling the fact that there was a child, or children, alone inside. She put a call through on the walkie-talkie to the bar and games room extensions, asking that an announcement be made. Another loud cry sounded from a chalet nearby. She pointed a little further along the path. 'I can't hear myself think, let's go and wait over there,' then put another call through.

'What happens if no-one comes?' he asked.

'I'll have to stay and keep putting out more calls until someone does come.'

He made a mental note to use this experience as an illustration in his next sermon; something along the lines of: although God is invisible, yet, for those who know they are His children, they have the assurance and comfort of knowing that He is forever present in their hearts and watching over their lives. 'I don't think I could leave my child alone, especially here,' he commented.

'No, nor me.'

'How often do you have to do this?'

'I don't normally have to. It's really the responsibility of the children's nannies, but one's on her night off and another's off sick; the other two are on duty in the ballroom.'

Footsteps could be heard running towards them. A young woman appeared, looking flushed and anxious. 'Thanks. It's alright, I'm staying,' she said, hurrying to attend to her distressed child.

Within seconds the crying stopped, however, the cries continued, unabated, from the chalet nearby.

'By the way,' he said, 'thought you'd be interested to know I'll be seeing Julia again next week.'

Before she could stop herself, she asked, 'Will you get Doreen to come and sit in?'

'No need. I'll be surrounded. The Ladies' Contact Club are having to use the manse lounge whilst the kitchen in the church hall's being decorated.' He looked over at the chalet, 'That child's sounding really upset now.'

Another cry went up from a chalet further along the same row. 'That's what happens when one starts,' she said. 'It wakes all the others up.' She put through another call.

'Will you be able to make it to the house group?' he managed to ask over the combined noise. 'We're about to start looking at the Trinity, especially at the Person and ministry of The Holy Spirit.'

'I'll try. It all depends on how things are going here.'

'Well, I hope you can. It would be a pity for you to miss the first week.'

'There's a lot about Him in the Bible, isn't there? I can't think how I kept missing Him before.'

'That's right. He's there, right at the start, in the very first verse.'

'I know this must sound strange, but I only really became aware of Him in **Luke**. You know, where it says about Jesus being full of the Holy Spirit?'

Just then a man appeared, staggering slightly, a cigarette dangling from his mouth and holding a bottle of beer. He saw them and grunted as he entered the chalet.

'Oh dear!' exclaimed Meredith. 'That doesn't look good. Tom wouldn't be too happy. Think I'll stick around a bit longer. But getting back to the Trinity, that would explain how Jesus could be fully human and fully divine at the same time.'

A woman walked past and went into another chalet with a handkerchief tied around the handle, but not the one with the crying child.

'Yes, that's right. But what about us?' he asked, glancing over at the staggering man's chalet.

She thought the situation strange. Here she was, trying to deal with crying children, and at the same time attempting to have a discussion about one of the great Christian doctrines. 'Well, according to John, Jesus breathed on His disciples, and said, **Receive the Holy Spirit,** just before He went back to Heaven. Anyway, the Bible makes it clear that Jesus, His Father and The Holy Spirit are One, so we don't worship three gods, just One. It's just that God reveals Himself in three different ways: a Trinity. And if Jesus is to be our example, then that means that we can have God's Spirit in us too, just like His disciples did, and that's what happens when we're born again. We still have just one spirit - our human spirit - only now it's joined with His Holy Spirit, He sort of…merges with our human spirit.'

Kingsley beamed at her, recognising that there was only one way she could have gained such knowledge: through the revelatory ministry of the Holy Spirit Himself. He had expected her to quote the usual answer, that The Trinity could be explained as water in its various forms: running, vapour and ice; three manifestations of the same element. He preferred the seed analogy: the seed in the ground, the roots becoming a young plant, then the mature, full blossom; three manifestations of the same plant.

'Well, let's hope you can get there. Maybe you'd like to share that with the rest of the group...'

Other voices and footsteps could be heard as more parents came to check on their infants.

'I was hoping to bump into Tom. How is he now?'

She knew straight away what he was referring to, and replied, 'He seems fine. I'm hoping he's too happy and busy to think about that Ouija thing again.'

'Good. But it's a pity that the people who were doing it haven't heard that everything's turned out alright.'

'They have. I felt very strongly that I had to tell them, so I wrote to their home addresses and sent a copy of *Journey Into Life* as well.'

'You did? Good for you!'

'You don't think that I was being a bit...heavy-handed then, do you?'

'Not at all! Quite the opposite; you've done them a favour, whether they recognise it or not. Just like you've done for Julia.'

The first baby stopped crying at last. The chalet door opened, and the man reappeared. He stopped to light another cigarette before stumbling away. Meredith called after him, 'Excuse me, but are you leaving your child alone again?'

'Naa, fetching the missus,' he replied, squinting at her through the smoke.

'Then we'll wait here until she comes,' said Meredith.

'Do what yer like,' he replied, offhandedly.

'I hope she won't be long?' she called after him, knowing that she *was* being heavy-handed now, but feeling justified in being so.

They heard him swear as he walked unsteadily away.

Kingsley looked at her, and realised that he was growing to like this young woman more by the second.

CHAPTER 15

The Bonnie Baby Competition was well under way. This was Julia's favourite shoot of the week. She loved children, and had all the time in the world for them, especially those who looked in any way neglected or hard done by. It was a wonder the shop made any profit, considering the amount of sweets, colouring books, crayons, bats, balls, buckets and spades she gave away. If she had to confess to any regrets about her chosen way of life, it would have to be the knowledge that she could never be a mother. Her only hope was that she could find a woman who had a child or two already. She thought she had found one, but the woman had recently gone back to her husband. It still hurt; she had grown to love those kids.

Hoping it would sweeten her mood, Tom had succeeded in talking Hilda Rodden, his mother-in-law, into going on the Norfolk Broad trip. She had been deeply unimpressed and personally offended by their choice of Zoe as the baby's name, and was making his life more awkward than usual. A measure of peace had eventually been achieved when they added Hilda as a middle name, which was just as well, because mother and child were due home from the hospital later that day.

It was Sunday evening, and despite hurrying to close reception, Meredith had just missed the quarter to six bus into town. Even if she ran all the way to church, the service would be half over by the time she arrived. She decided to go straight home instead and have a quick bath before going on to the Launchpad meeting. There would be no-one at home, her parents had gone to visit her brother, and would not be back until later that night.

Kingsley opened the meeting with prayer. Then he handed out several pages of typed notes, with the heading: 'What is the Occult?'

She had been looking forward to this, and felt more than a little curious to learn how he was going to handle the controversial topic. Glancing down the list, she found herself becoming even more curious:-

Amulet	Medium
Astral projection	Necromancy
Astral travel	Neopaganism
Astrology	New Age
Automatic writing	Numerology
Black magic	Omen
Blood pact	Ouija board
Chain letter	Palm reading
Channelling	Pendulum
Charm (+ good luck)	Pentagram
Clairvoyance	Psychic healing
Crystal ball	Reincarnation
Divination	Rune casting
Druidism	Satanism
ESP	Séance
Evil Eye	Shamanism
Fortune telling	Spell
Freemasonry	Tarot cards
Hex	Transcendental
Horoscope	meditation
Hypnosis	White magic
Levitation	Wicca

Everyone seemed more unsettled and excitable than usual, and Kingsley had to ask them to settle down several times before he could begin.

'We shan't be dwelling on this subject for long, but I think it would be sensible for us all to have an awareness of what the occult actually is. Let's begin by reading what The Lord has to say about it.'

They spent several minutes looking at various Bible passages. Then he started, 'You must have noticed that there's a lot more interest in anything to do with the supernatural these days, especially with all this New Age business going on. But who knows what the word *occult* actually means?'

'Devil worship,' someone offered, 'Satanism?' suggested another, followed by 'witchcraft and black magic.'

'In a sense, you're all right. But it's actually derived from the Latin word *occultare*, meaning, *secrete, conceal, to hide, covered over.* I suppose we could say, *hidden from view.* It usually refers to anything connected with some type of secret knowledge, or practice involved in a supernatural or psychic occurrence; the main aim being to gain personal power. Now we know that as Christians, we aren't seeking any kind of power for ourselves - quite the opposite. We are here to love and serve. That's not denying that there is power in love; God's love is the most powerful force we can ever encounter, and we, as his children, can often experience His love in powerful and super-natural ways. That's *super*-natural! *He* is our source of strength, not like the counterfeit demonic power experienced but those who dabble in the occult. Many of their practices rely on *unholy* spirits, in other words, demons, even though they would forcefully deny this, not wanting to acknowledge the truth of it even to themselves. We rely on God, and He works in and through us by His Spirit, His Holy Spirit - the very active and alive Spirit of Jesus.

Okay, let's make a start on the list. It's by no means complete, in fact, there were literally hundreds more things I could have added, but we'll focus on the more commonly known ones for now.'

He began, stopping to give a brief description of each item. When they reached *Neopaganism*, he explained that this was a modern form of *Druidism*, and dominated by *Wicca*. He told them that *Witchcraft* wasn't necessarily full of witches casting evil spells, then surprised the group by stating that committing evil was forbidden in that religion; that spells had to be cast only for the benefit of others, and should never cause any harm. He went on, 'Many profess to following *The rule of three*, claiming that they only cast good spells because they believe that any energy they send into the world will be returned threefold. But there's no such thing as a good or bad spell, or a good or bad witch, black or white - or whatever colour they give themselves! As far as The Bible's concerned, they, and everything they practice, are all absolutely forbidden.'

Again, everyone was surprised to learn that tarot cards contained a lot of Christian symbolism. He explained, 'That's why they can be easily digestible, even permissible, for those who've never encountered Jesus. Like everything else on the list, those involved can be deceived into a feeling a false sense of security. And that's why many of the main practitioners have been deceived into believing that they're doing a good thing, and actually helping others.'

There were plenty of questions when he had finished, including one about family members who were involved in any of the activities, and especially how it could affect others in the same family.

'That's a good question, and I'm glad you asked it. Our own curiosity in any of these can lead to accidental, or deliberate, involvement - ours or those close to us - including family members. Sometimes the harmful effects of such involvement - again by ourselves or a family member - may not show itself immediately, maybe not even until years later.

themselves

100

These can be manifested as poor health, difficult relationships, failed marriages, inability to make wise choices, unexpected and continual failure, or so called "bad luck". You've all heard people complaining that they must be jinxed? By being involved in any of the practices, we don't realise that the root cause, or origin, of any of these harmful effects, could be the way we - or a family member - may have opened ourselves, or themselves, up to some pretty harmful and nasty influences. That's not to say that all of life's problems are caused by doing anything on the list, but we often find that there is a connection. And from some of your comments, it sounds like many of you have been involved in some of them at some time or other. And you know what I'm going to say now, don't you? Please come and talk to one of us if you, or a family member, has been, or still is, involved in any of these activities. You don't need to feel embarrassed or scared. A session or two of prayer can usually sort things out.'

One item in particular had held Meredith's attention: *Freemasonry*. Kingsley had skimmed quickly past the subject, only saying that he could see no reason why any Christian should feel the need to join any secret society. But it wasn't until he stated that he knew of several churches which had either closed, or were unable to thrive, due to having members of the Craft amongst them, that she became alarmed. Disturbed, and unsure what to do, she remained uncharacteristically quiet for the remainder of the evening, and managed to slip away before the closing prayer, hoping that Kingsley hadn't noticed. How could she tell him that her father was a Freemason, and had been for as many years as she could remember?

CHAPTER 16

Meredith's parents returned home later that night. Obviously extremely tired, they soon made their way to bed, which was just as well, for Meredith had no idea how to broach the subject with her father. The thought that her lovely, mild-mannered Dad could be involved in anything even remotely occult was unthinkable. She just couldn't believe it. Still, she had to be sure.

She found him in the garden the next morning. Having spent a fitful night's sleep, she didn't feel too sharp, and hoped that she would have enough about her to be sensitive and diplomatic.

'Dad, can I ask you something?'

He bent to pull up a weed. 'Look at this! It's those fat balls your mother keeps putting out for the birds. They keep dropping seeds all around this area. I keep telling her they don't need them this time of year, but will she listen to me? Will she heck!'

She pulled a few weeds up herself. 'Yes, but look how much you both enjoy watching them. And they keep eating them anyway, no matter what time of year it is.'

He looked at his watch. 'Humph! Why doesn't she do some weeding then? Anyhow, it's not time to go yet, is it? Or are you wanting to go early?'

'No, ten more minutes. But I wanted to ask you something, about those meetings you go to, at the Freemasons.'

'Oh yes, why's that then? Are you interested in joining? I did hear that the women's group over in Brunston's been dwindling recently; they could do with some new members.'

'Women's group? I didn't know there was one! I thought it was just for men?'

He winked, 'Ah! There's a lot you don't know.'

'Such as?'

'Well now, that would be telling. But who do you think paid for that new toilet block at the school, and helped old Fred Turnbull out when he needed his roof fixing? Father Christmas?'

'Your group did, I mean, your lodge?'

He winked again. 'Mum's the word, or they'll have my guts for garters.'

'Really, are you serious?'

'Well, let's just say, we prefer not to broadcast what we do.'

'Why, what's the big mystery?'

He shrugged. 'It's just the way we are. You know, tradition.'

'Bit strange though, isn't it? What would be so terrible about people knowing how you're helping people? The Rotary Club and The Lions don't seem to mind. They're often in the paper.'

'Bully for them! But we like to be more...discreet. We don't feel the need to go blabbing to the press.'

This sounded reasonable enough to her, and she really couldn't see her father getting up to anything sinister, or underhand. Nevertheless, she went on to ask, 'So why are they thought of as being unchristian then?'

'*Unchristian?*' he repeated, sounding indignant. 'Who says?'

'Just...someone at church.'

'Ah! So that's what all this is about. Well, I shouldn't worry. What some people don't know, won't hurt them.' He turned and began walking back to the house. 'Anyway, what's good enough for my dear old dad, is good enough for me. And I've just remembered, we do need to get going, I need to fill up.'

❖

Meredith felt decidedly uneasy and grew more unsettled by the day. By Wednesday, she was determined to find out, one way or another, about the Freemason issue. The library was her first port of call, and she began searching the shelves for anything she could find on the subject.

The first book confirmed that it was indeed a secret society, and considered to be the largest one in the world. She read that the original founder had actually been a Jesuit priest, that its aim was to replace Christianity by a religion of reason, and that it had an internal disciplinary system which used mutual surveillance.

Another book gave explanations about the symbols used in Freemasonry, otherwise known as *The Craft,* the origins of which were drawn from the tools of stonemasons: the square, compass, level, plumb rule and trowel. It went into great detail about the eye in the triangle symbol, sometimes referred to as the *Third Eye of Illumination,* claiming that it had appeared on every United States one dollar bill since 1933. Now, she wondered, what on earth was that all about? She could only assume that there must have been some very politically powerful men around in America at that time to be able to influence such a thing - and still must be! She took a pound note out of her purse and examined it closely, and was relieved to find nothing on it resembling the diagram in the book. She continued reading. The symbol, which was still worn as part of the Grand Master of the Freemason's Lodges' jewellery, and referred to as *The eye of the Great Architect of the Universe,* was known by the Egyptians as the *Eye of Osiris,* or *Horus,* and actually represented the eye of Lucifer or Satan - the Devil himself. As for the triangle, that seemed to have originated from another secret society, the *Rosicrucian's,* whose teachings are still a combination of occultism and other religious beliefs and practices, and referred to as *The Law of the Triangle.* The book even claimed that the triangle with the eye symbol was clearly emblazoned on the front wall of

Hitler's bunker at Eagle Nest, and that it could also be found on many church buildings today - even on a wall in the church that is built over the supposed site of Joseph and Mary's house in the Holy Land.

So much for the history and architectural structure of the Craft. What she really needed to know was the influence and effect it could have on any individual involved in the organisation. She read on, and learned that any candidate has to declare a belief in *The Great Architect,* also known as *The Supreme Being,* but is still free to believe in the god of the religion he professes, including its holy book. How strange then, she thought, that with all its talk of reason and wanting to do good for mankind, as well as its pseudo-religious background, any discussion on politics and religion was apparently not allowed during any of their meetings!

Growing more perturbed by the minute, she learned about the significance of the pyramid, another well-known symbol. This was made up of *degrees,* or *levels,* the initiation rite to obtain one such level included placing a black hood over the initiate's head, and a rope with a running noose around his neck; pricking him by his heart with the point of a sword, and requiring him to repeat blood-curdling, witchcraft oaths whilst drawing his thumb across his own throat and saying things about having it cut and his tongue torn out if he divulged any of the Craft's secrets. She began to feel dismayed and yet fascinated at the same time. She read on.

There was some mention of *duality* being the reason for the black and white checked square patterns of the floor, or *pavement* as it was called, in every lodge building. As far as she could grasp, it was supposed to represent the ground floor of King Solomon's Temple, and symbolised the battle of good and evil present in all human life.

She went on to read that they even claimed that the Bible qualified their belief that, *Lucifer and Jesus were One and the same.* They justify this heresy by the misinterpretation of such

105

Scriptures as **Isaiah,** which states: **How art thou fallen from heaven oh Lucifer, son of the morning...** and Jesus's own words: **I am the bright and morning star.** However, she knew that a proper reading of the Scriptures teach that, due to pride, Lucifer was literally thrown out of Heaven and fell to earth along with a third of the angels. Whereas Jesus *chose* to come to earth and be born as a baby; He had certainly not been *thrown* out of Heaven! And so she realised that they had combined Lucifer's **son of the morning** title with Jesus's **bright and morning star** title: yet another instance of how the Devil constantly attempts to copy, or counterfeit, all things of God.

The article went on to detail the Craft's concept of *duality,* which they believe to be the two sides of divinity - in that Lucifer is the equal of God, having a dual character, made up of *The god of light and goodness,* and *The god of darkness and evil,* and that both sides are in constant conflict for humanity. Amongst the many quotes, she read:-

General Albert Pike, Grand Commander, sovereign pontiff of universal freemasonry, giving instructions to the 23 supreme councils of the world.

"That which we must say to the crowd is, we worship a god, but it is the god one adores without superstition. To you sovereign grand inspector general, we say this and you may repeat it to the brethren of the 32nd, 31st and 30th degrees - the Masonic religion should be by all of us initiates of the high degrees, maintained in the purity of the luciferian doctrine.

If lucifer were not god, would Adonay (the God of the Christians) whose deeds prove cruelty, perfidy and hatred of man, barbarism and repulsion for science, would Adonay and His priests, calumniate Him?

Yes, lucifer is god, and unfortunately Adonay is also God, for the eternal law is that there is no light without shade, no beauty without ugliness, no white without black, for the absolute can only exist as two gods,

*darkness being necessary for light to serve as its foil,
as the pedestal is necessary to the statue, and the brake
to the locomotive.*

She had to look up the word *calumniate*, and found out that
is meant, *to make false and defamatory statements about
somebody or something.* She could hardly believe it! Was The
Craft actually accusing God of making *false and defamatory
statements* about the Devil! What other way of taking it, was
there? This was all very confusing, especially when she had
found other statements claiming that Jesus and Lucifer were
actually brothers!

Mormonism also came into some of the explanations, and
she was surprised to learn that Joseph Smith, the founder of
that religion, and his brother Hiram, had been promoted to the
upper degrees of Freemasonry on the same day - and that their
doctrine teaches that Lucifer is the brother of Jesus.

Slightly confused and bewildered, she had to accept that
fact that everything she had just read confirmed the astonishing
and false claim that the Freemasons really did believe that
Lucifer is one side of God, and that *Adonay (the God of the
Christians),* was the other! Totally dismayed, now, even
alarmed, she slammed the book shut.

Now she really needed to find out how anyone could leave
the organisation. It took some finding, but eventually she came
across a helpful article, and learned that all a member had to do
was to write a letter of resignation to his lodge. As long as he
made it clear that he no longer considered himself a Mason -
and that he wanted nothing more to do with Freemasonry, now,
nor at any time in the future - he was free to leave.

She gathered up the small pile of books and articles, and
replaced them on the shelf. A stiff cup of coffee was needed.
She headed for her favourite café, and tried to put her thoughts
into some sort of order. It seemed that Kingsley had been right
to include *Freemasonry* on his list, and now it looked as

though she was really going to have to have a serious talk with her father. And to do that, she would need something to back her information up. But all the information was in the library's reference section, and, as such, was not allowed to be loaned out. Resigned, and not looking forward to the task ahead, she retraced her steps, and spent the rest of the morning making detailed notes.

❖

Instead of going to the house group that evening, she stayed home. She handed the notes she had made to her father, then went to her room to pray. Sometime later, and feeling that he'd had sufficient time, she went back downstairs and found him in his favourite place, the garden. He appeared to be absorbed in watching some butterflies dancing around a buddleia bush. The notes lay open on the bench beside him.

Slightly apprehensive, she went to sit next to him, and asked, 'Did you read those notes?'

'Hmm,' he replied, not looking at her.

'And? What do you think?'

'Stuff and nonsense! I don't take any notice of all that malarkey.'

'But it does go on, doesn't it? All that initiation stuff? The noose and hood, and the knife by the heart?'

'Just play-acting. I don't take it seriously. And, anyway, we're all about promoting peace and harmony around the place.'

'But what about those oaths? Have you had to say any of them?'

He was silent.

'And what about all that rubbish about *Lucifer and Jesus being one*, or that they're actually brothers?'

He shrugged. 'Nah! I just go through the motions, and let the rest of them get on with it.'

'But Dad, how could you even *think* of belonging to an organisation that teaches heresies like that? And grown men, carrying on like that - in this day and age too! It's awful. It sounds like something out of the Dark Ages. Does Mum know what you…what goes on there?'

'Nah! She's never been that interested, and I don't ask her what she gets up at the W.I. do I?'

'That's a bit different! Everything they do is above board; there's nothing secretive or sinister about their activities.'

He laughed. 'That's a matter of opinion! All those women, concocting deadly recipes…'

'Oh, come off it, Dad! You know what I mean. And why do you go there anyway? What's so special about it?'

He reflected, 'I have a good laugh sometimes, and they're a decent bunch of lads - supportive - you know?'

'But that's what you have at church, isn't it? The Men's Contact Group? And there's other places; places where they don't do…all that stuff. What about *The Lions*, or *The Rotary Club*?'

'No need! I've got some good friends there.' He paused, but still he would not look at her, then shrugged again. 'And I suppose I'm just used to going; and that other side of it doesn't concern me anyway.'

'Well it concerns me Dad. And I think it would concern people at church if they knew about it too!'

This seemed to unsettle him. He stood abruptly and walked over to the small pond. 'Leave it alone, Meredith! There's nothing for you to get all het up about. And I'm not leaving just because you've suddenly got all aerated about things you don't understand. You know I like to help out at church, and they'll be even more glad of me now that Charlie Somerville's moving on.'

'The Property Deacon? Is he leaving?'

'Next month. Wouldn't mind having a crack at it myself.'

'But…don't you think it's kind of contradictory… being involved with two organisations that have completely opposing belief systems? How can you mix the two?'

'Come off it, Meri! Don't be so dramatic.'

She recognised that he was on the verge of becoming annoyed now; he only ever used the shortened version of her name when he was feeling out of sorts with her.

'I told you, I don't take any notice of that side of things. And for the life of me, I really can't see what you're making such a fuss about.'

She went to stand beside him. It was warm evening, and they both stood for a while watching a green tench swim around and through the stone castle portals beneath the surface. 'I'm sorry Dad. It's just that I'm concerned about you, and I felt I had to speak up.'

He put an arm around her and gave her a hug. 'Don't you worry about me love. I'm fine. You just get on with your own life, and forget all about this nonsense.'

But she wasn't ready to drop the subject just yet, and determined that he should take her seriously, went on to ask, 'You know, I found out that they're easy to leave. They just need a letter…'

'Meri, shush now! Enough. I've told you to leave it alone.' He released her, sighing heavily.

She knew she had lost the argument, but there was one more piece of ammunition she had in her arsenal, although it was one she was loathe to use. But he was her Dad, and she was fighting for him now. Cautiously, she said, 'Apparently some churches aren't able to thrive if there's any Freemasons in the membership; some of them have even had to close.' She held her breath and waited.

'It's no good, Meredith. I've heard it all before, and it doesn't wash with me. Those churches were probably dying anyway. And if it's Reverend Pryce that been putting these ideas in your head, then tell him he's got nothing to worry about from us. He'll do okay. He's got the enthusiasm and drive; he'll make a go of the place.'

'Us! Are you saying that there's more of you…in the church? In *our* church?'

He recognised the alarm in her voice, but decided to ignore it. 'You just see to yourself, and let the rest of us get on with what we do best.' And with that, he turned and began to stroll back to the house, seemingly unconcerned, unhurried - and unchanged.

Disappointed and confused, she remained where she was; everything in her felt that he was wrong. And she had absolutely no idea what to do about it. No matter how much he denied having been involved in the ceremonial side of things, whatever he had done was still too much. Why couldn't he see how spiritually inappropriate and contaminating all those beliefs and activities were? How could such a lovely Christian man allow himself to be caught up in such devilish things, for there was no other word for it other than devilish - occult - hidden from view - concealed? And she had seen some of the effects of involvement in some of *that* recently, and knew that, one way or the other, and sooner or later, it would leave its mark on him, and maybe even on her and her mother and brother - if it hadn't already.

CHAPTER 17

Hoping that it would help her to stop dwelling on her talk with her father, Meredith went to watch the Bonnie Baby Competition during the afternoon break the next day. She was surprised when Kingsley came to sit by her.

'Mind if I join you? Wendy said I'd find you here. Just popped in to drop some stuff off for Sunday.'

'Please do.'

'What's going on here then?' he asked, looking at a long line of young mothers, bouncing their freshly preened babies up and down on their mini-skirted knees.

'Bonnie Baby Competition,' she replied, as one of the infants started to wail, quickly followed by another. Soon, two more had joined in; the combined din becoming almost unbearable. 'Although sometimes I think it should be called, "The Strongest Pair of Lungs Competition", she attempted to say.

Julia emerged from the shop holding a large, multi-coloured ball. They watched as she went over the one of the distressed infants and begin to shake it as she made all the soothing, cooing sounds she knew babies liked. Suitably distracted, the child soon stopped crying.

'It's got a bell inside,' explained Meredith, 'but she's definitely got a way with children. You watch, she'll try and calm the others down as well.' No sooner as she said it, than Julia began working her way along the line, successfully soothing the other babies en route.

A children's nanny took advantage of the peace to announce the start of the competition. The first entrant began to walk around the ballroom, before coming to stand in front of the stage, where she was asked several questions. The minute interview complete, she proudly held her baby up for all to admire as Julia took the official photograph.

'Expect Tom'll be entering his little one soon,' said Kingsley.

'Not allowed, he's staff; same as Jacko and his hair,' she replied.

'Fair enough. By the way, we missed you last night. I know that Doreen and Dave were hoping to see you to ask if you're free to go around theirs this coming Wednesday afternoon. They want to do some forward planning for the group. Jennifer's going, so it'll be just you four; I've got an appointment in Brunston.'

Another baby's wail filled the air. Julia went into action again, but despite her repeated efforts, this child refused to be soothed.

She stood and said, 'Let's go somewhere quieter.' What she had to say would need a calmer environment; somewhere where she would be able to think clearly and choose her words carefully.

Once outside, she glanced over at the Crazy Golf pitch. No-one was playing. She pointed, 'Let's go over there.' He followed, and she began, 'Actually, I've been having second thoughts about helping with the group. Something's cropped up, and I'll need some time to sort things out.' He frowned, and she knew he wouldn't be content to leave it at that, so she quickly added, 'To tell you the truth, Kingsley, I'm thinking I might not be right person after all.'

He looked disappointed. 'That's a pity; you sounded quite keen when we spoke about it before.'

'I am, I mean, I was. But…things have changed.'

The crying child and its mother emerged from the ballroom and passed them, leaving behind the smell of an obviously very full nappy.

'What things? More trouble here again? Something I can help with?'

She studied his face, and recognised real concern there. She did some quick thinking. Last night she had decided not to involve him, knowing that, as her father's minister, he would be duty-bound to intervene about his involvement with the Freemasons. And now she knew that, as the daughter of a Mason, she could well be spiritually affected - infected - by her father's involvement with something so occult. The awful thought had occurred to her that she may even have already been inadvertently passing some unhelpful things on to others. How did she know if she hadn't been a sort of hidden - concealed - rotten apple all this time? Now she felt almost overwhelmed with the seriousness of it all, and had no idea what she could do about it.

'You're looking worried, Meredith,' he remarked. 'You can tell me, whatever it is. You know that, don't you?'

She looked at him and tried to smile. Yes, maybe she should tell him. She really did need some advice, and from someone who knew what they were talking about. 'My break's almost over. It's a bit complicated, and I think I do need some advice. But I don't really want to go into it all here. Do you think I can come and see you again?'

'Of course! Why don't you let me give you a ring later on today, and we can arrange something?'

She telephoned her father that evening, feeling that it was only fair to warn him about her intentions. He tried to dissuade her, but she was determined. It had been a difficult conversation, and after the first ten minutes she felt that they were going nowhere; they just seemed to be going around in circles. Eventually, she decided to end the call herself.

'I'm only thinking of you, Dad. I *really* do believe you're mixed up in something unchristian. And I'm convinced now that it can't be good to have Masons in the fellowship.

Anyway, I'll see you on Sunday, but I'm not going to change my mind, unless you change yours in the meantime.'

'No chance of that!' her retorted, sounding very annoyed.

'Then, I'm sorry. I've got to do what I believe the Lord's telling me to do.'

He made no reply. All she heard was a nondescript grunt coming through the receiver as the line went dead.

The Farewell Concert was held later that evening. Meredith joined the other staff on stage to perform the usual set of late Friday night songs. She kept a large white handkerchief especially for the occasion, holding it up high, and waving it to the strains of *We'll Meet Again, Don't Know Where, Don't Know When; Wish Me Luck As You Wave Me Goodbye*, and finally, *Goodbye, Campers, See You In The Morning*.

Throughout the evening, Julia went around trying to sell any photographs that had not yet been bought. She spotted Meredith on one of her circuits, and went to sit by her.

'Cheer up, hun! It'll never happen.'

'I'm okay, just a bit tired.' She glanced at the pile of photographs in Julia's hands. 'Looks like you've got a lot left this week?'

'Yeah, tight lot. But you watch, there'll be a mad rush for them in the morning. Well, go on then, I know you're dying to ask.'

'Ask what?'

'About Kingsley and me, or should I say Reverend Pryce?'

Meredith felt momentarily nonplussed. Kingsley and her? What was she talking about? 'What do you mean?' she asked.

'Don't tell me you've forgotten? You know, I've been seeing him about my "little problem"'?

'Oh yes! Sorry, slipped my mind. How's it going?'

'Not bad. Been three times now. I can see where he's coming from. Suppose it makes some kind of sense to some kind of people.'

'But not to you?'

'Naa!'

'Why not? Have you been going with an open mind? Or aren't you even prepared to consider that there may actually be another way…'

'Hey! There's no-one more open-minded than me!'

'Are you sure about that? It sounds to me as though you've given up already.'

'Given up? Didn't you hear me? I said I'd seen him *three* times! That's *three* of my precious afternoons off used up!'

Then, deciding she had nothing to lose, Meredith added casually, 'Well, I think it's a shame. You know, it might help if you came along to church sometimes, or maybe to one of the film nights.'

Julia grimaced. 'Naa! Not for me, hun. There's enough hypocrites around the place. Everyone knows what your lot are like; all holier than thou on Sundays, then living like hell the rest of the week!'

'What! Is that what you think?'

'Too right I do!'

'Then…then I challenge you to come along and meet some of those "hypocrites" for yourself - instead of judging them from a distance? And I'm not denying that we have our faults; we never said we were perfect. But at least we *know* it. The Church is full of sinners; but sinners who recognise they need help.'

'Don't tell me you're actually *admitting* it? A bit condescending, don't you think?'

'I don't think so. Jesus said it's not the healthy who need a doctor, but those who know they're sick. And I *know* I need Him. There's plenty of things that need sorting out in me.'

'Bully for you! I just hope you won't be disappointed.'

'What do you mean?'

'You know, when you pop your clogs, and find that there's nothing at the other end. You can't prove your God exists anyway. Beats me why you all get so steamed about nothing but a…a fable.'

Meredith felt momentarily at a loss. Then, feeling that she really couldn't let such a statement pass unchallenged, replied, 'I could say the same about someone you hold dear, like your mother. You're always talking about her. And what if I said that you can't prove she exists either? And it beats me why you "get so steamed about nothing but a fable!" How would you feel about that?'

'I don't get you?'

'Well, I haven't met her, have I? Does that mean that I have the right to go around saying that she doesn't exist? And calling her "a fable"?'

'Don't be daft! Everyone's got a mother.'

'And everyone's got a God, if only they'd take the time to think about Him seriously. And just because I haven't had my own personal experience of your mother, does that give me the right to belittle your relationship with her?'

Julia smiled. 'Okay, I get your point. Although it would be easy to prove my mother exists, but I'm kind of curious to know how you can do the same for your God.'

'It's like I said, it all depends on how serious someone is about wanting to know Him. If they're really serious, they'll get their proof. But they have to be genuine. And I *can* prove His existence in my life by the things He's done for me, and the ways He helps me.'

'What's He done for you then? Apart from softening your brain so that you can't stop spouting on about Him!'

'I could give you a list. But there've been so many times when He's answered my prayers, especially when things don't look as though they're going to work out, or I haven't got a clue what to do about them. He's put people across my path who have proved to be true friends. Sometimes He's even healed me of various things. Remember that time I fell down the staff stairs and did something to my ankle? Remember how it swelled up like a balloon? You were there, you saw it. And then, after I'd prayed, you watched it go down in seconds, and I was able to walk perfectly alright. Then there was that time...'

'Yeah, well, that was a fluke. You couldn't have hurt it that bad. Anyway, here's a thing, I'm not trying to push you into believing in my mother.'

'Push? No-one's been pushing you. And, if I remember rightly, it was you who asked to meet with Kingsley. But what about you? Don't you think that you were a bit *pushy* about the way you propositioned me here that night, and again afterwards in the café, when I tried to apologise?'

Julia pulled a face. 'Come off it, hun. You're taking all this too personally. You're all so damned serious, like Kingsley with that flaming Bible of his. Gets on my nerves, spouting from it all the time. And what gives it the right to say that the rest of us are wrong, just because we don't go along with it?'

'You've got that the wrong way round. It's not right because it's in the Bible; it's in the Bible because it's right!'

'Oh, very clever! But those stories! They're crazy! Please tell me you don't go along with them all!'

'Stories? Are you talking about the parables? They're just earthly stories that Jesus used to explain Heavenly truths.'

'There you go again, spouting off! Anyway, everyone knows the damn book's full of contradictions.'

Meredith was well into her stride now. 'Really? So you *have* read it? Which bits are you talking about?'

'There's loads. You must have seen them.'

'No, I can't think of one. If you're talking about the parts that should be taken allegorically...'

'Liar!'

'No, honestly I haven't. The teachings of the Old Testament are explained and fulfilled in the New Testament, but as for contradictions...'

Julia held up her hand. 'Okay, okay! For God's sake, change the flaming record!'

However, Meredith refused to be browbeaten. 'You know Julia, you're very fond of shutting me up. You can't go around accusing me of being a hypocrite, and criticising my beliefs, and expect me to just take it. You'd be quick enough to accuse me of being narrow-minded and prejudiced if I kept belittling you, and criticising your way of life.'

'Sorry I spoke, I'm sure! That's it; I've had it! I can't go along with all this God stuff; it's really getting up my nose.'

Meredith felt exasperated. 'You sound almost suspicious about Him, Julia, and that's because you don't know Him. And I hope you don't speak like this to Kingsley?'

Julia gave one of her lopsided smiles. 'Kingsley? No. Now why would I do a silly thing like that?'

'So you will keep going to see him then? Even though you feel so…negative about everything he stands for?'

'Why shouldn't I? He's got a way with him; kinda cute.'

'Excuse me, but are you still selling those photos?' They were interrupted by a camper who wanted to make a purchase. Julia turned to attend to her.

Meredith stood and left, realising that this was becoming a habit. And that wasn't the first time that she'd heard Julia confess to finding Kingsley 'kinda cute'. Now, after the conversation they had just had, she began to think that her earlier suspicions had been right: Julia was making a play for him. After all, she did 'swing both ways.' But what could she do about it - apart from trying to find a way to warn him? And then, would he believe her? So now she had yet another difficult situation to deal with. It had always been like this, as soon as one problem was sorted out, along came another; only now they seemed to be coming along just that bit faster. Maybe there was some sort of concealed, negative force going on in her life. Maybe her father's involvement with the Freemasons really was having some detrimental effect on her after all. But

119

what could she do about it? Pray. That's what she must do. Definitely pray - and pray harder.

CHAPTER 18

'Your Dad's on the phone,' said Wendy, coming to take over the job of hanging a large pile of chalet keys onto their pegs. 'I've transferred it to your desk.'

Meredith returned to the office and picked up the receiver. 'Hello Dad?'

'Ah, Meredith. Sorry to bother you at work, only I thought you'd like to know that I've had a chat with Reverend Pryce.'

'You have! Oh Dad! Thank goodness…'

'Hang on! You might not be so pleased when you hear what happened. I…er…your mother and I have decided to leave the church.' He began to speak faster now, as though keen to avoid being interrupted. 'Your mother's been harking on about going to that Methodist church down Colemen Road for a while. Maybe we'll pop along there one Sunday.'

Dismayed at hearing the news, Meredith sat down heavily on her seat, her mind whirling. What had she done? All she had wanted to do was to warn him, and make him think about what he was doing. This was dreadful! Why hadn't she kept her big mouth shut?

Her father hurried on, 'You know she's been going to the W.I. there during the week anyway.'

'But Dad! Why? I don't understand. He didn't…'

'No, no, love. It wasn't his decision, it was mine. He wants us to stay, but I don't feel we can now. I think we'd be better to make a clean break of it; get a start fresh somewhere else.'

'You've decided to stay in the Masons - after everything I said - and all those notes I showed you?'

'Stop it Meredith! I told you, I don't take any notice of that side of things. We're right in the middle of a big campaign now, and I know I'll do more good by staying.'

'But what about all the good you could do as a deacon?'

'Well, that's just the thing. I can't be one. He was adamant about that. Says no Mason can hold any kind of office in his church.'

'Did he say that?' Somehow she could not believe that Kingsley would have said anything so hard-line.

'Not in so many words, but that's what he meant alright.'

'And...you can't go along with him...and see the reason why?'

'No. He seems to think like you. A bit over the top if you ask me. He's going to give himself a lot of headaches if he carries on like that. It's not just me who thinks he's too radical; a dangerous fundamental. He'll have to tone things down a bit if he wants to keep people.'

'What, become lukewarm you mean? Like Reverend Thomas was, and the one before him?'

'There was nothing wrong with them! Going to church was always nice and...comfortable then. This man's too challenging. Anyway, there you are. And you're going to have to think hard about what you're going to do now.'

'What do you mean?'

'Well, people are bound to start asking why we left. It could be difficult for you.'

'Difficult? How?'

'I don't know. Maybe he'll start casting aspersions, dropping little hints here and there.'

'What a horrible thing to say! You know he's not like that. He's said nothing about you. He doesn't even know I went to the library and spoke to you about it.'

'Well, I wouldn't be surprised if he'll be having a few words with you now.'

'It won't bother me if he does!'

'Oh yes it will, especially if you stay.'

'*If* I stay? What do you mean?'

'Er, well, it's up to you what you do, but I don't think I'd be too happy if you still keep going there - and allow yourself to stay under his influence.'

'*"Stay under his influence!"* What do you mean? I'm not under anyone's influence, only The Lord's!'

'Yes, well, be that as it may, enough said.'

'But Dad, if he's not told you to leave, obviously he's hoping you'll stay - if *only* you'd leave the Masons. Why don't you just wait a while, and give him another chance?'

'No Meri! Now let's drop the subject. My mind's made up, and that's that! Anyway, will we be seeing you later?'

She drew in her breathe, knowing she would just be wasting her time if she persisted. He sounded adamant. But she would have liked to have challenged him about why he should bother going to any church at all if he wasn't prepared to take his faith seriously. Instead, she said, 'I don't know. Maybe. I'll phone Mum later on.'

The call ended. She tried hard to focus on her job for the rest of the day, but failed.

She did not go home that night. Knowing that Kingsley was holding an open air down on the beach, she decided to go and see how he was getting on. Minutes later, she stood by the railings, peering down at the scene. Along with several members of Launchpad, he was singing and playing his guitar. One of the group gave a testimony about how he had met The Lord, after which they sang another chorus. Finally, Kingsley gave a short Gospel message to which two people responded. She turned and left before anyone noticed her, feeling glad that, at least, something seemed to be going right.

She didn't go to church the next day and telephoned home later that afternoon. Her mother answered, and sounded so matter-of-fact and almost relieved about the situation, that Meredith began to suspect that she had inadvertently provided her with an excuse to leave their church.

'But some big news!' her mother said, her voice becoming more animated, 'I bumped into Conrad's mother today. He's had an accident and hurt his leg. Did you know? They've had to operate, and they're sending him home when he's okay to travel. There's even talk of a medical discharge. Poor boy, it must be bad.'

She knew his parents' number off by heart, and quickly finishing the call, immediately telephoned them. His mother answered and confirmed the report, telling her that Conrad had been working underneath a heavy vehicle when the lifting mechanism had failed, and one of wheels had landed directly over his right leg. The nature of the crush injury was one that the British surgeons at the nearby RAF hospital had no experience of. However, thankfully, an orthopaedic consultant, on a year's detachment from the United States Air Force, had been called in, and had been able to perform some pioneering surgery. It was expected that Conrad would be flown back to the RAF Hospital in Ely in about ten days' time.

She returned to her chalet and sat down to write to him, hoping that someone in his camp's administrative office would forward it onto the hospital. Then, and still feeling too restless to pray, she quickly changed and went into the ballroom. She was just in time to hear Uncle Jacko finish his usual welcome speech with his usual warning: '… So don't be late for breakan on the morrow, or you'll have a great himpact and out-worry Nook the Chick if you ten up turn mins afore it tends.'

It was obvious that the family on the nearby table was having trouble trying to decipher the message. Taking pity on them, she leaned across, and explained, 'That's tomorrow's breakfast. Nick the Cook gets annoyed if anyone turns up ten minutes before it ends.'

They thanked her, and it was obvious that, like her, they found the mixed-up vocabulary neither clever nor amusing. She moved over to sit on one of the bar stools, hoping that Julia would keep her distance, and that the evening entertainment would provide her with all the distraction she felt she was in serious need of.

Tom was finding his mother-in-law's presence even more trying than usual. It was the same every time she visited; it would always end in tears - and always Sue's. Although there was no denying that mother and daughter loved each other dearly, it was also an incontrovertible, tried and tested fact, that the two women should never be allowed to live under the same roof for more than a few days at a time.

'I thought she was supposed to be leaving any day now?' asked a wary sounding Wendy.

'Next week, thank God! Sue's counting the days. The woman's such a fidget; always poking around, rearranging this and that. She's driving us crazy!'

'Maybe she's just bored,' suggested Meredith.

'Bored? Could be. Sue's coping fine now; and the old girl must see that she's not really needed anymore.'

'Then why don't you give her something to do? There must be something? Give her a job - or make one up? She probably only wants to feel useful,' Meredith said, an idea beginning to form in her mind.

Tom liked the sound of that. 'A job, eh? Such as?'

'Oh, I don't know. Maybe something here?'

Wendy immediately held up her hands in horror. 'What? Here? Not on your nelly! You'll have me off sick with my nerves.'

Tom's shoulders sagged even more. 'Wouldn't work, I'm afraid. Hilda's always had a downer on this place; doesn't think it's a "suitable environment for her daughter to be anywhere near." And now she's fretting about her granddaughter "picking up bad ways". She's always on at me to get another job, something with "a bit more class."'

'But she enjoyed the Broads Trip last week, didn't she?' Meredith asked.

'Huh! Till she got back. Then she found plenty to moan about.'

'Alright, then get her to go on it again. Only this time you could get her to do a…a sort of survey. She could ask the campers what they thought about it on the way back, and if they've got any suggestions about how it could be improved. You never know, she might even want to go on the other trips! She doesn't have to tell anyone that she's your mother-in-law; she could just say that she's been hired by, er, an independent body - quality control, that kind of thing'

Tom and Wendy stared at her, both trying to think of any possible flaw with the idea.

'Meri! You're a ruddy genius!' exclaimed Tom at last. 'That's a fantastic idea!'

Wendy opened her mouth, then closed it again.

'And I wouldn't put it past her to make out it was her idea all along,' he said. 'Damn! I think I'll give her a buzz right away.'

Hilda arrived hotfoot soon after, and within the hour, a middle aged lady could be seen, sensibly clad and striding around the camp in a pair of flat, comfortable shoes, with a pair of binoculars hanging around her neck, a clip board in her hand, and a plastic raincoat rolled up in her capacious bag. Hilda Rodden was on a mission. She was needed.

It was Jennifer's hen night, and she wanted to celebrate it at The Jolly Tar in Brunston. Meredith was amongst the guests. She was just passing the stairs leading up to the guests' bedrooms, when she noticed the two women coming down them: Julia and Fleur. Julia was dressed in her masculine mode black trouser outfit; Fleur in what could only be described as a little girl's dress, extremely short and with large, puff sleeves.

'Well, hello there hun!' said Julia. 'What's a nice girl like you doing in a place like this?'

Fleur halted on the bottom step, obviously unsure how to react.

Quickly recovering from her shock, Meredith replied, 'I could ask the same of you! And you too, Fleur. We haven't seen you at church for a while.'

Julia pulled Fleur down to join her, keeping hold of her hand. 'She's been too busy for stuff like that, haven't you sweetie?'

'I didn't know you two knew each other?' asked Meredith.

'Ah now, there's a lot you don't know about me, hun. Nor about this sweet child.'

Fleur looked at Meredith with a look of defiance. 'What's it got to do with you anyway? I can meet anyone I like, can't I?'

'Er, well, of course.'

'Hey! Nasty, nasty little girl!' interrupted Julia. 'Leave her be! And come on, I'm ready for my dinner. See you around hun.'

The two turned to leave. Unable to stop herself, Meredith caught hold of Julia's arm, and said, 'You know she's only eighteen?'

Julia smiled. 'Yeah! Good in' it? Old enough to know what she's doing.'

'Mind your own bloody business!' exclaimed Fleur, flashing angry eyes at one of the last people she had wanted to meet.

Meredith returned to the dining room soon after and found her companions already discussing the situation. She looked over at the pair. Julia appeared to be totally unconcerned by the looks they were getting, whilst Fleur cast frequent nervous glances over at her table. She avoided joining in the speculations, busy with her own thoughts, which were now mainly about Kingsley. In a few days she would be seeing him to discuss the situation with her father. It seemed to her that every time she spoke to him, she was having to deal with some problem or other. First, there had been all that trouble over the Ouija board, and how Tom had reacted, closely followed by the horoscope issue. Then she had told him about Julia and the trouble she was having with her. And now her parents had decided to leave the church they had attended for as long as she could remember, and all because she had made such an issue over her father being a Mason. She looked over at Julia and Fleur again, and wondered how long it would be before that situation found its way onto the list - and then made the decision that it would not. He was bound to hear about it; but it would not be from her!

CHAPTER 19

...Uncle Jacko can be a sociable and colourful character, however, he strikes me as being a touch coarse, especially when he makes inappropriate gestures and remarks when children are present. Is he a bit dated, I wonder? I feel that he has acquired all his jokes from Christmas crackers.

His appearance is rather unkempt, and he could do with a bib at meal times! Whilst I realise that he has to be sociable and approachable, he does seem to spend rather a large amount of time at the bar, especially at lunch times. This can't be doing him any good, and might account for his sluggish manner most afternoons.

Some campers struggle to understand that very peculiar topsy-turvy vocabulary of his. One family in particular are upset and have missed some events because of it. I've advised them to come and talk to you...

Although ashamed to admit it, Meredith was finding a perverse kind of enjoyment in typing up the first half of Hilda's report.

'Got much more to do?' asked Wendy, coming back into the office after dealing with a query at the counter. Most of the children had gone on the circus trip and the camp was quieter than usual, giving her a chance to update the booking registers: her own special and most favourite responsibility. Deeply curious, she leant over Meredith's shoulder and glanced at the top sheet.

'Crikey! Bit rough on Jacko isn't she?'

'Don't worry, everyone's coming in for a bit of stick.'

'Do tell!'

Meredith leafed through the completed pages and pointed at the relevant section. This bit's about us:-

...The two full-time staff in Reception are most polite. However, there was one instance when I had to wait nearly five minutes to be attended to, which was very frustrating. This occurred on Thursday morning...

'That's not fair!' exclaimed Wendy. 'You were off, and Tom was on his rounds. I had a queue half a mile long to deal with.'

'Tom'll know that, but I'll put a note in anyway.'

'Yeah, in red!'

Tom emerged from his office. 'Just off to the pool. Jacko's just phoned to say he's feeling rough and needs Murphy to cover for him.'

The two women looked knowingly at each other as he left. 'Looks like Hilda's hit the nail on the head,' commented Wendy, 'I saw him propping up the bar again at lunchtime.'

The reception bell pinged. 'I'll go,' Wendy volunteered, leaving the office just as the telephone rang. Meredith answered it.

'Hello Meredith. Kingsley here. Good, I'm glad I've caught you. I'm really sorry, but I've just been called to the hospital, and might have to be there for a while. Poor old Fred Turnbull's taken a turn for the worst and is asking to see me. Mind if we reschedule our chat for another time?'

She thought fast. She knew that Fred had been fighting a losing battle with cancer, and having only recently discovered his links with the Freemasons, she now felt some responsibility to share this piece of information with Kingsley. She didn't want to hear later how Fred had suffered any type of emotional or spiritual distress, which he might do if he had any unconfessed sin - or dark secret - preventing him from dying in peace.

'No problem, and before you go Kingsley, maybe there's something you should know, especially if Fred's...not long for this world. I think he might be a Freemason. Or was.'

'A Freemason? Are you sure?'

'Er, well, yes. It's just that I happen to have found out recently that they paid to get his roof repaired.'

'Did they indeed? I see. He might well be then; he was in middle management before he retired. Right, okay, I'll bear it in mind. Anyway, I'll have to go. And, once again, I'm sorry about having to cancel.'

The atmosphere at home was beginning to ease, partly because Meredith knew there was nothing she could say or do to change her parents' minds about leaving their church, but mainly because she had managed to have a really good prayer time. Feeling that she had gone as far as she was able, she had made a firm decision to trust The Lord to deal with the matter in His own way and time. So it was in this more settled and relaxed frame of mind that she went to answer the door later that evening, and found Kingsley standing there.

She noticed immediately how tired he looked. 'Kingsley! What are you doing here? Are you...is it over? At the hospital?'

He nodded. 'Fred was promoted to glory just over an hour ago.'

'Oh, I'm sorry! Was it peaceful? He didn't suffer did he?'

Kingsley considered before replying. 'Not as bad as it could have been. And you were right, he was a Mason, although lapsed. I just wanted you to know, and stopped by to thank you.'

'You're looking ready to drop. Do you want to come in? Mum's out, and Dad's still at work. Maybe I can get you something?'

'No. That's kind of you, but thanks anyway. I managed to grab a sandwich earlier. But I'd never have guessed if you hadn't told me. His family were there, but I did manage to have a few minutes alone with him. He denied it at first, but confessed towards the end, and was able to ask for The Lord's forgiveness. Anyway, okay if I call you tomorrow to fix up another time for us to have that chat?'

'If you like. There's no rush.'

He smiled. 'I like.' He turned and began walking away, 'See you on Sunday. And say hello to your parents for me. Bye for now.'

She watched him drive off, thinking again how different going to church was going to be from now on. It had always been the three of them; four when her brother, Allan, was home. Now she would be going alone.

Hilda left on Friday afternoon, but not before handing over the second part of her report: all thirteen pages of it. Once again, Tom gave it to Meredith to type up. This was no hardship as she found the task both interesting, and, at times, highly amusing.

The report was very comprehensive, not only covering Hilda's findings and suggestions on the excursions she had been on, but her ideas on such things as the external fencing of the camp, and the beach itself, where she advised:–

> ...I strongly recommend that the relevant department of the local council is informed that the hover flies are being particularly troublesome around the beach. For the sake of your more delicate and senior campers, they should also be instructed to erect a sturdy hand rail by the steps.

The kitchen fared better than most other areas:-

...I was not able to observe the kitchen as the Cook would not allow me access to the area. However, I understand that he is an ex-service man, so there should be nothing to worry about there. The dining hall, which I assume is also his responsibility, is adequate, although possibly a more imaginative table layout would not go amiss, and bulging cleavages are not an appetising sight!

The report went on:-

...The bicycles are unfit for purpose. Several campers complained to me that their derrières were extremely uncomfortable and the tyres needed to be blown up. It is obvious they are not regularly serviced.

...If you find it necessary to continue having a beauty competition, I strongly recommend that you incorporate into the questions a few more worthwhile topics for the entrants. It is my firm opinion that a young woman should strive to possess a good moral character and a reasonable education as well as an attractive appearance.

The first item in the next part particularly interested her:-

...The Sunday morning church service was rather unusual, and I feel that a more traditional style would be better attended. The young minister holds rather radical views, but I expect is well meaning, and one is able to hear that he has rather a pleasant voice when he stops playing on that unsuitable stringed instrument of his!

...The shop is well stocked and the assistant most attentive, especially with the younger children. The opening hours are adequate. However, I feel that all

chewing and bubble gum products should stop being sold as a matter of urgency. Not only are these items a potential choking hazard, they are most unpleasant to put one's foot on, especially on a hot day.

...The café is a problem area that requires your immediate attention. The tables are left cluttered and unwiped for hours at a time. I need to make you aware that one of the young assistants, I believe her name is Christine, has a most disrespectful manner. She regularly disappears when she is alone on duty, when, I suspect, she goes behind the scenes to indulge in a cigarette. Items such as muffins and crumpets would be a most acceptable addition to the menu, especially for the more mature campers.

...Both children's play areas appear to be well used, but a few more benches positioned nearby would be appreciated by the watching parents, also a rubbish bin.

...The paddling pool is a delightful amenity, although on two separate occasions I was disturbed to witness some teenagers running rampage through it and frightening the smaller children.

...The games room also suffers from the same fate. The darts and snooker cues seem to hold a particular draw for the more rowdy elements. May I recommend that a time limit for certain ages be implemented and policed, thus keeping the teenagers at bay. Maybe some quieter games, such as dominoes, backgammon, ludo, monopoly and chess, even the odd jigsaw, would be welcome additions, and might help to calm things down a bit.

...The swimming pool is well attended and I found a life guard on duty at all times. My only criticism, once again, is the wild and inappropriate behaviour of the teenagers, especially the boys. However, I am able to

report that on the two occasions I witnessed such mayhem, the life guard on duty was quick to stamp it out. I shall not mention the attire, or lack of, of some of the teenage girls, as I am sure you are well aware of the situation. The Swimming Gala is obviously much enjoyed by the younger campers. However, I found it all a bit too noisy, as I suspect a few other, more mature campers did as well. The loud, almost hysterical announcements were very intrusive for those of us wishing to find a bit of peace and quiet.

...The bar appears to be very well supported. I found the staff efficient and polite, and the young Jamaican man extremely personable. Small bowls of crisps and peanuts on the counter would be a nice touch, especially during the evening entertainment. However, children would need to be kept well away to avoid the danger of choking.

...Regarding the evening entertainment, much of which, as you are aware, I was unable to attend due to exhaustion. However, most of what I observed was perfectly adequate, and, I suppose, what your average camper has come to expect. Personally, I found the quiz, whist drive and afternoon tea dance more enjoyable. The ballroom dancing exhibition deserves special mention and was quite delightful.

...Unfortunately, I feel it my duty to provide you with additional information with regard to Uncle Jacko. As I have mentioned before, in my opinion, he spends far too much time at the bar, particularly at lunch times. The effect of alcohol was particularly obvious when he conducted the concert auditions on Tuesday and Wednesday afternoons, when his speech was noticeably slurred and incoherent. The situation is exacerbated by his insistence upon using that topsy-turvy grammar of his, which is not particularly clever, and I have

overheard several comments from some campers who became increasingly irritated by it as the week wore on. I have already mentioned this to you in the first part of my report, and do hope that you will give this matter your immediate attention.

...The chalets are far too basic for this day and age and I do feel for the campers, especially with regard to the poor quality bedding. Although the ex-army blankets are warm and serviceable, I do wonder if the campers appreciate being reminded of the war, or their National Service, or their life in married quarters when they are on holiday? The counterpanes are very faded and some have worn very thin and should be replaced immediately. Why aren't the chalet maids on top of this situation?

...Some of the chalet maids most definitely need more supervision, although there were a few efficient exceptions, especially amongst the more mature in age, who know how to get down on their knees. I found several of the younger ones smoking behind the chalets, and some were hardly cleaned at all! Many campers leave them in a good and orderly state, but even so, every sink and floor should always be thoroughly bleached. Certainly, I could detect no smell of the use of any sort of disinfectant when I inspected them afterwards. One must always be wary of verrucas and other unpleasant conditions which can so easily be caught...

The task completed, Meredith put the finished version in a buff folder and handed it to Tom.

'What did you think?' he asked, giving the document a cursory glance.

'I think Marcus would be delighted to know that she thinks he's a Jamaican! But she's not your typical camper, is she? I suppose we can't expect her to understand all the ins and outs of life on a holiday camp, but I think she's made some good points. And this bit about the chalet maids was a bit worrying.' She showed him the section:-

... You will recall that I asked you for one £1 note and one pound in mixed change, as well as some of the older, more valuable items from your collection of items left behind by careless campers. I secreted the items in the following chalets, making sure to put the loose change in places where it could not possibly be mistaken as a tip. Here are my results:-

Chalet 3: One gentleman's watch with brown leather strap. (Not handed in).
Chalet 22: Eight and sixpence in loose change. (Not handed in).
Chalet 49: One small black leather writing case. (Not handed in).
Chalet 74: Five shillings in loose change. (Not handed in).
Chalet 90: £1 note and three and sixpence in loose change. (Only the loose change handed in).
Chalet 101:Three shillings in loose change. (Not handed in).
Chalet 116:One ladies diamante broach in an edelweiss pattern. (Handed in).
I hope you will take immediate action to dismiss the culprits.

Tom closed the folder. 'Looks like she's left me with a few headaches. And do you know, the old biddy's only gone and told Sue that she intends to come back, and do the whole exercise again later on!'

'Well, tell her to stay away from us,' retorted Wendy. 'We work flipping hard and don't need anyone cracking the whip. Or it'll be talons at high noon!'

CHAPTER 20

Meredith was to be a bridesmaid at Jennifer's wedding. It wasn't often that she took a day off for personal reasons, but she felt no qualms about doing so the following Saturday. Although not an ideal solution, and one that Wendy would have cause to moan about for the next few days, a children's nanny was coerced into helping behind reception.

The wedding was a joyful occasion, after which the whole assembly, consisting of over a hundred people, strolled around to the church hall for the reception. Kingsley left soon after the speeches, having been called away to attend another sick bed.

Meredith returned home later to change. Her father had been on a ten day course and was due to return later that day, and she had set herself the task of tidying up the garden.

'Come in, Meredith! There's someone to see you,' called her mother from the open French doors, her voice sounding more melodic than usual.

'Who is it?'

'You'll find out when you come in; he's in the front room. Don't keep him waiting. I'll put the kettle on.'

'What's the big mystery? she asked, washing her hands and putting a comb through her hair, as Pamela arranged an assortment of biscuits on one of her best fancy plates.

'You'll see,' she replied, opening a fresh packet of custard creams. 'Now go along! You've kept him waiting long enough.'

She didn't recognise the back of the man's head when she entered the room, but her eye was quickly drawn to the sight of a large, white plaster, resting on a pouf in front of him. She nearly tripped over the pair of crutches, lying on the floor beside him. 'Conrad! You're back! Why didn't you let me know?'

'Hello Meri. Glad to see me?'

'Yes. Of course! What a surprise!'

'For everyone, including me. But here I am.' He strummed his fingers on the plaster, 'All of me!'

She moved the crutches away from the door and went to sit on the nearby armchair. She looked closely at him. He looked older, and his hair, always cut in the typical short back and sides, military style, was longer than usual.

'I was really sorry to hear about the accident. How are you now?'

He grimaced. 'Not too good, it's bloody painful. Couldn't have come at a worse time. I'm up for promotion, or was.'

'What happened? All we heard was that you'd had some sort of accident with your knee.'

He stretched his other leg out on the pouf, both feet now protruding over the edge. 'Got stuck under a wagon when the lifting gear failed. Snowdrops still haven't found out how it happened, the b......'s wouldn't stop bugging me. I'm glad to get away from them.'

She knew he was referring to the military police with their white covered hats, and asked, obviously shocked, 'Why? They don't suspect foul play do they?'

'More like carelessness. Not mine, you understand. We'd had a group of apprentices in, and I'm damned sure one of them had been messing about. But proving it's another thing.'

She wanted to ask if anyone had thought to check the equipment after they had gone, but thought better of it.

Just then, her mother came bustling in with the hostess trolley. Fairy cakes and scones had been added to the biscuit selection.

'Well now Conrad,' began Pamela, sitting down and beginning to pour the tea. 'I expect your parents are glad to have you back safe and sound? And it'll be nice for you having

Meredith close by; she'll be able to keep you company. But it's a shame Allan's spending his summer holiday in Skegness.'

'What's the attraction there then?' he asked, as Meredith looked on, wondering at the sight of the trolley, which was only ever wheeled out for very special occasions.

'His girlfriend! Oh, she only went and got them both jobs at Butlins. Didn't Meredith tell you?'

'Er, oh...maybe.'

Pamela looked accusingly at Meredith as she handed him his cup, and said, sounding pleased with herself, 'Five lumps. See, I remembered. And Meredith, why didn't you tell him? I don't know...'

'Actually, I did!' interrupted Meredith, 'I wrote and told him ages ago. Anyway, are they going to hold some sort of enquiry? Have they interviewed everyone that was there?'

Pamela, who already knew the answers, having previously telephoned his mother to find out such things for herself, snapped, 'For goodness sake! Leave the poor boy alone! Can't you see he's had enough? Of course they've looked into it.' She turned her attention back to Conrad. 'Help yourself, dear, and I've had a word with Simon, and he's happy about letting her have the car on her days off.'

Conrad took three of the custard creams. 'That's handy, I've got a two o'clock appointment at the hospital tomorrow.'

Meredith looked on, realising that the pair had already spoken and made plans. It was a pity they had not thought to check with her first; her talk with Kingsley had been rescheduled for that very time.

'Well now, that's very convenient! She's off tomorrow afternoon,' announced Pamela.

Meredith spoke up. 'Er, I'm sorry, but I've got to be at the church then.'

'At the church? What do you mean?' Pamela asked, making the location sound somehow distasteful.

'I've got an appointment myself...'

'An *appointment!* At the *church!* Well then, you'll just have to cancel it, won't you!'

'No Mum! I won't. It's already been rearranged once. But what about your mother, Conrad, can't she take you?'

Becoming flustered, Pamela retorted, 'I've never heard anything like it! Of course you'll take him. Who are you seeing there anyway? I can't imagine they'd be very impressed to hear that you've refused to help someone in need.'

'It's with the minister, and it's been put off once already...'

'Oh, for goodness sake! Don't you see enough of *that* man? I've got a good mind to ring him and cancel it myself...'

'Okay ladies!' interrupted Conrad. 'I'll ask around and get a mate to take me. Pass me a scone quick, Pamela. A man could die of hunger around here.'

Pamela passed him one of her best Spode tea plates and offered him the selection of cakes as she shot an angry glare in Meredith's direction. 'I'm very disappointed in you, my girl. I'd drop everything if I could drive.'

Meredith had been doing some quick thinking. Although she had been looking forward to seeing Kingsley again, she now felt that there was no great need for her to go through any special time of prayer, or counselling, about her father's involvement with the Freemasons. She had already prayed, and used the same words that she had used over the horoscope problem - at least as much as she could remember. Maybe her mother with right, and Conrad's needs were greater than hers.

'Alright. I'll take you. But I'd better ring and tell him right away.'

'And I should think so too!' exclaimed Pamela. 'I don't know! Making all this fuss.'

Meredith went out into the hall to make the call. Behind her, she heard her mother ask, her tone of voice sounding almost appealing, 'Does this mean that we'll be seeing a lot more of you now, Conrad?'

'Of course! Got to keep my main girls happy.'

Kingsley was obviously out. Meredith left a message and returned to the front room.

Conrad was talking, '...there's some talk of a medical discharge. It's put paid to Germany, and all other overseas postings. I'm not A1 fit anymore.'

Pamela replaced her cup with a crash. She looked almost ready to cry. 'Oh you poor boy! What an awful thing to happen!'

'But you'll be okay won't you? You'll be able to walk properly again?' asked Meredith.

He shrugged. 'They reckon so. But it's going to be a long old job. And this damn thing's uncomfortable.'

'Yes, it looks it.' She studied the thick tube-like plaster, and her heart went out to him. He was - or had been - such a fit, healthy person; a sportsman at heart. Being so constricted and weighed down by such a cumbersome looking object must be really hard for him.

'And it's not a straightforward case,' he continued, 'Apparently, they had to take the whole knee cap out; it had shattered anyway, and use one of my thigh muscles to make some sort of bridge in my knee instead.'

Pamela gasped.

Meredith imagined ligaments and tendons, muscles and cartilages, all flapping about, having no central fixed point. 'Goodness! That sounds fantastic!' she exclaimed. 'I've never heard of anything like it! I didn't think you could walk without a knee cap?'

'Yeah, they reckon that the Yank that did it is a bit of a maverick. His detachment's over and he's back to the States, but he wants progress reports.'

'What a good thing he was there,' remarked Pamela, almost recovered from her dismay now.

'Huh! Having my leg restrung isn't exactly what I need at my age! And it's going to be a long haul before I can get back

143

on my feet and get going again. I may have to reconsider my options.'

Meredith asked, 'What options?'

'They've offered me a job at the RAF careers office in Brunston, but I'm not sure that I want to get other lads to join up and live the life I can't anymore. Dad's offered to take me on at the garage to do the office side, but...' he sighed, 'Office work? *Seriously?*'

Obviously close to tears now, Pamela reached out her hand and patted his. 'Oh, you poor, poor boy! It's dreadful, dreadful!'

He caught hold of her hand, and looked up at her with a woeful expression. 'I think I'll be able to bear it, knowing that you...and Meri ...are here for me. It'll help me to face things.'

Pamela's face flushed. 'You just say the word, Conrad, and we'll be there for you. Day or night. Whatever you need. It's the least we can do for you, you poor boy.'

He smiled and kissed the top of her hand, then, letting go, reached out and helped himself to a few more custard creams.

Meredith attended the house group that night and was slightly anxious at seeing Kingsley there, feeling that Conrad's arrival would complicate things even more, although she was not exactly sure how, or why. Even without her mother's interference, it was obvious that he was expecting her to keep him company for the duration. But then, that was nothing unusual, he always had on his visits home.

The group was still studying the Person and ministry of The Holy Spirit. Frances, the house group leader, and a grammar school teacher, had a natural way of explaining the great Christian truths in a clear and concise way, and began by giving a brief summary of the previous weeks' discussions.

'Just a quick round-up for those who weren't here last week. We've discussed the nature of the Holy Spirit, and how He's often referred to as *The Third Person of The Godhead.*

I'm not surprised that some of you are still struggling with the concept, but I would ask you not to become anxious about it. Remember, our faith holds many mysteries, and if we understood them all, then we'd be God! It's enough to know that The Lord works in a multitude of ways to reach each one of us with His love.

We've already covered the gifts, so tonight we're going to make a start on the nine fruits of The Spirit, looking at the first two: love and joy.' She paused to look around, 'Meredith, would you open in prayer for us?'

Meredith had been re-reading **Genesis**, and with it still fresh in her mind, she began: 'Heavenly Father, we thank You for Your living Presence within us. We read at the very beginning of Your Word how You created light and order out of darkness and chaos, and we thank You that we have experienced Your creative-Genesis work in our own lives. Forgive those of us who may still have some dark places; places where your light still needs to shine.'

Kingsley raised his head and looked over at her, as she continued, 'Please help us to be willing to open every door and allow Your healing light to shine in. May we hear You speaking to us tonight. May we be willing to let You clean and recreate and us in those dark, secretive places. For we ask it in Your Son's precious name, our Lord Jesus, Amen.'

Several heartfelt 'Amens' were echoed. The study progressed, followed by a time of prayer, and finishing with another drink, before everyone began to go their separate ways. As usual, Jennifer was giving Meredith a lift home.

Kingsley went to speak to her as she was leaving. 'I had your message. You sounded a bit upset; is everything alright?'

'Yes, sorry about that. And I'm fine thanks,' and then, hoping that he wouldn't ask for any details, quickly went on to ask, 'How did the beach outreach go?'

'Okay I think. It would be good to see you there one of these evenings. We're planning on doing a barbeque next time. I'll be announcing it on Sunday.'

'That sounds like fun. I'll try and come along.'

'Excellent. By the way, we still need to reschedule for that other matter. If I wasn't a Christian, I'd say "Third time lucky!"'

'Well, actually, I don't think I need to bother you about it now. I've done some praying and...things are sorting themselves out.' Her speech faltered, had she just told a lie? 'And my friend's back, you know, the one I told you about - in the Air Force? He's had a bad accident and his leg's in plaster; he may even be back for good.'

'Ah! I see.' He was silent for a moment. 'Then why don't you bring him along to the barbeque too? It would be good to meet him.'

'Er, alright. I'll ask him. Anyway my lift's waiting, I'd better go. See you soon,' and with that she turned and left, wondering if she had just told a lie. It was true that she had prayed about her father's involvement with the Masons, but for the past few days she was beginning to suspect that things were not 'sorting themselves out', as she had just stated. But then it was just a little white lie - wasn't it? Knowing that there was no such thing, for a lie was a lie - no matter how little or big it was - she realised that she would need to spend a bit more time doing some confessing during her quiet time tonight.

CHAPTER 21

Pamela had a new mission in life: to help Conrad - 'the poor boy' - get through this awful patch. And to do that, she needed the assistance of her husband and daughter. Especially her daughter. She began to invite him to tea; always on Meredith's day off. The hidden motive behind her endeavours was obvious for all to see: she was matchmaking. Conrad appeared not to mind and co-operated fully, although he wasn't going to tell her that he was all for keeping his options open. Meri had always been his back-up plan anyway; she would do nicely if no-one else came along by the time he was ready to settle down. But he wasn't ready - just yet.

Fully aware of her mother's machinations, Meredith asked her to stop interfering, and had even found it necessary to ask her father to aid her cause. However, he merely shrugged and gave his usual reply, 'Don't let it get to you, she doesn't mean any harm. And you know your mother, will she listen to me? Will she heck!' He had already been nagged into getting a lift into work organised for Thursdays, thereby releasing the car so that Meredith could take Conrad out on her day off.

On two occasions Meredith had suggested that they call in at the camp, but Conrad had refused, saying that he was too embarrassed about 'the damn thing on his leg' - which he had begun to hate, and stating that he would prefer to be taken to some of the quieter, country pubs around the area. Knowing that he had been in the Boys' Brigade as a youth, she asked if he would like to go to church with her, or to any of the beach open-airs, especially the barbeque. But once again, he had refused, claiming that, 'He had grown out of all of that years ago.'

As a result, her own church attendance dropped dramatically over the coming weeks.

The Gospel Service in the ballroom had become a regular feature, and Kingsley would always find time to call at reception and have a few words with her before he left. He never commented upon her sporadic attendance at church, and she was grateful to him for his understanding.

Wendy invited them both for a meal one Thursday evening. 'It's our fifth wedding anniversary, and I want to try out a new curry recipe on someone before we get Neville's boss over on Saturday. You don't mind, do you?'

Once again, Meredith had to telephone Frances and excuse herself from the house group. She had missed the previous three, and knew that the series on the Holy Spirit would soon be drawing to close. Somehow, she would have to try and make it to the final one; she was really beginning to miss her friends and routine by now.

They arrived at Wendy and Neville's in time to witness Wendy burn one of the chapattis she was making to accompany the chicken curry. Neville ushered them into the lounge and brought out the first of the bottles of wine he had carefully selected for the evening.

'Thanks mate,' said Conrad, taking a large sip as he sat on the edge of an armchair. Taking another, he reached down to grab the bottom rim of the plaster, and swung his leg up onto a nearby stool.

The two men seemed to be getting on well, so Meredith left them to it and returned to the kitchen to help Wendy. Shutting the door behind her, she asked, 'Didn't you tell Neville that Conrad's not supposed to drink?'

'He knows, but we'll need to keep an eye on him. You know how he gets carried away when he's had a few.'

The curry was a great success, and gasps of appreciation were made when Wendy took a large strawberry pavlova out of the fridge. Conrad looked flushed as he remarked, 'Blimey! That's fancy. I'm impressed!'

'Wish I could lay claim to this one, but Neville brings them home from work,' confessed Wendy. 'But I'm still perfecting my technique.'

Neville was struggling to open another bottle. '*When* you remember to get them out of the oven! She forgot last time, and it was in for eight hours instead of five. Mind you, turned out great; the best yet.'

The two women decided to wash up before having coffee. The men went back into the lounge, and it wasn't long before the pungent smell of cigar smoke began to pervade the whole house.

They had almost finished, when Meredith spotted four empty wine bottles behind the kitchen bin. Pointing at them, she asked, 'I had two glasses, and not full ones either. How many did you have?'

'Er, two I think. Neville had...maybe four?'

'So that's eight accounted for; that's about two bottles.' They looked at each other, then Meredith exclaimed, 'Don't tell me Conrad's had the others? I didn't see him fill his glass up that much.'

'Well, he did. I saw him at least four times, then I lost count. I didn't know he was a drinker?'

'He's not. He only ever has a couple of halves when we go out.'

'He'll be on the brandy now,' warned Wendy, tossing her head towards the lounge, and knowing her husband's drinking habits.

Meredith looked concerned. 'He'll be risking it then, what with that cigar on top of the curry and pavlova. And I noticed him take another pill at eight.'

149

Wendy hurriedly took her plastic apron off. 'Right then, let's get in there. Put the kettle on. We'd better get some black coffee on the go.'

They found the two men deep in slurred conversation when they joined them.

'Enough you!' ordered Wendy, taking the empty glass away from Neville. He looked sluggishly up at her with glazed eyes, and gave her a sheepish grin. "Ello, bootiful. What you doin' rest a my life?'

Meredith held out a mug of strong coffee to Conrad.

'You can take that 'way, woman!' he said, pushing her hand away roughly, causing her to spill the hot liquid on her dress. She gasped and ran into the kitchen, quickly followed by Wendy.

'Serves 'er right,' he said, 'comin' 'ween a man an' 'is drink. Mustn't do that. Never, never, never!'

'Poor show, old boy,' slurred Neville. 'Got to 'pologise.'

"Pologise? Bloody 'ell, no! Woman's got know 'er place. Man and 'is drink…'portant. Good job not bloody married. Hell no!'

'Not going marry 'er then?'

Conrad smiled and lifted his glass. He took a long drag of his cigar and blew the smoke out to form a series of rings. He winked, 'Might do, if nothin' else fancy comes 'long.'

A gentle snore came from Neville's chair.

Meredith came back into the room, a large wet stain covering the front of her dress. 'I think it's time we made a move,' she said, determined to put an end to the evening. 'You've had too much already, and I'm soaking wet.'

'Sod off!'

Wendy came in, stared at the scene, then uttered something about needing to clear up. Meredith attempted to prise the nearly empty glass out of Conrad's hand.

'Gerr'off! Bloody women! Leave us 'lone. Bloody 'ell…'

'That's it! You've gone too far. Give me a hand to get him up, would you, Wendy?'

It took almost ten minutes for the two women to pull and push the towering six foot two figure, hampered by the heavy plaster, out of the room and through the front door. Once the fresh air hit him, he staggered, and would have fallen, if it had not been for the firm hold they had on him as the first stream of vomit shot out of his mouth.

Eventually, and obviously very much the worse for wear, they managed to get him onto the back seat of the car. Meredith couldn't apologise enough, and offered to stay to wash the mess off the path and garden, but Wendy wouldn't hear of it. She just wanted the man gone.

Twenty minutes later, Meredith delivered Conrad back to his parents' house. She felt deeply embarrassed as his father looked upon the grim scene, before helping her struggle to get his semi-conscious son out of the car and into the house. Afterwards, his mother stared with disgust at the large wet patch on her dress, then glowering at her, told her to leave, slamming the door noisily in her face.

She waited all the next day to hear from him, but there was no call. Anxious now, she telephoned later that evening and asked how he was.

'He's not here,' replied his mother, a hard edge to her voice.

'But he's alright, isn't he?' she asked.

'Yes, but no thanks to you! I'm surprised at you, Meredith Sanderson. You were a decent girl before you started working on that camp. I shall certainly be having a few words with your mother. Fancy letting him get him in that state! You could have killed him! Disgusting carry-on. Just you leave him alone from now on, and don't call here again. He can do without the likes of you dragging him down.' The receiver was slammed down, hard.

'Who was that?' Simon asked, coming through from the kitchen.

'Conrad's mother. She's...not too happy with me.'

He frowned, 'Why not?'

'She's blaming me for the state he was in last night.'

'What, when he got drunk?'

'Yes. Thinks I'm a bad influence, and told me to stay away from him!'

Pamela had just emerged from the bedroom, and was on her way down the stairs when she overhead Meredith's last statement. 'Stay away from who?'

'Conrad. You know, last night, when he got drunk. His mother's blaming me.'

'Well, you were silly, you know. Why didn't you stop him? You know he shouldn't drink when he's on those tablets.'

'Thanks Mum! I knew I could rely on you. And I did try to stop him, but he wouldn't have it. And why should I be held responsible for what he puts in his mouth anyway? He's supposed to be an adult.'

'That's a selfish attitude to take, my girl! You know he's in a very vulnerable state, and it's up to us all to look out for him now. You'd better go around there and apologise to his parents. You can't afford to lose a nice boy like that.'

Meredith stared hard at her mother. 'If there's any apologising to be done, it's him who should be doing it! He behaved badly around Wendy's, and...and...' she stopped short, not wanting to add fuel to the fire by revealing that Wendy had asked her, 'Never to take *that man* to her home again!' Instead, she went on to say, 'And it would be nice to have some support from you sometimes.'

'That's enough Meri,' interjected her father, upset at hearing his wife and daughter at cross purposes. 'Let it drop now. I'm sure Conrad will straighten things out when he's up to it.'

'Do you think so, Dad?' she asked, 'I hope you're right, but he's taking his time about it. And I'll tell you now, I'll be having a few words with him myself when he finally has the courage to face me again!'

'You'll do no such thing! You'll have to change that attitude, and get off your high horse, my girl!' Pamela exclaimed, pushing past them both, 'Or you'll end up like Freda - fat and frigid - and all alone in the world. And don't say you haven't been warned!'

Meredith had grown up hearing all about Freda, her mother's young sister, alias 'the black sheep of the family'. Exasperated, she rolled her eyes, and looked at her father.

He gave a secretive smile, and said quietly, 'That's not what I've heard!'

'What? What was that?' Pamela asked.

'Nothing,' he replied, winking at Meredith, 'only your Freda doesn't do too badly for herself.'

If Meredith had not been a Christian, she would have given in to her curiosity and asked for details - but she was a Christian.

After a lengthy prayer time, calm, and now full of feelings of forgiveness, she went back downstairs and hugged her mother.

'What's that for?' Pamela queried, shrugging her off, not being much of a hugger herself.

'No reason. I just felt like it.'

'Does that mean you've changed you mind? That you'll go and apologise to his parents?'

'No Mum. That's not going to happen. Anyway, are you two going to church tonight?'

'Don't think so,' replied her father, fishing in his pocket for the car keys and offering them to her, 'I've got a report to finish by tomorrow.'

Pamela tutted loudly and walked out of the room, knowing that now the unpleasant task would have to fall to her. But she wasn't surprised; the girl had always been a disappointment.

Meredith drove to church. She tried to remember how often her parents had been to their new church since leaving Plover Baptist. Certainly, they were not going as regularly as they always had been. She didn't know much about the Coleman Road Methodists, only having met a few of their young people when they came along to the film nights. They had always struck her as not being on the same spiritual wavelength as her own fellowship. Resigned, she knew that this was yet another thing she was going to have to add to her prayer list.

CHAPTER 22

'That man's out there to see you,' said Wendy, returning to her desk, and sounding none too pleased. 'I thought you said he didn't want to come here?'

'Who? You don't mean Conrad?' asked Meredith, hardly able to believe it.

Wendy inclined her head towards the open door, 'Doesn't look too good either. Still on the pop is he?'

Meredith hurried out. 'Conrad! What are you doing here?'

'Pleased to see you too!' he replied, sarcastically. 'Got a mate to drop me off. I'm bloody cheesed off, and thought I'd come and see what's so special about this place.'

'But I'm working!'

'I know that!' he replied, testily. 'They give you a break, don't they?'

She looked at him, trying to decide where she could take him that didn't involve drinking, and hoping that it was his obvious need to rest his leg that was making him so tetchy. She called out to Wendy, 'Just going to the pool. Back in a minute. Come on, Conrad, let's get you sitting down.'

'How far?' he asked, following unsteadily on his crutches.

'Just two minutes.'

She said the odd word of encouragement as they made their way across the forecourt; the things she really wanted to say to him could wait for now. Their progress was slow, and the short two minute walk turned into almost five. Arriving at last, he groaned as he hurled himself down on the nearest vacant sun lounger.

'I'll fetch you a coke. Ice?' she asked.

'That'll do,' he replied, repositioning himself.

He looked more relaxed and comfortable when she returned a few minutes later. 'Can't stay, I'll have to get back. Will your friend know to come to reception when he comes back to fetch you?'

He shrugged, 'Expect so.'

'See you soon then.'

An hour passed before she was able to join him again. He lay with his eyes closed, his face and body appearing to be more relaxed. 'You're looking a bit brighter. How's the pain?'

'Not so bad, but it'll be back. I jolted it when I tripped over yesterday.'

'Ouch! Have you been and had it looked at?'

'No. It'll calm down. I've done it before.'

She wanted to say that he should be more careful, then held back, knowing that that would have been stating the obvious. Instead, she went on to ask, 'Did you know that I phoned your house when I didn't hear from you after the other night?'

'Yeah, well, I phoned yours too.'

'You did? When?'

'Today, this morning. And a little bird told me it's your birthday on Thursday and said you'd not got any plans. So I came hotfoot to invite you out for a meal. I quite fancy that old pub we looked in on the other week, remember, over at Gorsham Broad? Their menu looked alright.'

Meredith guessed the identity of that 'little bird', and decided she would have to have a few more words with her mother.

'And I happen to know that your dad's car will be available,' he added, 'so that's the transport sorted.'

This was true; her parents were due to go away on a mini coach tour of the Lake District the next day. 'Well, I suppose - okay. But, I think we really need to talk about the other night at Wendy and Neville's…'

'Hey! You're not going to harp on about that are you? Could I help it if he kept filling my glass up? It would have been antisocial to refuse.'

She stared at him. 'That's pathetic! They warned you not to drink on those tablets. Honestly, Conrad, it was really embarrassing. And Wendy's still upset about it.'

'Come off it Meri, can't a chap have blow-out once in a while? You wouldn't deny me that now, would you? After all I've been through?'

'Yes, I certainly could! Especially in your condition. She pointed at the plaster. 'You could have fallen and cracked it. You said that you'd tripped over again, and that's when you're sober - or were you?'

'Talk about the Spanish Inquisition! Yes, I damn well was! The damn cat shot out in front of me.'

'Cat! Where?'

'At home.'

'I didn't know you had one!'

'Well, there you are then. There's a lot you don't know about me.' He scowled hard at her.

She scowled back just as hard. 'And there's a lot you don't know about me either! And why did your mother blame me for the state you were in? She was really quite rude when I phoned up. Haven't you told her what happened yet?'

'Bloody hell! Can't you give it a rest? You know what mothers are like.'

'So you haven't told her?'

He evaded her look, and her question, only replying, 'She'll come round.'

'What, like my mother! She blamed me as well, you know!'

For some reason he found this amusing.

'And you won't go round and put her straight either, will you?'

'Cool it, Meri! It'll blow over; they'll have forgotten all about it next week. You're getting all bitter and twisted. You need to get away from this place more. And what about your birthday? I'll be ready to be picked up at seven.'

So, now she knew that he had no intention of apologising, or explaining his drinking behaviour to anyone. Disappointed in him, and yet quickly coming to terms with this newly discovered side of his character, she gave in, although determined that he wasn't going to have it all his own way, she replied firmly, 'Too early. I shan't be able to get away till eight.'

'Who was that handsome guy I saw you with by the pool?' Julia asked, coming to sit opposite her on one of the staff tables in the dining room later that day.

'Just a friend,' Meredith replied, dismissively.

'Friend, eh? I take it that it's all off with you and Kingsley then?'

'All off? What do you mean? It was never on!'

Julia's already arched eyebrows raised even higher. 'Pull the other one, hun. I know you like him, and I kinda got the impression he likes you too. And I suppose this *friend's* the reason you've stopped going to your church lately?'

Meredith looked down to study her ham salad. 'I have been going, but not quite so much? Anyway, how do you know?'

'Kingsley told me. Remember, he's been trying to de-sex me? And don't pretend you aren't flattered. Why else would he keep asking after you if he wasn't interested?'

'He asks after everybody who's not been for a while. And he's certainly not *interested* in…any other way.'

'Oh yeah! Is that right? Well then, you'll have to tell him to ask about you from someone else from now on. I've put a stop to it. He's just wasting his time, and mine. The sessions were getting a bit heavy, and I'm not like you, hun, I don't need any God.'

Meredith looked at her, concern written all over her face. 'But you do, Julia! You really do. We all do. It's just that you don't recognise it now, but one day you will.'

'Nah! Got by okay so far; why go spoiling a good thing?'

'Spoil what, your...lifestyle...and having relationships with girls much younger than you?'

'Say it like it is, hun!'

'Alright, I will! You know that's one of the Devil's oldest tricks: to make us think that we don't need God in our lives? And that we can get along okay without Him?'

'Speak for yourself. I'm just fine and dandy as I am.'

'But what'll you do if you wake up one day and find that you're not so "fine and dandy"?' Conrad's image came into her mind, 'You don't know what's round the corner. What if you find you can't fend for yourself anymore?'

Julia shrugged and bit into her ham, taking her time to chew. 'I'll find a way. Make sure I've got plenty of cash behind me; take out insurances. There's always ways and means.'

'But money doesn't solve everything.' The noise level around them grew. Meredith knew that this was not the most suitable place to have this type of conversation, but felt strongly that she should speak up, even in this environment.

'Goes a long way, hun. You can touch it, and make it work for you. I guess that's the difference between us. Sounds like you use your God like an insurance policy. I'm more honest about things; more realistic.'

Meredith had to think about that. Did she use Jesus like some sort of insurance policy? Did she only want Him in her life just so that she could call upon Him when things went wrong? - like some sort of divine back-up? No. She knew the answer to that. She wanted - needed Him, because she loved Him. It was true that she relied on Him when things weren't going too good, but she also knew that she wanted - needed Him, just as much when things were going well.

'You're wrong. I want Him in my life because I love Him, and I know He loves me, and I want His love, no matter what's going on. And stop shifting the focus onto me when we're talking about you. I think you're really going to have to watch yourself, Julia. You might find yourself getting bitter. You know how things can chip away at you in life.'

'Rubbish! A good night out always sorts me out. You should try it sometime. Get that *friend* of yours to take you out. What's he done to his leg anyway?'

'You're shifting the focus again. He had an accident and damaged his knee badly. And how can a night out on the town, or a drinking session in Jacko's room, solve anything?'

'Oh, you'd be surprised! I was born free, and that's the way I'm gonna keep it.'

'But you're not free Julia. Can't you see that? You're just marching to the beat of the Devil's drum.'

Julia laughed out loud. The campers on the nearby table looked across, then around, trying to find where the entertainment was coming from. Jacko was nowhere to be seen. Disappointed, they returned to their meal.

'Yeah! Well, reckon it's a damn sight more fun than the one you're marching to!' She grinned her lopsided smile. 'But I'm kinda glad for you, hun. Truly I am. And I'm touched that you tried to show me your...way. But the world's a different place now, and you'll have to come to terms with the fact that the rest of us just aren't interested in joining your club.'

'That's because they don't know; they haven't heard how much God loves them, and it's up to us to tell them. That's what Kingsley's doing: in the church, out of the church, in the ballroom, on the beach, anywhere and everywhere he goes. And you've seen for yourself how people react when they take the time to listen, and think about what he says.'

'Oh, admitted, he catches a few. But he gets up a lot of noses as well. You're cocooned in that office, but I hear the comments. They laugh at him when he's gone. One day he'll wake up and smell the roses.'

'Yes, I know people laugh at us, and mock us. They did to Jesus. In a way, I've come to expect it.'

'Well then, why don't you stop trying? Why don't you just go along to your little gatherings, and leave the rest of us alone? Can't you see it's not working?' There was a tone of genuine concern in her voice now.

'I can't Julia. It's like I've got a big bottle of medicine and I want to give it to everyone around me. But they don't realise they're sick. I get so...frustrated.'

'Meri, Meri! You sweet girl. We're not sick!'

'But can't you see, that's why you all go around doing the things you do, and trying so hard to find some sort of happiness or peace? You just don't give yourselves a chance. You won't allow yourselves to look in the right place.'

Julia stirred her tea. A thoughtful expression on her face as she began to shake her head slowly. 'You're heading for a lot of heartache if you keep banging your drum to a beat no-one else wants to march to. One day you'll really get up some wrong noses, and then you may find yourselves being forced to shut up, or you'll end up getting locked up!'

'Everyone's free to make their own choices. We've made ours. And no-one's forcing you to change. And it was you who asked to see Kingsley, remember? And anyway, why should we be forced to be quiet, or change our beliefs? Aren't we entitled to the same freedom everyone else has? Look at all the worshipping that goes on at pop concerts and football grounds - even at political rallies! Why don't you go and tell all them to be quiet, or change their beliefs?'

Despite herself, Julia recognised that Meredith had made a good point, and one that she couldn't think of any argument against right now. 'Can't win with you, can I? But if it was up to me, hun, you'd all be left alone to get on with it - as long as you stay away from me!'

Meredith pushed her plate away, and with a real note of sadness in her voice, said, 'Well, thanks for being honest with me. But, you know, we aren't Jesus. We're all just trying; we're sinners, saved by grace. Please don't judge Him by our standards. But I really hope you'll think about Him again one day.'

'Can't see it, hun.' Julia stood, and reached over to pat Meredith's head as though she was a little girl. 'But bless you child. I know you mean well.'

Not caring what the people around her would think, Meredith caught hold of her hand and held it tightly. 'The door's always open, Julia. You'll always be welcome. Please try and remember that He loves you; He loves you so much, and He always, *always* will.'

Without a word, Julia pulled her hand away and left.

CHAPTER 23

She had just reached the gate when the front door opened and Conrad emerged. He looked as though he had made an effort: his hair had been cut, and he was wearing what looked like a new shirt. Around one arm he had looped the handles of a plastic carrier bag which swung in time with his unsteady step; both hands gripped the crossbars of his wooden crutches.

'You look very nice,' he said, shuffling into the car and hauling his leg across the back seat.

'Thanks, you do too. How are you today?'

'Same. Here,' he un-looped the bag and held it out to her. 'Happy birthday. Had to rely on Mum to get it.'

She opened the bag and took out the box of chocolates, *Black Magic*. She wasn't a fan of dark chocolate, and had seen them on offer in the local supermarket; nevertheless she made an effort to sound grateful. 'Thank you. You shouldn't have.'

They drove on, arriving at the restaurant in good time for their booking. The meal was pleasant, but not exceptional, and Meredith was relieved to find that he was the same agreeable companion she had always known: gregarious, funny, and likeable. It had been a shock to encounter that other side of him; all she could think of was that the accident must have sent him temporarily off-kilter.

After they had eaten, he took a small brown plastic bottle out of his pocket and popped one of the pills into his mouth. For a moment, she became concerned, and hoped that there would be no adverse side effect, not relishing a repeat performance of the night around Wendy's. But she relaxed when she remembered that he had only had one pint of lager.

A waitress began clearing their table. She ordered coffee to be taken in the garden as he excused himself and went off to find the toilet, leaving the bottle of pills on the table. She put the bottle in her handbag and made her way outside.

Passing the car park, she noticed a familiar red sports car with a familiar registration. What was Jacko doing here? She hadn't heard anything about him having the evening off. She thought no more about it as she went to sit on a bench near the shade of a large beech tree. A young woman with fine, long blonde hair, was sitting at a table a few yards away. Although she had her back to her, Meredith was sure it was Fleur. Young Fleur! A thought struck her, and she immediately tried to dismiss it as being too absurd to even contemplate: Jacko and Fleur - here together! Conrad broke into her thoughts as he returned. The waitress arrived with their coffee at the same time, and there was no sign of Fleur when she looked again.

They chatted amicably for a while. She yawned, then he did, and they both decided to call it a day soon after. They were reversing out of the car park when she saw a figure in dark slacks and a neat, fitted black jacket walking towards Jacko's car. It was Julia. Then she saw Fleur running towards the car and jump in. Fleur and Julia - together again. She really must start getting used to the idea. And that was all she could think about as she drove Conrad back, and deposited him, safe and sober, by his front gate.

She needed to stop for petrol on the way home. The garage was owned by Conrad's father, but she knew he would not be there; he never was at this time of night. A van pulled up at the next pump. An Asian youth hopped out and began to fill up his tank. A few seconds later, the screech of car brakes could be heard as two cars came to a noisy halt on the road, some yards away. Doors were flung open, and within seconds a gang of skinheads ran shouting onto the forecourt.

Meredith was replacing her fuel cap, and watched with horror as two of the skinheads charged at the Asian youth, the first head-butted him, whilst the other, heavily booted, began kicking him from behind. The van door opened and what looked like half a dozen Asian youths spilled out. She was relieved when she noticed one of them go and replace the still gushing fuel nozzle.

A full scale fight between the two gangs soon broke out. Meredith looked with horror at the fallen, crumpled body of the attacked Asian youth, and before she knew what she was doing, she began pushing and shoving her way through the melee of fighting bodies. Reaching him, she knelt and saw that he was conscious, although his eyes were half closed, and in obvious distress. Wetness began to seep through her stockings and dress, and she realised that he was lying in a pool of petrol; somehow she would have to get him, and herself, away from there as quickly as possible. She put her arm underneath his shoulders and tried to raise his head. Something gripped her shoulder. She looked up into the face of one of the skinheads, glaring menacingly down at her.

'P... off you nosy cow!' he snarled, some of the ash from his cigarette falling onto her as he dug his fingers hard into her flesh.

'Get off me!' she shouted back, trying to shrug herself free.

He raised his other fist, but was prevented from doing her any damage when he was thumped hard from behind - for which she was extremely thankful.

The minutes passed, and despite being constantly barged into by the brawling mob, she was not directly targeted again herself. Despite repeated efforts, she was unable to get the injured youth to sit up. He remained as he was: his eyes still half open, moaning and breathing hard. She was hardly aware when the level of noise around her began to die down, and when a hand gripped her again, exasperated, she grabbed and

165

hurled it away from her before looking up - and into the face of a police constable glowering intimidatingly down at her.

The sequence of events that followed was of a nightmarish quality for Meredith. Whenever people asked what had happened afterwards, she would reply, 'You won't believe it! I still can't. The injured youth was taken away in an ambulance, and the rest of us were piled into vans and taken to the police station. I don't know about the others, but I was put in a room by myself. They took my handbag away and then left me alone for ages. I had no idea what was going on. Then a policewoman came in and began questioning me. There was a tape machine on the table, but I don't think it was switched on. I made a statement and signed it. I didn't feel too bad, just shaken up a bit. I felt sure they'd realise what had happened and let me go. I kept expecting them to, especially when the policewoman went off somewhere with my statement.'

At this point, she would hesitate, always uncertain if the next part of her story would be believed.

'After a few minutes, I heard her talking to someone outside the room. I could hear them clearly; she'd left the door slightly ajar. I'm sure it was another police officer. I knew they were talking about me, especially when he said that, "It would be easy for them to get the girl for assault." As far as I knew, I was the only girl involved. Then he said that, "They could pep things up, and make it a bit more interesting, and make it look good for them by getting the numbers up." I heard her agree. Then she went on to suggest that I could be done for possession! I got really worried after that.

She came back a few minutes later, and her attitude was much harder, more official. I asked her if I could make a phone call and if I was entitled to a solicitor, but she just ignored me, saying we'd discuss that later. She told me that I could be in serious trouble, and that I had better start to co-operate, and tell them about the drugs they'd found in my handbag. I asked what she meant. Then she pulled the bottle of pills out of her pocket - but they were Conrad's painkillers! I couldn't believe it! She accused me of possessing an illegal substance, and said that I could make life a lot easier for myself if I confessed. I told her about Conrad, and that they were just painkillers, and about how he'd left the bottle on the table in the restaurant - and how I'd picked them up. She emptied some on the table, and, I suppose, if you'd never seen them before, they would look suspicious: big pink, round pills. But the label was clear enough on the bottle, and with his name and instructions on how to take them. Now I demanded that they get me a solicitor. But she got up and left me alone again, and this time she was gone for ages.'

And now, whether her listener was a Christian or not, she would say, 'All I could do was pray. I knew the situation was bad and that I was in real trouble now, but I believed that justice would prevail. I knew I'd done nothing wrong. All I had to do was to stay calm, and keep trusting in God. He'd vindicate me. He was more powerful than any false accusation - or bent police officers. Then, after when seemed like hours, she came back with my handbag, and told me that I could go, and that I'd be contacted again soon. Anyway, I didn't stop to ask why. I know I should have, but I just wanted to get out of there, and get as far away from the place as possible.'

Meredith had never had a birthday like it, nor did she ever want to again. She would often look back and remember the long walk back to the garage to collect the car; part of the route was along dark, country lanes. The dawn was just beginning to break by the time she reached her home. At least she didn't have to face her parents. She made a hot drink, threw her stockings away, put her dress in to soak, then bathed all the petrol off her skin. Finally, physically and mentally exhausted, she set her alarm and went to bed. But she could not rest. The sights and sounds of the past six hours bombarded her mind. It was only when she remembered to pray, and thank Jesus for her deliverance, that they began to release their hold on her, and finally fade away, allowing her to fall into a desperately needed sleep.

❖

The cold light of day brought some unpleasant realisations with it. Similar thoughts had occurred to her throughout the ordeal, but she had managed to push them to one side, wanting to concentrate fully on what was happening to her. Knowing that the consequences of the incident would have to be faced, she made a mental list of people she would need to tell, and her parents were at the top. It was only a matter of time before they found out about the whole thing anyway, and she would rather them hear her own version of events than anyone else's, especially as the incident had happened at the very garage owned by Conrad's father. She would definitely have to tell Tom, who, apart from being her employer, regularly used the same garage. And Wendy was bound to hear about things. She wasn't sure about telling her friends at church; that would mean telling Kingsley - and what on earth would he think of her then? Every time she saw him, she seemed to have some problem or other.

No doubt, Conrad would have heard all about it by now. Conrad - his painkillers! He would be needing them. She would have to take a detour to his home on her way to work. It might be a good idea if she asked him to go to the police station, and confirm that they really did belong to him.

An hour later she rang his doorbell and waited. No-one came. The seconds turned into a full minute. She looked at her watch; it was ten minutes past eight on a Friday morning. His father must already be at the garage, or the police station, but his mother should be in: she didn't go out to work. The net curtain moved slightly by the side of the large bay window. Still no-one came. Disappointed, and finding it hard to believe that Conrad would deliberately ignore her like this, she left the bottle of painkillers on the doorstep, and turned to leave. Out of the corner of her eye, she saw the net curtain twitch again.

She told Tom and Wendy everything when the morning rush was over. Both listened intently, Wendy with her mouth open, only shutting it when any mention of Conrad was made. She had heard of things like this happening before, and knew that there was some sort of law that dealt with such interracial disturbances: something to do with Race Relations. However, she decided that, for now, she would keep her thoughts from Meri, but she would definitely be having a quiet word with Tom about it later on.

CHAPTER 24

Meredith went to collect her parents from the railway station later that evening. The atmosphere was tense in the car, and she recognised the symptoms: they had been 'having words'. From the continuous stream of acerbic comments her mother made, she learned that, instead of sitting with her, her father had spent every evening at the hotel bars, associating with the driver and a small group of other male passengers. As a result, Pamela had found herself obliged to sit with the stranded wives, most of whom were, 'not her type at all'. Meredith knew this latest misdemeanour of her father's would be added to the already lengthy list of other unforgiveable grievances her mother had against him; a list that Meredith had heard so many times that she knew it off by heart.

She was relieved when they went upstairs to unpack. She put the kettle on, then the radio, in an attempt to drown out the sound of the ongoing argument. She took some tea up to them a few minutes later.

Her mother looked disapprovingly down at the mugs when she opened their bedroom door. 'Did you use white sugar?'

'Yes, as always.'

She took a sip and grimaced. 'Doesn't taste like it, and his is too strong.'

Eventually Pamela came down, her arms full of clothes for the washing basket. 'Look at this! He wore a clean shirt *every night!* I wore the same blouse three times, but then, *I* wasn't trying to impress anybody!'

Meredith took the sandwiches out of the fridge and began uncovering them.

'What's in those? Not cheese I hope? You know we can't eat anything heavy after travelling.'

'Ham and tomato, and egg and cress. Will Dad be down soon?'

'Oh, *he's* lying down. Says he's worn out. And no wonder, after all that beer swilling! I hope you haven't overdone it with the salad cream. And you might as well put some soup on.'

Meredith took a can of vegetable soup out of the cupboard and began to open it.

Pamela pushed her to one side, accusing her of being slovenly as she straightened the remaining cans in the cupboard, the top one having gone slightly out of alignment, '…and it won't cook by itself, you know.'

Meredith looked at her, puzzled.

'The gas! Turn it on! For goodness sake, what's the matter with you? You'll have to buck your ideas up, my girl, or Conrad will be putting a ring on someone else's finger!'

'Give me a chance! I was just about to. And there's no chance of *that* happening!' Her mother had only been in the house less than half an hour, and already the browbeating had started. She began to stir the soup, slowly, methodically, forcing her breathing to follow the smooth motion of the spoon.

Pamela let out an exasperated sound. 'No, there won't be, if you carry on like this. And will you never learn? You've used the ends of the tomatoes! I don't know, I despair of you. No wonder Conrad's taking it slow. Poor boy, he must be wondering what on earth he's letting himself in for.'

That was it! Meredith had had enough. 'Oh, I shouldn't worry about him, Mum. He'll do okay. I'm sure he'll find someone good enough. I just hope she's as fussy and nit-picking as you! But it definitely won't be me, especially after what happened last night!'

'What do you mean? What happened last night? You didn't let him get drunk again, did you? Didn't you learn anything from the last time?'

'No! I did not "let him get drunk again". And since when have I been responsible for what he puts in his mouth? Don't you think that "poor boy's" old enough to control his own alcohol consumption?'

'Now, now Meri,' came her father's voice from the kitchen doorway. Neither had heard him come down the stairs. He had heard the two women at cross purposes, and had forced himself to rally. He looked weary, almost defeated, as he went to sit down at the table. 'There's no need to take on so.'

Pamela pushed Meredith out of the way and began to stir the soup with quick, angry movements. 'You'll be pleased to know that your daughter's upset Conrad again. Well, go on then, madam, tell us the worst. What have you done this time?'

And now, for the second time that day, and despite constant interruptions, Meredith attempted to describe the previous night's unfortunate sequence of events. And, as she knew it would be, this time the response was vastly different. Her father appeared to have trouble assimilating the news as he sat horrified, silently staring down at his soup. Her mother was anything but silent, declaring over and over again that she could not be more mortified if she tried. As far as she was concerned, the police must have had good cause to act the way they did. Meredith must have aggravated the situation in some way, and, no doubt, brought the whole thing on herself. What was she doing filling up the car at that time of night anyway? And why didn't she get in it and lock the doors, or drive off, as soon as she saw there was going to be trouble - or at least take refuge with the garage attendant? Didn't she know that she was only asking for trouble by going over to the injured Asian? What was she doing taking Conrad's pills anyway? And why didn't she give them back to him in the pub? The poor boy must have been in dreadful pain. How could she be so thoughtless?

The pills were something that Meredith had wondered about herself - before remembering how distracted she had been at the sight of Julia and Fleur - a fact which she now chose to keep to herself, only stating to her parents, as she had to the policewoman, that she had 'just forgotten all about them.'

The last straw came when her mother sarcastically summed up her feelings on the matter. 'Well, you can kiss anything to do with Conrad goodbye now! He won't want a wife that's been involved in such a thing, and Heaven knows what his parents must be thinking! I can just hear his mother holding court in the W.I. now. What a meal she'll make of it!'

Almost in tears, Meredith looked from her father - who was holding his bowed head in his hands - to her mother, who was standing erect, with her arms folded tightly across her chest and glaring fiercely at her. She couldn't help comparing how Tom and Wendy had reacted when being told the same news. They had believed her, and had not shirked from immediately offering their support and friendship; neither had blamed or judged her in any way. And yet, here were her parents - her family - the very ones who should be there for her, the ones that she should be able to rely upon and lean on. But they were not here for her in any shape or form, in fact, they seemed to be making matters worse. Quietly, she said, her voice breaking, 'You know, Mum, I did nothing wrong. Why are so angry with me?'

'Angry? Angry?' her mother shouted. 'Well of course we're angry! Anybody would be after learning that their daughter has been stupid enough to go and get herself mixed up with the law. To think of it! One of my own, getting a criminal record! I've been warning you for years, my girl, but would you listen to me? No, not Little Miss Know-It-All! Hell bent on going your own sweet way. Well, you've made your bed now, my girl, now you'll have to lie on it. And don't expect any help from us! I thought Freda was the black sheep of the family, but it looks like she's got some competition!

You're going to end up like her: fat, frigid and alone, you mark my words...'

'Come on now, Pam. That's a bit rich,' interrupted Simon at last.

'A bit rich! *A bit rich!* You're a fine one to talk, Simon Sanderson! If you hadn't been so...so indulgent with your precious "little girl", she wouldn't have gone off the rails like this. You've always been too soft with her. Now look what you've done! I hope you're satisfied. She's turned out a bad one; sneaking around at all hours of the night, up to goodness knows what.' She turned her furious stare back onto Meredith. 'And haven't we always tried to show you the right way? And all for nothing. You've thrown it all back in our faces! When I think of what you've put us through...' And then, as usual, she began to recite her other list, only this one contained all the unforgiveable grievances she had against her daughter, finishing with a few recently added items, '...and you spend too much time at that church, and Conrad, that poor boy - from such a good family - and good prospects too.'

Now Meredith knew what she must do. She couldn't bear to stay under the same roof as her mother any longer. She faced her, and said as calmly as she could, 'I'm sorry I'm such a disappointment to you. And by the way, you forgot to mention how slow I was to potty train, and that I only got seven 'O' levels, and am rubbish compared to Allan, and that I'm only wasting my time at that camp. You know Mum, you've always made me feel like nothing but a nuisance and an embarrassment to you. So, let me do something right for a change. I'll go and stay at *that camp,* and then you can give Conrad my room! That way you can really help *the poor boy.* I'm sure he'd be delighted; he'd be much nearer the pubs here. Then you can monitor his drinking to your heart's content! And you won't have to put up with the shame and inconvenience of having this criminal around the place - and polluting your perfect, proper home.' And with that, she turned to march up the stairs - and began to pack her bags.

She could hear their muffled voices below. She fully expected her father to come knocking on her door, but there was no sign of him.

He was still sitting at the table, holding his bowed head in his hands, and still staring down at his soup - now cold - when she opened the front door and left the house ten minutes later.

CHAPTER 25

Meredith thanked The Lord that she had somewhere to go that did not involve anyone else. She was just 26, and knew that most women her age would have left home years ago, or were married with children. It just hadn't happened for her. She had never been an ambitious type of person, and up until recently, had always been content with her job and way of life.

She could hear the band leader introduce the Conga as she passed the ballroom. Soon the campers would be spilling out to settle down for their first night. She unlocked her own chalet and began unpacking. She knew she was a disappointment to her mother - who had never made a secret of her resentment about her close relationship with her father. But Meredith had never tried to take her parents, nor her home, for granted. She had always helped around the house and paid her way. Now that she was a bit older, she had come to appreciate the few evenings a week she was able to spend away from the frenetic atmosphere of the camp. She knew she would have to leave home properly one day, but never had she dreamt that it would be like this - under these awful circumstances. Could things get any worse?

Six people stayed behind to talk to Kingsley after the service in the ballroom the next morning. Five took the *Journey Into Life* booklet; the sixth decided to hold back and seek out the local vicar when he returned home. As a result, Kingsley needed to hurry away in time to take the half-past ten service. He was disappointed; he had been hoping to have a few minutes with Meredith before he left.

She did not attend the evening service later that night, nor did she turn up for Launchpad. When she failed to attend the following Wednesday evening's house group, he made his mind up to call her home the next morning, remembering that Thursday was her day off.

Her mother answered, and informed him, none too politely, that 'the girl's moved out.'

Taken aback, he asked, 'Moved out! Where to?'

'The camp of course! Where else would she go?' she replied, caustically.

'Is she okay? There's nothing wrong is there?'

'Nothing wrong! Nothing wrong! Not if you don't call getting yourself involved in fights and being arrested "nothing wrong!"'

He could hardly believe his ears. 'Pardon?'

There was a heavy sigh. 'I'm surprised you haven't heard. Half the town must know by now. She only went and got herself arrested. To think that a daughter of mine would behave in such a way! And what her boyfriend must be thinking of it. It's just too awful to contemplate. She's broken her father's heart, and...'

'Arrested!' he interrupted, becoming more alarmed by the second. 'What for? When?'

'I really don't want to talk about it. It's too painful. And I'm so concerned about that nice young man - just waiting for her - she's kept him dangling for so long. And now she's got herself into all sorts of trouble with the authorities. Goodness knows what will become of her! I wouldn't blame him if he decided to look elsewhere; it would serve her right. She'll live to regret it, mark my words! I'm at my wits end. She went off in a high-huff the other night. Wouldn't listen to me, nor her father. Well, she can jolly well get on with it. I've washed my hands of her.'

This was sounding bad. Poor Meredith, obviously something serious had happened, and he began to regret not trying to contact her before now. 'Er, right. Thank you Mrs Sanderson. I'll try and reach her at the camp.'

'And unless she shakes her ideas up and begins to realise what side her bread's buttered, she's better off staying away. And it's her boyfriend I feel really sorry for. The last thing he needs now is all this upset on top of everything else the poor boy's been going through!'

Kingsley wondered at the fact that this mother's support was sounding very misplaced. Curious, he went on to ask, 'Things aren't going so good for him then? I did hear that he'd been injured.'

'Yes, and you'd have thought that she'd want to be there for him. But oh no! Off she goes, swanning around at all times of the night; getting involved in goodness knows what, and getting herself taken off by the police! Dreadful! Poor Conrad. I bet he doesn't know if he's coming or going with her!'

Feeling strongly now that one of them should start speaking up for Meredith, he said, 'That doesn't sound like Meredith at all.'

'And the shock we had! It'll take me years to get over it, if I ever do!'

'But something must have happened? I haven't known your daughter long, but long enough to know that she's no trouble-maker.'

There was a long pause. 'We certainly didn't bring her up to bring trouble home.' A sob broke through her voice. 'But what will we do if she's really gone off the rails? It's dreadful, dreadful!'

'Alright. Look, I'll try and see her, and find out what's been going on. Maybe there's been some sort of misunderstanding. Let me get back to you later.'

'She's such a hot head...'

His doorbell sounded, giving him the excuse to end the call before hearing any more unpleasant criticism about a young woman he had grown to like and admire.

'Trevor! Hello, what are you doing here?'

Trevor Fosdyke, a friend and church member, stood there, and he was not looking too happy. 'Just passing through. Got a minute? There's something I think you ought to know. I haven't got long; got to be on the other side of town soon.'

'Yes of course. Come on in.' Kingsley showed him into the lounge.

'I'll get right to it. Have you heard from Meredith lately?'

Kingsley felt jolted. Meredith again. 'Meredith! No. Why do you ask?'

'Looks like she's in a spot of trouble. One of our reporters was doing his usual trawl of the police stations the other night, and got to hear of a Paki-bashing incident at Fenton's garage. Seems that Meredith got caught up in it.'

Kingsley's stared at him. Trevor was the sub-editor of the local newspaper, and, as such, was often the first to hear about anything newsworthy going on in the area.

Trevor continued, 'Most of the youths have already got previous convictions, and now it looks like the police have decided to go to town on this one.'

'She didn't get hurt, did she?'

'No, she was lucky there. She'd only just stopped to fill up when the fight broke out. One of the Asians ended up in hospital with concussion and a couple of broken ribs.'

'But why should she get arrested? It must have been obvious to anyone that she wasn't involved?'

'It's the law, you know, Race Relations? Everyone involved has to be charged. And it was just Meredith's bad luck to get caught up in it. But, er, I'm afraid there's more bad news.'

'More...about Meredith? Are you sure she's alright   not hurt?'

Trevor sighed, a look of resignation on his face. 'Not that we've heard. But whatever sentence is handed down to the youths - and that could mean a custodial sentence - will have to be dished out to her as well.'

'But...that's just plain ridiculous!'

'I agree. Let's just hope that it goes before the Magistrates and not the Crown Court. It's a damn shame; she must be worried sick. Anyway, thought I'd stop by to tell you in case you run into her. And, er...' he paused. Kingsley held his breath. 'You might want to warn her that the editor's thinking of making it a centre page spread in the next issue. He was all set to put it on the front, but there's just been another bad crash on the A140, and I reckon he'll run with that instead.'

'Well, let's hope so,' said Kingsley, recalling the mother's obvious sense of outrage and embarrassment. 'Was she alone, do you know?'

'So they say.' Trevor sighed again and shifted his weight from foot to foot, debating with himself about revealing even more unpleasant news.

Kingsley recognised the signs. 'There's something else?'

'Afraid so. Apparently, there's some talk of drugs being involved.'

Kingsley gasped. 'Drugs! The youths...?'

'No, on Meredith. A suspicious substance was found in her bag.' He drew in his breath, 'Don't think that'll help her case.'

'What! For goodness sake! I just don't believe any of this! There's got to be some sort of mistake.'

'Yeah, but look where she works? They get some pretty shifty characters working there, you know.'

'Rubbish! Meredith's too level headed to get mixed up with anything underhand or illegal.'

'Be that as it may, the police obviously think they've got something to go on. I just hope you're right; I'd hate to see her get locked up.' He looked at his watch, 'Sorry, but I'll have to get going. You'll...er, try and see her and warn her then...about the paper?'

'Of course. And I appreciate your coming to me first.' Then, thinking again of the mother's critical attitude, added, 'She's going to need us now Trevor; our friendship and support, especially our prayers.'

Trevor nodded. His expression even more grim.

Meredith returned to her chalet after watching a particularly well attended Knobbly Knees Competition, thankful that it had helped her to forget her troubles for a short while. Someone knocked on her door a few minutes later.

'Conrad! At last! Where have you been?'

He stood awkwardly, attempting to balance on his crutches. 'And hello to you too! Thought I'd drop by. They told me in reception that you'd probably be here.'

She stood and looked at him. All week she had played out in her mind the speech she would make and the questions she would ask when she finally saw him again.

'Hey, what's that look for?' he asked.

'I've been waiting to hear from you all week. Why didn't you phone?'

'I did! I spoke to your mother; she's not too happy with you, you know. Poor woman, she sounds really upset.'

Meredith could hardly believe her ears. 'Poor woman! *She's* upset! I don't believe you! Don't you know what's been happening?'

He scowled at her. 'Of course I do! All that bloody nonsense at the garage…'

'"Nonsense"! Is that what you call it?'

He shrugged. 'Sounds like a storm in a teacup to me. And no need to go all dramatic on me.'

She stared hard at him. 'Just "a storm in a teacup!" Then it's a shame you weren't there to share in the…the drama, especially the bit when I was arrested and held for hours at the police station! And, I might add, accused of possessing drugs - because I just so happened to have your pills in my bag! By the way, I hope you've already been to the police station and told them that they were yours?'

He gasped; this last piece of information was obviously news to him. Then he laughed. 'You what? Drugs? My pills? Flaming hell! That's...that's fantastic! No-one told me about that! And there's no way I'm going to any bloody police station; they'd have to inform the RAF., and then I'd have the bloody Snowdrops on my back again!'

She knew he was right; as a member of the Armed Forces, any involvement with the civilian police meant automatic involvement with the military police. Still, she had hoped that he would have done this one thing for her.

'Conrad, please, can't you...even if your father...'

'No, sorry. No way!'

'Well, thank you for all the support!'

Knowing she was beaten, she went on to say, 'You know I brought them around yours on my way to work the next morning, but it seems that no-one was home. No-one answered the door to me anyway. I suppose your parents still think that I'm a bad influence on you and leading you astray? And you're letting them?'

'Come off it, Meri! You can't blame them; they're entitled to their opinion.'

'Actually, I'm not concerned about what they think of me anymore; their opinion is not one that I'm too bothered about. And as for you, turning up here - *seven* days after the - the *drama*, I don't think much of that either!' Anyway, where've you been all this time?'

'Hey! Don't take on so! I've had a rotten cold all week.'

'Oh? Too weak to pick up the phone then? But obviously not too weak to speak to my mother!'

'Couldn't talk much, could I? Throat's been really rough.'

He made a choking noise to emphasis the fact. The truth was that he'd only had a slight chill, and had seized upon it as a convenient excuse to lie low and wait for the fuss to die down.

His father had played merry hell about the incident, especially about the slur it was having on the business. And the fact that 'The Sanderson girl' had been involved, only served to add more fuel to the fire.

It had been a long and boring seven days, but now he was ready for some action. Surprisingly, he had enjoyed that first visit to the camp, and felt that it might be a good place to find a few new drinking buddies - amongst other things. But Meredith was his only contact there, and he needed her to gain access to the place. It went against the grain, but he knew he was going to have to eat some humble pie now. Lowering his eyes, and affecting an uncharacteristically apologetic tone, he said, 'Yeah, maybe I should have rung, but I knew you'd be alright. You've got plenty of friends...and that church of yours.'

Meredith hesitated, trying to read what was really going on behind his downcast countenance. He did sound sincere, and she had to admit that he did look a bit peaky.

He coughed. 'I'm gagging for a drink. Come on, Meri, my throat feels as rough as hell. Let's go to the pool, like before. It's your day off, isn't it? What else are you going to do?'

She thought he had a point. She had spent the past week working, or wandering aimlessly around the camp, reluctant to contact anyone at church because she had started to feel ashamed, and even guilty, which was very frustrating, because she knew she had nothing to be ashamed or guilty about. But the vivid memory of her experience in the police station, and the way she had been treated, had left her feeling somehow tainted. The only thing that was helping to alleviate the unhappy feelings was when she prayed. Wendy had been kind, and had invited her home for tea on several occasions, but she couldn't even face that, especially Neville's inevitable curiosity. Tom was as supportive as he could be, caught up as he was with his new role as father to his new baby daughter, Zoe.

'Oh alright!' she conceded, reaching behind her for her key, 'But just for a bit then,' reminding herself to make sure to steer him well away from anywhere near the bar.

CHAPTER 26

Just a few teenagers and adults were enjoying the warm water and sunshine when they arrived. As before, she settled him on one of the vacant loungers before going off to get him a drink. Passing one of the wash blocks, she noticed a familiar looking car parked in one of the visitors' spaces in front of the main building.

'Talk of the devil, here she is!' exclaimed Wendy, spotting Meredith approach the reception counter.

Kingsley swung around. He looked keenly at her, trying to spot any signs of obvious distress. 'Good. Got a few minutes, Meredith? I've called in especially to have a word.'

A range of emotions swept through her as she stepped closer: apprehension that he must have heard the unpleasant news by now; dismay at what he must be thinking of her, and lastly - relief. Relief that, at last, here was someone she really could unburden herself with; and someone who would listen to her with a Christian heart and mind.

Kingsley noticed the fleeting look of anxiety cross her face and the dark shadows under her eyes, and his heart went out to her. 'How about a stroll on the beach?' he suggested, casually, 'I feel like some fresh air.'

'Go on Meri,' urged Wendy, 'it'll do you good.'

'Well, alright. But can you give me a minute? There's something I need to do.'

'That's fine. I'll pop in to see how Julia's doing and meet you back here in a few minutes.'

Meredith hurried off to the café and bought a cola.

She found Conrad talking and laughing happily away with Murphy when she returned to the pool; there was no sign of his 'rough' throat now! Handing him the bottle, she said, 'Something's cropped up and I've got to go. I'll be back later.' Not waiting for any reply, she turned and walked back to reception.

Conrad hardly noticed; he had been wondering how he could get rid of her so that he could get pally with the lifeguard anyway.

She met Kingsley coming out of the ballroom and they immediately set off towards the beach path. 'Julia's been seeing Fleur. Did you know?' he asked.'

She inhaled sharply. So now he knew. 'Er, yes. We bumped into them at Jennifer's hen night,'

'Yes, I heard about that. And I saw them in the Jolly Tar the other night; I often go for the odd half. That could explain why she's not been to church lately, and probably why Julia's stopped coming to see me.'

'What will you do about it?'

'Nothing. Fleur's eighteen, and old enough to choose her own path. But I have managed to have a word with her. She knows that we'd be glad to see her back at the group. I don't want her to think she's got to stay away.'

'Really?'

'You sound surprised?'

'I am! You'd welcome her, even though…you know…'

'She's probably having a relationship with someone of the same sex?'

'Well, yes.'

'Hmm, well if that is the case, then we need to pray that she'll come to realise what damage she's doing to her spirit. If she wants to have an open and honest relationship with The Lord, then she'll have to make her mind up, and end any inappropriate one she's having with Julia.'

'Can't see Julia being too happy about that!'

'No, neither can I. But we all have to make some hard choices sometimes.'

By now they had reached the beach. No-one was swimming, and only a few children were paddling. 'Not many around again,' he commented.

'It's one of our quieter days. It's nearly lunch, and a lot of them will be going on the Broads trip this afternoon.'

'What! The whole camp?'

She laughed. 'I wish! No, just a hundred and eighteen this week.'

'What's on for those that don't go?'

'There'll be a film show in the ballroom, and a long nature ramble if there's enough interest.'

'Plenty of choice then.'

'Yes.'

They walked on, passing the area where the twice weekly open air services were being held.

After a while, he asked, 'We haven't seen much of you at church recently. I expect your RAF friend's still keeping you busy?'

'You could say that. And other things keep cropping up and...and just seem to keep getting in the way.'

'Yes, so I've heard.'

Her pace slowed.

He looked at her and gave her a reassuring smile. 'I know about the trouble at the garage the other night, Meredith. I phoned your home this morning, and your mother...mentioned it. And, actually, that's why I'm here now - in case you need to talk to someone.'

She looked at him, her eyes full of anxiety. He had a strong urge to put his arms around her; instead, he reached over to touch her forearm. 'I understand you're staying here now, and not going home on your days' off?' They walked on. She remained silent. 'We're here for you, you know that don't you? Your friends are missing you, and I've been concerned as well.'

At last she spoke. She thanked him, and then began to tell him everything. Once she started, she found it almost impossible to leave anything out, even the most insignificant detail seemed to take on paramount importance as she emptied herself of all the unhappy and distressing information. They had walked some distance by the time she had finished. He listened closely, nodding and making assenting, encouraging noises when she faltered. Not for one second did he disbelieve her; somehow he simply knew that she had told him the whole, unadulterated truth. When she did eventually finish, he suggested that they retrace their steps and head for the beach café, having decided that he must now tell her about Trevor's visit.

'Trevor called in to see me this morning. You know that he's a sub-editor on The Bugle? I'm afraid you must prepare yourself for some more difficult news, Meredith. It seems they're going to print the story in this week's paper.'

She gasped. 'Oh no! I hadn't even thought of that!'

'Well, let's hope they get their facts right. He's hoping it'll be on inside, and not on the front.'

'This is awful! Now...now everyone will know about it.'

'Everyone will know that you just got caught up in someone else's fight - and that you did what you could to help. That's not a bad thing.'

She nodded, 'I know, but I feel so...so ashamed. The way they treated me, and then what I overheard them saying - even trying to pin something on me because of those blasted pills!'

'I can't see that sticking. But they're probably having to take the whole thing seriously because of The Race Relations Act. You know about that, don't you? They did tell you about it?'

She had to think. 'No. No one mentioned it. Was it because there were Asians involved?'

'Yes, but...no-one explained it to you?' He sounded surprised.

She shook her head.

'Well, they should have! It's a darned shame you didn't have a solicitor. I can't understand that.' He paused, knowing that what he was about to tell her now would be like a hammer blow, but she had to be told. She had to be warned. 'According to Trevor, it'll end up being a court case, hopefully in a magistrates, and under The Act, everyone involved - and found guilty - has to face the same...consequences.'

She stopped and stared at him, shock written all over her face. *'But I'm not guilty! I didn't do anything!'*

'I know. It's just that it seems that a lot of the youths were already well known to the police.'

It was some time before she was able to make any type of coherent response. 'Are you saying that...those consequences...if they're found guilty, and get some sort of...sentence, that I could get it *as well?'*

He nodded.

They walked on, he praying quietly, she struggling to assimilate this truly awful news, before asking, 'Kingsley, you aren't talking about...prison...are you?'

'Let's hope not. It all depends which way they go. But they must take you into consideration. Hopefully, there'll be some others involved who've never been in trouble before too. I'm not well up on this sort of thing, but there are people who are, and that's another reason why I wanted to see you, to advise you to see a solicitor, if you haven't already.'

'A solicitor! I hadn't...it hasn't crossed my mind.'

'Right. Then I think you'd better, and soon. I imagine you'd be entitled to legal aid. And I wouldn't hang around, Meredith; you'll probably be served with a Summons any day now; that should say exactly what the charges are.'

By now they had reached the steps to the café. He paused on the top step and turned to look at her, a serious expression on his face. 'You're going to have to be very brave. But you know you'll have The Lord on your side; He'll be with you every step of the way. And I'll be here for you too, and your friends in the fellowship. There's no way that we're going to let you go through this alone.'

She couldn't speak.

'Come on, you look as though you could do with a sit down.'

He took her arm and led her into the café. He guided her to a corner table, then went to join the small queue at the counter. Feeling dazed, she looked around, and was surprised that everything appeared to be normal; the bottom might have just dropped out of her world, but in here, people were still behaving as though nothing had changed: the expresso machine was still hissing, cutlery was still clinking, and people were still chatting. He brought over a large beaker of hot chocolate, stirred it, then pushed it in her direction.

'Here, drink! And let's decide on our next move, which has to be going to see a solicitor. And I think I should go with you.'

She took a sip of the rich, dark liquid, and attempted to smile. 'Yes, alright. But only if you really want to. You're so kind...I hadn't expected...' She was forced to stop, feeling tears begin to prickle at the back of her eyes.

Kingsley reached out and put his hand over hers. He sat and spoke comfortingly to her, and by the time they left, a full hour later, she felt more in control of her emotions - and even a measure, albeit a very small measure - of reassurance.

She returned to the pool. Conrad appeared to be enjoying the attention of two young bikini-clad women, one of whom had her arm linked through one of Murphy's, who was standing close by.

'I'm going back to my chalet now. What are you going to do?' she asked.

'I'm staying. Murphy's offered to give me a lift when his shift ends.'

'Good.'

'See you around then,' he said, dismissively, not even bothering to look up at her, being far more interested in the navel area of the semi-naked girl's body near him.

CHAPTER 27

Even before she had taken her jacket off the next morning, Wendy put the newspaper down in front of her. 'Here, look in the middle.'

Meredith opened it and began searching through the pages, stopping abruptly when she reached the centre. She began to read:-

GANG FIGHT AT LOCAL GARAGE: FIFTEEN ARRESTS MADE

And below it, for all the world to see, and surrounded by a mass of fighting youths, a picture of her, kneeling beside the wounded youth. She skimmed through the article quickly, then forced herself to read it again, only this time slowly and deliberately. To her enormous relief, there was no mention of drugs.

'Did it really happen like that?' asked Wendy.

'Yes,' she closed the pages. 'That's what happened, at the garage anyway.'

'Not a bad picture of you though. Are you going to show it to Tom when he gets in? He'll need to know.'

'What?'

'Tom, he'll need to know. You know, in case someone spills the beans to the trustees; you being an employee here, and all that.'

'Oh! I see.' Wendy was right. Why hadn't she thought of the trustees before? 'You don't think...he won't...do you think they'll make him get rid of me? Maybe I should offer...'

'Well, I don't know, I'm sure. But knowing Tom, I doubt if he'll be pushed into doing anything he doesn't want to do.'

It was agonising waiting for Tom. Thankfully, he arrived just a few minutes later and appeared to be his usual self. She took his coffee into his office and tried to sound matter-of-fact as she told him about the article. 'I'll leave it with you, shall I?'

'Yes, okay. Thanks for the coffee.'

There was nothing obvious about his tone or manner to concern her when he asked her to 'step back in' soon after. The paper lay open on his desk. He tapped it with his forefinger.

'Wondered how long it would take them. Juicy bit of local news. Surprised it didn't make the front page.'

'I'm glad it didn't.'

'Expect we'll have Nick roaring in here any second now, demanding to know what I'm going to do about it.'

She nodded.

'Bad do this Meri.' He tapped the paper again, 'Must make you feel sick to your stomach.'

'Yes,' she replied, quietly.

'And your parents, things still difficult there? You haven't been home yet?'

'No, not yet.'

'Hmm,' privately he thought that was a bad show. Her family should be there for her now. There was no way he would leave little Zoe to cope with a thing like this alone.

'Kingsley came to see me yesterday. He thinks I should see a solicitor.'

'Sounds like good advice.' He glanced at the article again. 'Smith and Bartrum on the High Street are sound enough. I hear old man Bartrum's a bit of an old codger, but he's supposed to be the best in town at this sort of thing. They call him "The Bloodhound" because of his antics in court.'

'Okay. But...I was wondering how this could affect the camp, you know, our reputation? What if the trustees get to hear of it? Do you think I should leave? I'd really understand if you think it would be for the best.'

Tom raised his eyebrows and his hand at the same time. 'You can put *that* idea right out of your head *straight away!* And the campers'll probably find the whole thing very titillating, that is if any of them bother to read the local rag.'

'But the trustees…'

'What about them? You know what they're like; they'll just tell me to "deal with the matter." And my way of dealing with it will be to continue to benefit from your hard work. Apart from which, I think Wendy'd give me hell if I let you go!'

She stared at him. And again, for the second time in as many days, tears almost came to her eyes. Tom and Kingsley: her employer and her minister, two very different men. One had known her for years, the other for just a short time, but both had not hesitated to step forward to offer their support. Overcome with relief, she tried to thank him, and promised not to allow the whole affair to interfere with her work.

'Think you're going to find that impossible,' he said. 'And look, you're going to have to speak up when you find it's getting too much for you. You know what I'm like, I won't see the warning signs. I'm sure Wendy'll cover for the odd time you need to be off, and I can always ask one of the nannies to do a stint behind reception.'

Once again she thanked him. The discussion over, she turned to leave, knowing that, by now, Wendy would be almost beside herself with curiosity.

'Thinking about it, hang on a minute!' he said. 'Might as well strike while the iron's hot.' He began spinning his index carousel. 'Smith, Arth - Adolphus - Charles - and Doug - where the hell is it?'

Realising he was searching for the solicitor's card, and knowing how he used a very hit and miss alphabetical system, she suggested, 'Try the B's, Bartrum.'

He spun the device and quickly found the relevant card. He snapped it down loudly by the telephone. 'Wouldn't do any harm to give 'em a ring right now; try and set something up. I'll leave you to it, and thrill everyone by doing an early round.' And with that, he left. She heard him speaking to Wendy, before being ambushed by what sounded like a very upset Jacko in the foyer a minute later.

She was able to make an appointment to see Arthur Bartrum for the morning of her next day off. Wendy looked up when she re-entered the office. 'Kingsley phoned, wants you to call him back.'

'I'll do it now, we seem to be quiet.'

'Humph! It would be if Jacko'd belt up about the bingo machine going berserk again.'

Kingsley picked up the phone after the first ring.

'Hi Kingsley. Wendy said you'd called. Sorry, I was on the other line. Actually, I was making an appointment to see a solicitor.'

'Excellent! Who with?'

'Smith and Bartrum, they're by the museum.'

'And when's your appointment?'

'Thursday morning, eleven o'clock.'

'Okay, just let me take a look.' There was a long pause. 'Yes, that'll be fine, and I'll meet you there.' He paused, then added, 'I assume you've seen the paper?'

'Yes.'

'Did they get it right?'

'More or less. But I wonder who took the photo? I can't remember seeing anyone there with a camera. And I'm so relieved they didn't mention anything about drugs. That would have been *really* awful.'

'I think we can praise God for that! And I'll ask Trevor about the photo when I see him again. What did Tom have to say about it?'

195

'He was great! I offered to leave, you know, the camp's reputation and all that, but he wouldn't hear of it. And it was him who made me phone the solicitor's just now.'

'Good for him! Now try not to worry too much, Meredith, I know that sounds easy, but I've got a feeling you'll come out of this okay. You know the old saying, *This too will pass?* I don't know why it's happened to you, but I'm convinced that you'll be able to look back one day and see just how The Lord helped you through it all. I feel absolutely certain about that. And remember what I told you, about the Summons? You might get served with it any day now. They have to hand it to you personally. Give me a ring when that happens.'

'Hmm, I'm not looking forward to that.'

'Don't worry, it's just procedure. See you at Smith & Bartrum's at eleven on Thursday morning then?'

'Yes, and thanks Kingsley.'

'Peace and grace to you till then, Meredith.'

'And to you.'

The summons arrived the next day. A man, soberly dressed in a black suit, and with a blank expression on his face, approached the reception counter. 'Is there a Meredith Sanderson here?'

'That's me,' she said, feeling thankful that she had been forewarned. He handed her a large, buff envelope, and asked her to sign a form. Then, without a word, he turned and walked away. She watched him go, wondering how anyone could bear to spend their working life performing such unpleasant tasks. She returned to her desk, opened the envelope, and began to read the list of the charges against her:

...The Race Relations Act of 1965.
...actions likely to cause a breach of the peace.
...possession of a suspicious Class B Substance.

...the use of offensive language against a member of
H.M. Police Force in the commission of his duty.
...assaulting a member of H.M. Police Force by knocking
his helmet off whilst he was in the commission of his
duty...

Horrified, she clutched her stomach and gasped, feeling that some invisible fist had just punched her hard there, especially when she read who it was that was bringing the charges against her. She had been expecting to see Conrad's father's name, but it wasn't there - instead it was the police themselves - and *only* the police.

'What is it,' asked Wendy, realising that something was not quite right, 'What've you got there?'

'The Summons. But I...I don't understand. It's all wrong...I didn't do any of these...'

Wendy rushed over and grabbed the document. She skimmed through it, and let out a series of loud exclamations. 'Whoa! Blimey! Flippin' heck, Meri! They've really put the boot in. And the *Police!'*

Meredith looked at her, dismayed. 'I don't know how to...how can I fight them? Who's going to believe me now?'

CHAPTER 28

'You're going on the trip, and I won't hear any more about it! It'll do you good to get out of here, and the girls'll be glad of your help.'

Tom was well meaning, but the thought of trying to control a double-decker bus full of excited children - and then keeping them safe and out of trouble for the whole afternoon - was the last thing Meredith felt like doing right now, but two children's nannies had come down with a heavy summer cold and Tom was in need of another responsible adult to go on the excursion. 'You've done it before, and if it doesn't help to take your mind of things, then nothing will!'

She knew there was no point in arguing. He had made up his mind: good, kind Tom - good, kind - and *very* stubborn Tom. As far he was concerned, that was it; the matter was settled.

'Go on now and have an early lunch. Ah, hang on a minute.' He jangled the keys in his pocket and walked back into his office. They heard the safe being opened and the petty cash tin being unlocked. Returning, he handed her a small plastic bag containing several ten pounds notes. 'Ice cream money.'

Meredith didn't feel up to arguing any more, the fight had gone out of her. She began tidying up her desk. 'Alright, but I won't be much fun to have around.'

'That's what the animals are there for,' remarked Wendy. 'And try and find out if Suzy pooped that girl's ring out, and if she's wearing it again.'

Tom grinned, 'And try and leave a few kids behind. Hilda's arriving this afternoon, and I'll be looking for a good excuse to get away.'

'She not coming in here again, is she?' Wendy asked, sounding alarmed, not relishing more interference from his imperious mother-in-law so soon after her last visit.

'Afraid so. Wants to see what progress I've made with her report. Don't worry, I'll try and keep her out of your hair.'

'You should hire her out to the other camps,' Meredith quipped, not thinking for one moment that anyone would take her seriously.

Wendy suddenly became animated. 'Hey! Like a spy! Industrial espionage. Get her to infiltrate some of the other camps as a day visitor - and do some poking around there too!'

Tom looked at her, wide-eyed. Several expressions rapidly crossing his face, before he said, sounding enthusiastic, 'Wendy! That's *brilliant!* Why didn't I think of it?'

The double decker arrived, and the two nannies aided by a handful of accompanying parents tried in vain to control the constantly moving mass of over one hundred excited children. The din was all pervasive, and Ann, the senior nanny, had to blow her whistle loudly several times before she was able to make herself heard. Meredith took her position on the upper deck and tried to create some order as a steady line of children filed in and began jostling each other for a seat.

The journey took less than half an hour, but this was too long for some children, a few of whom began to complain of feeling sick. From the sound of the loud and overdramatic 'E-e-rs!' and 'Yucks!' coming from the deck below, Meredith guessed that this unfortunate event had happened, and not once, but several times. They arrived at the zoo, and then, with some difficulty, were split into four groups. At last, and with nearly everyone in high spirits, they set off, each group heading in a different direction.

Meredith's group encountered the owls and other large birds first. The sight of the caged birds always disturbed Meredith, who felt nothing but sympathy for the poor creatures, trapped as they were behind cruel, manmade bars - their own artificial prison. They made their way past cages and compounds of wallabies, various breeds of sheep, lemurs, llamas, wolves, marmoset and tamarin monkeys, deers, small cats, flamingos, and other wading birds. The boys seemed particularly interested in the vultures and leopards, although the penguins, tigers and giraffes proved to be popular with almost everyone.

At break time they sat on a grassy slope near the café. Meredith and one of the mothers went off to purchase twenty seven tubs of vanilla ice cream, three large bottles of orangeade, and a large tube of plastic cups. Later, all successfully toileted and refreshed, the group set off again.

The camels were next, and a few of the children were disappointed that they only had one hump. The long maned wolves caused much howling, and the cart horses were obviously the highlight of the trip for one of the fathers. They entered the reptile and invertebrates section and jostled each other to gain a better view of Suzy, the eighteen foot Burmese python, who lay coiled and seemingly oblivious to all the faces peering in at her through the glass wall of her tank. A commotion broke out behind them when one older brother thought it would be fun to terrorise his smaller sister by looming over her, waving his arms about frantically and moaning loudly, pretending that he had been bitten by one of the tarantulas, and was in the process of turning into one.

The chimpanzees were in a particularly lively mood and did a good job of entertaining the children for several minutes with their antics. Cherry, a four year old girl, was almost hypnotised by one that kept pointing in her direction and appeared to be signalling for her to go over and join them. Meredith had to spring into action quickly and grab the child by her cardigan just before she plunged headlong over the railings and into a stretch of deep water, situated directly in front of the animals' area.

Next came the cockatoos and parrots. Meredith made enquiries, and learned that the ring Wendy had asked about had been 'passed naturally,' and returned to the newly engaged member of staff, 'after a good clean up'. Then came the small red pandas and spider monkeys, followed by the zebras. Cherry's older sister regularly abdicated her responsibility and left the young four year old to fend for herself. Since the chimpanzee incident, the little girl had taken a shine to Meredith, and came to stand beside her now, putting her small, sticky hand in hers.

Looking up at her new protector, she asked, 'Please Miss, who painted those lines on the horses?'

'Well, Jesus. He made all the animals.'

'Did he make parrots too? How did He catch them?'

'I expect they didn't need catching. They were His friends, so I expect he just had to call them over to Him.'

'I'd like to be their friend too. Mummy read me a story about a horse…and there were lots of pictures…but it didn't have stripes like these ones.'

'These are different types of horses, Cherry. They're called zebras.'

'What have they got stripes for?'

'Er, I think they must have them to help them to hide in the long grass.'

'*I* can see them.'

'Yes, but you're not in Africa are you? They've got very long grass there.'

'But why haven't they got any spots?'

'Well, I suppose Jesus knew that stripes would be better to help keep them safe from other animals.'

'What other animals, Miss?'

'Lions, leopards, hyenas, and maybe even crocodiles in some places.'

'Have they all got great big teeth?'

'Yes, I think they have.'

The little girl looked pained. 'And do they bite them, and have them for dinner?'

'I'm afraid so. But they have to eat too, don't they? And they have babies to feed as well.'

The little girl considered this piece of information. 'Jesus is naughty!'

'Why'd you say that, Cherry?'

'Making them nasty, and eating nice stripy horses.'

'But He didn't make them nasty. They were all friends at the beginning. He made them just to eat plants and grass, and things like that.'

'Why don't they eat it now?'

Meredith paused. This was getting a bit more complicated than she had expected. Still, she felt that the child deserved some sort of explanation, simplistic though it would have to be. 'A lot of them still do. And have you heard of The Garden of Eden?'

The group started to filter away. Cherry looked around, 'No, is it here?'

'No, but it was a lovely place, a long way from here, where all the animals were really good friends. Jesus made them first, then He made a man and a woman called Adam and Eve. He told them to look after the garden and all the animals. But they were naughty. Then all the bad things started to happen, and lots of animals started to be afraid. And that's when a lot of them stopped eating plants and grass, and started to eat each other.'

'Naughty man and woman!'

The group had already reached the next enclosure. 'Yes. They were. Anyway, come on,' Meredith said, leading her away, 'we need to keep up with the others.'

Cherry grasped her hand tighter. 'Dave Dee's got a big white stripe.'

'Who's Dave Dee?'

'Candy's goldfish. She got him from the fair. But Dozy hasn't, he's got a black spot, and so has Beaky and Mick. But I like Titch best, he's my favourite. He's really pretty.'

'Did Candy win them all at the fair?'

'No, Mummy got them from the pet shop. Poor Dave Dee was all alone and Mummy said he needed some brothers.'

'Well, that's good. Oh look! Can you see that otter? He's upside down, and what's he got in his hands?'

At last, the visit came to an end. All the groups assembled in the coach park. As far as could be ascertained, all one hundred and eleven children and accompanying adults were present and correct. Cherry had kept close to Meredith's side for the remainder of the afternoon and continued to ply her with questions. Meredith was no animal expert and found some of the little girl's enquiries challenging, nevertheless, she did her best to give answers that a child of her age could easily understand.

The zoo was not a major one, and some of the children were disappointed not to come across some of the larger animals. However, it was easy to spot the children who came from homes where there was no television set: like Cherry, they were the most interested and delighted.

She found a note from Wendy pushed under her door when she returned to her chalet:-

Meri, Hope you had a good time.

We had a bit of a do when that horrible bald rude man from Sheffield played hell and twisted his ankle playing miniature golf! I had to bandage him up because Ann had gone off with you lot. Talk about cheesy feet and now he's threatening to sue us!

Your Dad called but didn't leave any message. I told him you'd ring him back.

See you day after tomorrow.
Good luck with Cheesy Feet and Hilda. W. x.
PS. He says he won't be asking her to do that spying.
Reckons we'd get into trouble.
PSS. Tom's done the wages, yours are in the safe.

At last! For days she had been expecting her father to call, and had become increasingly unsettled and perplexed at his silence. She immediately went over to the public telephone box in front of the main building and joined the queue. Her turn eventually came, and she entered the box.

'Hello. Sanderson residence,' came her father's usual response on the other end of the line.

'Dad, it's me. Wendy said you'd phoned. How are things?'

'Ah, yes, Meri. Er, how are you dear?'

'Fine thanks. I suppose you've seen the paper? Mum too? How is…everything?'

'We're alright. I'd have been in touch before, but, well, I thought it best to let things cool down a bit.'

'I had been wondering. What's Mum got to say about it?'

There was a long pause, then, obviously trying to choose his words carefully, he said, 'Oh, you know your mother, got to make a meal out of everything. It was a bit of shock you see, we didn't expect it.'

'No, neither did I!'

'No, well, anyway, it's just that I was thinking that you might be needing some things. You left in such a hurry. Your mother reckons it's getting colder, and your white coat's here.'

'Well, yes, I do.'

'Thought so. She's going on an excursion with that club of hers tomorrow and won't be back till late. I could come and fetch you on my way back from work if you like.'

She looked behind her. No-one was waiting. She was free to talk. 'I'm surprised she can bring herself to go, after what she said about being so ashamed of me!'

'Don't be like that Meredith! That's not like you. And I was thinking, maybe it's best that you stay there for the time being, at least till all the fuss has died down.'

'Then we might have to wait for some time.'

'What do you mean?'

'It seems that there's going to be a court case, and that could take months to come up.'

'A court case?' He sounded horrified. 'But...that won't involve you...will it?'

'Yes, I'm afraid it will.'

'But...why?'

She hesitated, then realised that he would find out sooner or later. It would be better that he heard it from her, at least she could give him the truth, and he wouldn't have to rely on local gossip. She told him about the Summons and the false charges made against her by the Police.

It was obvious that he was having trouble trying to assimilate the information. She noticed that there were several people waiting behind her now, and decided to end the call. 'Look Dad, I'll tell you all about it when I see you. I'll stay in the office until you come. About six'ish?'

'Er, could be a bit later. But Meredith...'

'I'd better go Dad. There's someone waiting to use the phone. Till tomorrow then.'

She hung up. Poor Dad. If only she hadn't stopped for petrol; if only she hadn't given in to Conrad and gone with him that night; if only her mother hadn't told him it was her birthday. If only Dad wasn't such a worrier...

CHAPTER 29

Cherry's family were due to leave. Assuming that the little girl had told her parents all about her time at the zoo, Meredith had been half expecting them to turn up and demand that she apologise for filling their daughter's head with 'a load of nonsense'. However, her concern proved to be unfounded when both parents declared that they were more than satisfied with everything to do with the holiday when they came to hand in their chalet key the next morning.

'You've got something for her, haven't you Cherry?' said her mother.

Looking very shy, the little girl reached her small hand up and placed a folded sheet of paper on the counter. 'I did this all night, Miss.'

The father tousled the curly hair, 'Silly billy! Trying to join the monkeys' gang! She can't stop going on about it. And now she wants a parrot!'

Meredith opened the sheet and smiled broadly as she recognised the rough shape of a zebra, only this animal had purple, yellow, red and green stripes, as well as spots. 'Oh, wow! Thank you so much, Cherry,' she exclaimed. 'What a pretty zebra, and what super colours! I shall put this up on my wall.'

The little girl seemed pleased with her reaction. 'Will you tell Jesus to make it?'

'Ah well, I think He's finished making all the different types of animals now. But you never know, maybe He'll paint one like it when it dies and arrives in Heaven!'

Cherry beamed, obviously taken with the idea. 'And will He make another one...green and red...and...like a parrot? I can help Him; I'm good at colouring.'

'Maybe one day you can; but I don't think you'll be able to for a long time. But why don't you draw some more pictures? Or how about making some animals yourself? You could even make your own little zoo! Do you have some Play-Doh? That would be fun, wouldn't it? You could make your very own multi-coloured zoo!'

Big, brown eyes stared up at her with wonder.

'Nah, she likes to stick plasticine all over the place. Especially on my David Essex posters!' said the obviously disgruntled older sister standing behind them, and coiling one of her long plaits impatiently between her fingers.

'Well, maybe Cherry won't do that anymore if she's got a really big project to do? Will you Cherry?' asked Meredith, encouragingly.

Cherry nodded as she reached out to hold her mother's hand, her eyes looking troubled now. 'No-o-o Miss!'

Meredith wished she could rush off and buy a couple of packets of Play Doh there and then. 'They sell it in the shop here. Have you seen it?'

'That's an idea. Would you like that Cherry? An early birthday present?' the mother asked.

The older sister was tugging very hard at the unfortunate plait now. 'That's not fair! You wouldn't let me have another hula-hoop.'

There were some impatient sounds coming from the queue behind the family, and Meredith knew she had to bring this discussion to an end. 'Well, anyway, thank you so much Cherry. It's a beautiful picture. But I have to get on with my work now.'

The father quickly thanked her again, then led his family away. Out of the corner of her eye she noticed some discussion going on between them. Minutes later, they passed the counter: the older sister rolling a hula hoop triumphantly beside her, Cherry skipping along excitedly and clutching a carrier bag to her chest. She ran towards Meredith, and said breathlessly,

'Miss! Miss! I've got lots! There's lots of pink, and…and…yellow, and lots and lots of blue, and green, and…and…'

Her father came to pull her way. He turned back to give Meredith a thumbs-up signal, before disappearing through the main door.

'…and…and yellow…' called Cherry behind them, desperate for 'Miss' to know all her good news.

Later that night she unpacked the items she had brought from home. The small locker wasn't big enough to hold everything, so she had to leave some in the suitcase under her bed. The best of the summer seemed to have passed, and she was glad of the extra layers of jumpers and her thicker coat.

It had been good to see her father again, brief though the time had been with him. He had looked and sounded preoccupied as she told him more about the garage incident and its possible consequences. All he could say, after hearing everything, was an almost angry sounding, 'Just tell them straight!'

He hugged her tightly before leaving. She watched him drive off, and wondered how long the stalemate between her and her mother would last, and which one of them would give in first. She had a feeling it would have to be her - if not for her own sake, then for her father's.

'Just goes to prove that the quiet ones are always the worst,' Julia remarked when she came to reception the next morning. 'Seems our little Meri's got herself tangled up with some crims. How exciting!'

Most of the younger staff never bothered with the newspapers, however, this wasn't the case with all the staff, especially the older ones, and Meredith had become accustomed to ignoring Jacko's not-so-amusing comments, and defending herself against a continually scandalised Nick. As

Tom had warned earlier, he appeared to have taken the report personally, even hinting that 'The girl should be told to go, or at least made to work out of the public's eye.' Thankfully, Tom had made it his business to explain the true facts of the matter to him, but still he eyed Meredith with disapproval and regularly passed critical comments whenever they had any dealings with each other.

'I'm surprised it's taken you this long to bring it up!' replied Meredith, handing over the shop float to Julia.

'Didn't see the paper till last night. So, what happened? And who's that bloke you were kneeling by? He looked kinda dark; bit different from your other...er, *friend.*'

'Yes, well, there you are. I'm sorry, but I just couldn't stand by and watch someone being beaten to death in front of my very eyes! And who are you talking about anyway? What *friend?*'

'Con...whatshisname, Con...the one with the leg. The one you were with by the pool the other week. He's been knocking around with Murphy lately. A fine old time they were having of it last night. Seemed to find the whole thing hilarious.'

'Conrad? Here's been here?'

'Regular. Didn't you know?'

'No! And what thing was he...so amused about?'

'You know? That trouble at his father's garage.'

Meredith chose to ignore this piece of information. Somehow, she wasn't surprised. 'I didn't even know he was coming here!'

'Well, he has. And he's a typical male! Told us all about you two being old pen friends, and how you'd been hanging around, waiting for him all this time. Poor Meri! Take my advice and dump him; he's a rotter! You'd do better with Kingsley. I'll do it for you, if you like.'

Meredith had to stop to think, realising that Julia seemed to be more than a little interested in her relationship, or, to be more accurate, her *non*-relationship, with Conrad. 'Er, no, don't worry,' she said, 'actually; we've never been that serious. Just friends.'

Julia looked surprised. 'Is that so? Anyway, look at the time, must run. See ya' around.' She turned and left, feeling that this needed some thinking over. From the way Conrad had been talking about Meredith, and despite his very obvious wandering eye, he had sounded to be more than a little serious about his intentions towards her - certainly more serious than just a friend would be.

Meredith's thoughts were interrupted when Tom arrived with Hilda. It was obvious that they were having some sort of heated discussion, and it sounded like Zoe's christening was the hot topic.

'I'm dead against it!' snapped Hilda, marching past Meredith, before turning back and glaring at her. 'And *you, young lady!* What have you got to say for yourself? I hope you realise how lucky you are, having such a soft-hearted employer?'

Some campers looked over as Meredith felt her face grow hot.

'That's enough, Mother!' Tom said, taking his imperious relative's arm, and guiding her, none to gently, into his office.

One young male camper looked at Meredith with renewed interest. Business-like, she ignored his questioning stare, and began to work her way through the queue.

Kingsley arrived a few minutes later. He came over and rested the sketch board and guitar case against the far edge of the counter. 'How are you doing, Meredith? Holding up?'

The queue had cleared again. She looked at his concerned and kind expression, and felt her frazzled nerves begin to melt away. 'Sort of. I wish everyone would shut up about it. You'd think I'd murdered someone!'

'Hmm, vultures picking over dead meat. Part of the human condition I'm afraid. It can't be pleasant, but you know it'll pass when they find something else to pick over. Anyway, are we still on for Thursday?'

Grateful that here was someone who didn't find the whole thing interesting, entertaining or disgusting, she replied, 'Yes. If that's still okay with you?'

'Of course it is. You're my priority.' He tilted his head towards the ballroom, and asked, 'Are you able to join us today?'

Another queue began to form just as Tom and Hilda reappeared. Tom greeted Kingsley warmly, before introducing him to his obviously still annoyed mother-in-law.

Kingsley held out his hand. 'Good to meet you, Mrs Rodden.'

Hilda hesitated, and not making any effort to hide her reluctance, held out her own hand very begrudgingly. This young minister was a protestant, and a free churchman at that - and, as such, didn't warrant a firm handshake. Her back stiffened as she stared fiercely at the cause of her current distress. 'So, *you're* the person I've got to thank for putting ideas in his head and causing all this upset!'

Kingsley looked from one to the other, as did the remaining queue of campers.

'Leave him alone Mother!' ordered Tom.

'You must be thrilled with your little granddaughter?' Kingsley asked, hoping to diffuse the awkward situation.

'Well of course I am! And I'll be even more thrilled when she's *decently* christened!'

Kingsley read between the lines. 'I see. Well, I'm sure that will happen, Mrs Rodden. The Lord welcomes all children: sprinkled or dipped. Anyway, I'd better get on. And I hope you'll be able to come in at some point, Meredith?'

'Oh, I think we can spare her for a few minutes,' said Tom, seeing a way to end this embarrassing scene, and maybe even do something to show Hilda just how unjustly critical and judgmental she was being. 'In fact, now here's an idea, why don't you go in with her Mother, and see for yourself how harmless he is?'

Hilda stared at him in horror, then fixed her glare on Kingsley's neck area. 'But I know what he's like. Remember? In my report?'

Kingsley felt around the open neck of his shirt. 'The service tends to be less formal here, but I'd be delighted if you could join us, Mrs Rodden.'

'Then that's settled,' beamed Tom. 'Wouldn't mind coming myself, maybe next week.'

Hilda's eyes narrowed. She was thinking fast now. Yes, maybe she should go in; then she could back her objections up with some actual knowledge. 'Alright. But, I'm warning you, young man, I'll be the first out if you insist on playing that...that instrument too loudly.'

Kingsley smiled with such grace that Meredith wondered how anyone could take offence at him, or, at least, not respond favourably to him. 'Understood. Just give me five minutes to get set up, would you?'

CHAPTER 30

Meredith and Hilda took their seats near the back of the small gathering. Kingsley opened with a short prayer before introducing the first musical item, *Morning Has Broken,* which just happened to be one of Hilda's favourite hymns. The words were printed on the sketch board and nearly everyone joined in, quietly and shyly at first, then gathering in confidence and volume as the hymn progressed. Taking their seats again, Hilda turned to Meredith, and whispered loudly, 'Not the same without an organ.'

Kingsley placed the guitar back on its stand and introduced his theme: 'How can we find peace and balance amongst all the pressures of life: the ones we put on ourselves, and the ones put upon us?' And then, in between drawing quick illustrations on the sketch board, quoting from various sources, and singing more choruses, he invited his listeners to consider the place of God in their lives.

At one point, Hilda turned to Meredith, and commented sarcastically, 'The man's full of gimmicks!'

'Remember, this is a holiday camp, he has to do things a bit differently here. And what's so wrong about finding different ways to tell people about God's love for them anyway?' replied Meredith, growing a bit tired of the other woman's negative attitude.

Hilda harrumphed loudly but remained where she was. After a while, her caustic remarks became less frequent.

Kingsley continued. 'Here's some things to think about. Do you have an attitude of gratitude? Are you grateful and content with what you have, or are you discontented, and always feeling that the grass is much greener - only to discover that that's not the case when you do manage to get over that fence?

Do you lie in bed at night and count your cash, and not your blessings? Do you judge others by their material wealth, not realising that they're worth infinitely more than their bank balances? And you parents, do you know that your presence...' he stopped to spell the word, '...is more valuable and essential to your children than those presents...' once again, he stopped to spell the word, '...you try to fob them off with, and try to ease your conscience with?'

'Is this supposed to be the sermon?' Hilda asked, sounding almost indignant.

Meredith replied patiently, 'He doesn't do sermons here, just short talks.'

'You know, the Bible says that, **It is more blessed to give than to receive,** and, **...how does a man benefit if he gains the whole world and loses his soul in the process?** And I'm sure you've all heard the saying, *When is enough, enough?* How many of us are truly satisfied? The more sea water we drink, the thirstier we become. Now, don't get me wrong, I'm not saying that it's a bad thing to have aspirations, ambitions and goals. Far from it! But we shouldn't let these things dominate our every waking moment. We should always be on our guard against them trying to possess us.

For those of you who want the world to be a better place, and may even be actively involved in trying to make it that way, I would ask you to consider this: someone has said that communism can put a new suit on every man, but Christianity can put a new man in every suit. Can changing an outward system really get inside a person and change their basic human behaviour - permanently? I'd like to suggest to you that it would be far better to rely on, and find your security, in Someone who won't ever let you down, or leave you; Someone you can always trust. Not something that will rust, or change every time there's a new headmaster, or boss, or relationship - or even a change of government. When you discover just how much God loves you, you'll find your focus will shift from

214

temporary things and onto eternal truths. Money can buy a bed, but not sleep; it can buy acquaintances, but not a true friend; in some parts of the world it can buy an unearned certificate, but not an education; it can buy a crucifix, but not a Saviour...'

The service ended soon after. Meredith was pleased to overhear some positive sounding remarks coming from the campers as they filed out of the ballroom. Hilda, however, looked preoccupied, as, without another word, she walked straight past reception and out of the building.

Kingsley came through into the lobby soon after. He had a young couple with two small children with him, and Meredith noticed that the man was holding the *Journey Into Life* booklet in one hand. They spoke for several minutes before going their separate ways. Then, turning to her, and pointing at his watch, he called, 'Take care, Meredith. Hope we see you later. Grace and peace to you till then.'

She returned to her chalet after the evening meal and began to flick apathetically through the latest issue of the local newspaper, scanning the *Accommodation to Rent* columns. The season was fast coming to an end, and she would have to start thinking seriously about finding somewhere else to live. She knew that Tom wouldn't put any pressure on her to vacate the chalet, but she didn't want to impose on his kindness any more than she had to.

Closing the pages, she remained on her bed, trying to drum up some enthusiasm to get changed and go to church. Somehow, she really didn't feel up to it. Maybe she should go into the ballroom for a short while. Then she remembered what Julia had said about Conrad. What if he turned up tonight? She wasn't in any mood to face him, and she knew she wouldn't be able to remain passive if he began to drink himself silly again. His parents' bad opinion of her must be set in concrete by now, especially if he had been going home half inebriated after being here. Blow Murphy! Why did he have to go and get involved?

She glanced up at the wall. There was young Cherry's picture; it always made her smile. She could hear again the little girl's innocent questions, and remembered how accepting she had been of her answers. So different from Hilda, who had been nothing but negative and critical about the Gospel Service. If only people could somehow keep that same childlike, uncomplicated and delightfully innocent curiosity, interest and non-critical attitude towards Jesus when they grew up, how much happier they, and the world, would be!

She thought again of Tom and his wish to have Zoe dedicated and not christened, and wondered what Sue's wishes on the matter were. From what she had witnessed of the disagreement between Tom and Hilda today, it sounded as though they wanted to have her 'done' soon. Maybe she should look out for a christening card next time she was in town. Or should that be a baptism card? Then again, if Tom had his way, it would have to be a dedication card.

The polka-dotted and multi-coloured striped zebra looked down at her. It was bright, colourful and cheerful. And then she had the idea. But what a strange one! Yes, why not? All it needed was some suitable words - and there was no law against it! But first, she felt like a good soak. She gathered her toilet bag and towel and headed for the staff corridor in the main building. There would be no ballroom for her tonight. Instead, and feeling energised and inspired now, she would spend the remainder of the evening designing and making a card for Zoe's dedication, or should that be christening - no - dedication. Yes, definitely dedication!

CHAPTER 31

The worship tape Meredith was playing on her cassette recorder helped to lift her spirits. She sang along enthusiastically to the choruses as she worked on her card-making project and didn't hear the first knock on her door. It was only when Conrad knocked louder and called out her name that she realised he was there.

'You sound cheerful! What's that you've got on?' he asked, stepping in before being invited.

Disappointed that her pleasant state of mind had been interrupted, especially by the very person she wanted to avoid, she replied sharply, 'Do come in! I only live here.'

'And whose fault is that?' He looked around him, which didn't take long, because there wasn't much to see. 'Bloody hell! It's worse than my room in the barracks; at least I've got ablutions at the end of the corridor.' He peered down at her artwork, 'What's all this then? And turn that down would you. A bloke can't think straight with all that racket going on!'

'It suits me, and I'm working on a...a project.' She adjusted the volume, but only slightly. 'And to what to do I owe this pleasure?'

'Thought you'd be glad to see me. Especially now. By the way, nice shot of you in the local rag.' He gave a small, sarcastic laugh as he lowered himself clumsily onto the bed and put his leg up. 'That's my Meri, always getting stuck in when anyone else would have run a mile; a real Florence Nightingale!'

'Do we have to talk about that?'

'Why not? It's all the rage in my house!' He spread his crutches out before him, their rubber-stopped ends touching the opposite wall.

She sat on the chair. 'In that case, I hope it's entertaining you all. And is that the only reason you're here now?'

'Bit touchy, aren't we? Should have thought you'd be glad of a bit of company.'

'Well, actually, I'm not!' She thought for a moment, then added quickly, 'Unless you can fill in some blanks - and tell me who took that photo and gave it to the press? And what your father intends to do about it all?'

'Do about what?'

'What do you think? What happened at the garage, of course!'

'Oh, he's leaving all that to the police. But he's flaming mad, I can tell you!'

'I'm not surprised, but what about the photo? Who took it?'

'The attendant.'

'And he gave it to the papers?'

He rolled his eyes, 'How should I know? And what is this? A cross examination? I'm not the one who...who...'

'Who what? Was stupid enough to get caught up in the middle of someone else's fight? And accused of goodness knows what - and by the police! And was stupid enough to have their name dragged through the mud?'

'Hey, hang on a minute! What are you getting on at me for? Bloody hell! I only came to see you, and to let you know I'm off tomorrow.'

'Off? Where to?'

'That's better. A bit of thought about what I've been going through wouldn't go amiss, and I don't need you yelling at me right now.'

She bit her lip and tried again. 'Okay, so where are you going?'

'Oh, you are interested then?'

Exasperated, she exclaimed, 'Conrad! For goodness sake! You're not the only one with problems, but from what I've heard, you've still been able to get out and about. So what's going on? Are you being sent back Germany?'

'No, one of their hospitals over here. RAF Nox...Noxmand, or something - to have this off.' He tapped the plaster. 'Thank God! I can't wait! Driving me bloody crazy. Itch, itch, itch! Poking a knitting needle down's the only thing that helps.'

'And you're going tomorrow?'

'That's my orders. They've warned me I'll have to be there at least a month. Got to go through a whole regime of remedial gym - or some such palaver. Something about needing to get the muscles built up again, and get the knee bending. The whole thing sounds like torture to me. And they've said that it might not work anyway. This type of operation's only been done a few times before, in the States, and not everyone's been able to walk again after. Bloody typical if they've cocked me up.'

'But you told me that the operation went well?'

'So *they* said. But they would, wouldn't they? All I know is that it's been bloody painful.'

Now she felt some sympathy for him. Whether the accident had been his fault or not, she could not deny that he had been suffering with the leg; and maybe he had good reason to feel sorry for himself with the threat of a possible permanent disability looming on the horizon. Attempting to sound reassuring, she said, 'I'm sure they'll do all they can to get you walking again. After all, they arranged to get that American specialist in for you, didn't they?'

He glared at her, 'And why shouldn't they have? It's their fault I'm in this bloody mess to begin with. And another thing, you might be interested to know that I've decided to refuse their pathetic offer of working in their stupid careers office. I've had enough of the Forces and being told what to do every minute of every bloody day.'

She was surprised, and went on to ask, 'Are you sure? You're not being too hasty, are you? It sounded like a really good opportunity to me.'

He smiled, a secretive type of smile, and tapping the side of his nose with one finger, said, 'I've got other ideas. I'll do alright. As long as I don't end up in a bloody wheel chair!'

'What ideas?' The incongruous thought suddenly struck her that he had decided to find seasonal work on a holiday camp. Maybe that was why he had been hanging around the camp lately.

He leant back on his elbows, his eyes resting on Cherry's picture. 'Think I might take them up on their other offer.' He paused, wanting to, and enjoying, keeping her guessing.

'What other offer?'

'Lump sum, or a pension.'

'They offered you a pension?' she exclaimed. 'What, you mean for life?'

'Of course, for life! What other type is there?'

'But you're so young!'

'Can't help that. And it's called a War Pension. Only paid out when you're twenty percent disabled, or something. Huh! Feels more like fifty. But I couldn't do much with that; a bit each month, drip, drip, drip. Wouldn't amount to anything useful. Anyway, I've decided on the lump sum.' He rubbed his hands together, looking almost gleeful, as he continued, 'Quite a generous amount really. And a bit of ready cash'll come in very handy right now.'

She still could not get the idea of the life pension out of her thinking. 'But Conrad, are you sure you're making the right choice? What if you somehow, you know, get through the lump sum, and then find yourself left with nothing? At least with a pension, you'd have some sort of steady income coming in?'

He sat up, annoyed at her unwanted advice. 'Belt up, woman! Don't you think I've thought of that? You sound just like my mother; driving me bloody crazy. Your mother too; they've been getting my flaming goat.'

'*My* mother?'

'Oh yes, didn't I say? I've been popping around. Doing her nut, she is. You're being very selfish, and worrying her sick, walking out like that, and not contacting her. She's got no idea when you'll be back.'

She felt like asking him to leave then and there. Instead she replied, 'Actually, I'd appreciate it if you'd leave my mother out of this.'

He shrugged. 'Huh! Someone's got to try to cheer the old girl up.'

She could just imagine him settling back on the settee as her mother rushed around, fawning and pandering to his every whim. 'That's what my father's for! Why don't you tell her what's really been going on, and what you've been like since you came home?'

'What do you mean?' he asked, looking genuinely puzzled.

'Well, for a start, that night at Wendy and Neville's, and how your parents blamed me for the state you were in.'

He rolled his eyes dramatically and sounded exasperated, as he exclaimed, 'For pete's sake, are you still going on about *that?* Why don't you belt up about it and change the record?'

'So, they still do? And my mother too? And you just sit back and let them? Thank you very much! What a good friend you are!'

Knowing she was right, he pressed his lips together and studied his plastered leg, deciding to make a show of experiencing some pain.

Frustrated at what she considered to be his dishonourable and evasive behaviour, she went on to say, 'Oh, and by the way, maybe you'd like to tell my mother - next time you happen to "pop in" - that I'm staying away because it's what I believe is best for her and Dad.'

He looked up. 'You're crazy!' He glanced around him and grimaced, making it clear what he thought of her surroundings. 'You can't stay in this dump forever.'

'Who said I was? For your information, I intend to find a place of my own when the season's over.'

This piece of news seemed to interest him, and he visibly perked up. 'Oh yeah, and where to?'

She shrugged. 'Somewhere around.'

Now he had a thoughtful expression on his face, and said, watching her closely, 'That's interesting. I'll be looking for a place too, when I get back.'

'You won't go back home? But what if...if things don't go so well at the hospital?'

'Shan't rush it. But I don't want to hang around too long. I'm needing my own space.'

She sighed. 'Yes. I should have left home myself, ages ago.'

'Too right! Got yourself into a rut, haven't you? Need someone to help you get out of it.'

She studied him, wondering at his change of tune. A few seconds ago he was criticising her for leaving her home, now he was agreeing with her that she should have left long ago.

He smiled across at her. 'Here's an idea. Why don't we join forces - kill two birds with one stone - and solve both out problems?'

'What? I hope you're not suggesting that we move in together?' she retorted, finding the very idea more than a little unpleasant.

'Well, why not? I'm not talking about sharing a bed - just expenses. And what if I'm needing a bit of your Florence Nightingale touch afterwards?' He reached across and grabbed her hand, 'Come on, Meri! I know you're a Christian and don't sleep around, and I'd respect that. Haven't I always?' Then, as an afterthought, and with a sly smile, added, 'Although, I'm sure I could accommodate you in that area if you ever changed your mind...'

She pulled her hand away. He really was incorrigible. 'Er, what's happened to "needing your own space?"'

He tried to look disappointed, but failed miserably as far as she was concerned. Nodding, he said reflectively, 'Yeah, well, I'm sick of people telling me what to do, and who I can do it with. And I know you'd respect my privacy. And if you think about it, you may change your mind, especially if I find a decent enough place somewhere near town. I'll be able to put a good six month's rent down - that would help you out - you get paid a pittance here. You could find another job. I'd be doing you a favour; help you get out of this dump.'

She sighed. Poor Conrad. He had no idea who she really was. 'No Conrad, I don't think so. You'll have to go ahead without me.' And then, wanting to change the subject, went on to ask, 'And what are you going to do about earning a living anyway? Have you decided to work for your father after all?'

He seemed to come to life as he sat up, his whole countenance becoming animated. 'Nope! Going to open a motorcycle dealership. Dad likes the idea. He's been thinking of knocking down the back wall of the toolshed and extending out the back anyway. I'll start small, maybe a dozen bikes - and some parts.'

'Motorcycles! But...are you sure? What if...'

He looked at her defiantly, and interrupted, 'Don't you say it! Don't you dare say it! Whether I come back in a wheelchair or on my own two feet, I'm damn well going to do it!'

Ignoring his defensive manner, she went on to ask, 'But wheelchairs and motorbikes don't mix! Why don't you wait and see how you are before committing yourself?'

'No!' he shouted. 'And you and my mother can go and hang! I'm sick of hearing her bleating on and on about it. Dad's sick of it too. Even told me I can move into that large storeroom above the garage as soon as I like!'

'But Conrad, if you're in a wheelchair…'

'Stop talking rot! It'll be crutches - if anything.'

'So why did you just say about being in a wheelchair?'

'I don't know! For God's sake, why'd you go hanging on every word I say?'

She decided to stay silent, realising that he was struggling to keep some sort of hope and purpose alive. On the one hand, she was glad that he had something to focus his mind on: on the other, she felt that selling motorbikes was not the most suitable of things for him to be planning on as a career move right now.

The moment passed, and he seemed to calm down. 'There's a kitchenette and a loo up there, and I can manage the stairs with these.' He picked up his crutches and began to raise himself to his feet. 'It'll get me away from all the nagging till I get something else. Anyway, I'm needing a drink. Can't persuade you to get yourself decent and come with me then?'

'No thanks, I'm not in the mood tonight.'

'You're daft, woman! You'd rather stay here and listen to that mumbo-jumbo. And what's that you're doing anyway?' He tilted his head towards her unfinished card.

'I'm making a card for someone.'

Swaying back and forth on his crutches, he lowered his face towards her, and said, 'You're a strange one, Meri! I can't fathom you out. But I think you'll change your mind when you start looking around and see what crap's on offer out there.'

'Then don't hold your breath!' she replied, standing to open the door.

He stepped outside. 'Well, wish me luck!'

She watched him expertly negotiate the balcony step. She didn't like the man anymore, nor could she rely on him, or even trust him. But she did feel some sympathy for him. 'I really hope everything works out for you Conrad, and you know that I'll be praying for you.'

'Yeah! Like that'll help!' he commented sarcastically with his back to her, keen to down another pint.

CHAPTER 32

Kingsley was waiting for her when she arrived at the offices of Smith and Bartrum. She had been looking forward to having the opportunity to tell her side of the story to someone official.

At precisely eleven o'clock they were shown into Ernest Bartrum's office. Her heart sank at the sight of the untidy and gloomy room. An elderly man sat behind a large desk, his trays were full, and a miscellany of legal looking documents lay scattered indiscriminately on the surface. Stacks of other paperwork leaned against the sides of the desk, and rows of black box files covered the shelves behind him.

They were invited to sit, as the solicitor, whose appearance she thought was as dark and foreboding as his surroundings, began searching through one of the trays.

'One moment,' he mumbled, selecting one, and bending his grey head low to study its contents.

Since entering, Meredith had felt a definite sinking of her spirits; this old man didn't look as though he could barely grip the pencil he was holding, never mind be sharp witted enough to be effective in a courtroom situation. He and his environment looked as though they had stepped straight out of a Charles Dickens' novel. And yet, this was the man Tom had recommended. Oh well, she decided, she was here now, so she might as well find out what he could do for her, and, if needs be, try to find another solicitor afterwards.

Kingsley sat back and crossed his legs. He studied the man. If his age was anything to go by, then he must have many years' experience behind him. He hoped that that would prove to be the case. The house group had put a lot of prayer into this meeting, and he was curious to see how The Lord was going to answer them all.

At last, the grey head lifted to peer at Meredith over some half-moon glasses. His voice, when he spoke, was sharp and high; every syllable articulated with the utmost precision. 'Well now, Miss Sanderson, it seems that you've landed yourself in a spot of bother!'

Mildly irritated at the banality of his opening statement, Meredith told herself to remain calm, and asked, 'Yes, I know that, but can you help me?'

'That all depends,' he replied, putting his pencil down with a slow, deliberate action, before holding out one hand towards her. 'Summons?'

She opened her bag and handed him the document. His eyes skimmed over it. Then he returned to studying the papers in front of him.

Meredith's impatience and agitation grew as the agonising seconds passed. At last, unable to stop herself, she exclaimed, 'I didn't do any of it...' only to be interrupted by a raised hand, as he continued reading.

After what seemed an eternity to her, he looked up and began tapping the document with one thin finger. 'According to this, you hurled abuse at a constable before knocking his helmet off.'

She lost no time in denying the charges. 'I honestly have no idea what all that's about.' Not knowing what else to say or do, she turned and looked, wide-eyed and appealingly at Kingsley. 'Why would they accuse me of doing something like that? Was it *just* because they weren't busy that night, and wanted to get the numbers up? That's what I heard them say. Even that they could easily get me for assault and possession. I heard them plan it all!'

Kingsley reached over to squeeze her hand, then addressed the solicitor. 'We haven't been introduced; I'm Reverend Kingsley Pryce, Meredith's Minister and friend. We're hoping that you can fill us in, and advise us about the next step.'

The man harrumphed and looked keenly at him, focusing for several seconds on the dog collar. 'Fill you in? Very well, if you insist.' Then, without any change in his facial expression, he began to read out the document before him, his voice remaining steady as he quoted, verbatim, the tirade of abusive and foul language Meredith had been accused of saying.

She was aghast. Such words and expressions were not part of her vocabulary - nor had they ever been. In fact, there were several she had never even heard before.

'I take it that you deny all these charges?' the solicitor asked, matter of factly.

'Of course she does!' retorted Kingsley, surprised that the man had felt the need to ask such a question.

Unruffled, the solicitor replied, 'I need to hear it from Miss Sanderson herself.'

Meredith was quick to respond. 'Yes, I do deny them! All of them. I didn't say any of those…things. And I certainly didn't knock anyone's helmet off! That…that's just…ridiculous!'

Used as he was to hearing similar, passionate denials, the solicitor sat back and studied her face. She remained motionless as she felt his gimlet eyes attempting to bore deep into her mind. Defiantly and unwaveringly, she stared right back at him. Let him, she thought, I've got nothing to hide.

Slow nods came next. He flashed the briefest of smiles at her, then opening one of the side draws of his desk, he drew out a small, brass bell. 'Coffee, I think,' he said, ringing it loudly.

Just over half-an-hour later they emerged from the claustrophobic environment, wincing at the daylight brightness, and relieved to be back out in the fresh air.

'Man of few words, but I've got a strong feeling that there's a wise old fox lurking beneath that bleak exterior,' remarked Kingsley.

Meredith took a deep breath, thankful that the ordeal was over. 'I hope you're right, although I've got to admit that I'm feeling a bit better than when we went in. I felt like bolting when I first saw him.'

'And I wouldn't have blamed you; you did well to sit tight.'

'Do you think he believed me?'

By now they had reached the car park. He began searching through his pockets for his keys. 'That's the feeling I've come away with, and I got the distinct impression that he warmed to you after a while.' He unlocked the car. 'Still feel like lunch at Doreen's? Remember, I've got to shoot off soon afterwards.'

'Yes, I think I do.'

They joined the line of traffic waiting to go onto the main road. How safe she felt in his company; he was so calm and reassuring. If only she could always feel like this.

'And you understand your position now, don't you? All you have to do is wait for the court date to come through, and leave him to get on with all background legal stuff. I can't imagine it's going to be easy, but keeping to a routine helps.'

'That's what I've been trying to do,' she replied, half-heartedly. 'But I feel so…like I've lost control of my life, especially now I know what things they're saying about me - and by the police themselves! I…I really don't know what's coming - what's ahead of me.'

He heard the anguish in her voice. 'Yes, that's understandable, I think I'd feel the same. But try to remember that The Lord knows everything, and He's still in control. He has a plan for your life, and knows exactly what your future holds. And I don't think that's going to include anything to harm you, Meredith. Try to keep trusting in Him.'

'But it's so hard having to sit back and do nothing. If only the case could be heard tomorrow, or next week, but he reckons it'll take months! I just want to get it over and done with and get on with my life.'

'Then maybe what you need is a challenge; something else to focus your mind on.' He knew that this could prove easier said than done, especially now that they had heard that there really was the threat of a prison sentence hanging over her head.

She remained silent. He turned to look at her. 'Meredith?'

'Challenge? I've got a few of those on my plate already. Things are still tricky with my parents, and I need to find somewhere else to live soon.'

'You don't want to go back home then?'

'No, it's time I found my own place. And there's no guarantee that the agency will want to take me back on their books, not now...with all this going on.'

He nodded. 'Looks like we've got a lot to pray about.'

Doreen was comforting and encouraging. Meredith was relieved that the lunch was a simple affair, consisting only of vegetable soup and rolls. She doubted if she could have faced anything else. Kingsley made his excuses and hurried away within minutes of finishing, but not before stressing, once again, that he and the fellowship were there for her.

Doreen went to put the kettle on. Alone in the lounge, Meredith picked up the local newspaper and turned to the *Accommodation to Let* section.

'Looking for a place?' Doreen asked, returning with the drinks.

'Thinking about it. The season's almost over. My boss has offered me one of the staff rooms in the main building, but I don't really fancy the idea.'

'Why's that?'

'I tried it once, but I couldn't settle with the thought of all that dark, empty space underneath me. And I kept hearing noises, even though there was no-one else around.'

'Don't blame you! I get spooked when Dave's home late. So what are you after? Something near the camp, or a bit nearer town?'

'I'm not fussy. As long as it's on a good bus route, and clean and affordable. And I wouldn't mind sharing.'

Doreen sat, stirring her tea slowly. 'W-e-ll, there is Fred's old static, you know the one, it's just behind his house? He always let it out in the summer, and I expect it'll be free soon. Maybe the family would be glad of someone to keep it warm and aired over the winter. I can't imagine they'd want much, and it's not much further along from the camp. His niece has moved into the house. She's been on the council list for years and has just had a baby, so I expect it's come in just right for her. Poor old Fred. I do miss him.'

'I do too, especially those corny old jokes of his.'

Doreen nodded and smiled. 'They were awful, weren't they? Anyway, what do you think? Do you like the idea?'

'I more than like it!' Meredith replied, enthusiastically.

'Well, okay, we could give her ring and sound her out now, if you like. I've got the number. Ah, thinking ahead, the family'll probably want to start letting it out to holidaymakers again come spring. Then you'd have to move out.'

'That's no problem. I could move back on camp.'

'Well then, I suppose there's no time like the present - although - maybe we should ask The Lord what He thinks about it first?'

'Of course! You're right,' agreed Meredith, seeing the wisdom in the other woman's suggestion.

And so the two women spend some time in prayer. When neither felt any sense of foreboding at the idea, Doreen recommended that she should be the one to make the call, having already had some dealings with the daughter in the past.

Linda Turnbull was at home, and although initially surprised at the proposal, promised to think about it and contact Meredith in a day or two.

The rest of the afternoon was spent pleasantly, and Doreen invited her to stay for the evening meal, but she refused, feeling that she had imposed herself for too long already.

❖

Crowds of campers were returning from the Broads trip when she arrived back at the camp. Negotiating her way through them, she felt an almost overpowering sense of gratitude for the care and concern that was being shown towards her by her Christian family - and then a heavy sadness as she remembered how very different things had been, and still were, with her own mother, and to some extent, even with her father.

Determined not to allow herself to wallow in self-pity, she opened her Bible and began reading. By now she had reached the book of **2 Samuel**. The first few verses of Chapter 22 seemed to speak directly to her:-

> **David sang this song to the Lord after he had rescued him from Saul and from all his other enemies:**
> **"Jehovah is my rock,**
> **My fortress and my Saviour.**
> **I will hide in God**
> **Who is my rock and my refuge.**
> **He is my shield**
> **And my salvation,**
> **My refuge and high tower..."**

Yes, a *high tower*. She liked that, and somehow she knew that God was promising that He would be her *High Tower* too. She prayed, and like a comforting, warm blanket, the image stayed with her throughout the rest of the cold night.

CHAPTER 33

'"You'll never get anywhere in life - not the sharpest tool in the box - a dimwit - a bit slow." Ring a bell with anybody?'

Silence followed. 'If that is your image of yourself, then let me tell you today that it's wrong. Utterly and completely wrong. And it's not what God thinks of you. The Bible...' he held up his copy, 'says that we are all - *all* - made in the image of God, and *He's* certainly none of those things! Apart from that, you are all absolutely, totally, and one hundred per cent unique. There has never been another human being like you, nor will there ever be. Even identical twins have some differences.'

Meredith walked towards the group of people sitting on the sand. Several members of Launchpad were sitting on the steps, near the front. This was the last beach outreach of the season, and she had made a special effort to get there before it ended. An offshore wind was disturbing the large sheets of paper on the sketch board behind Kingsley, causing them to flap about noisily. She picked up a few pebbles and went to place them on the narrow shelf in front of the pages, then went to sit on the steps, near a group of teenagers.

Kingsley smiled across at her, 'Thanks Meredith.'

She sat back on her elbows and began to wonder what type of image she had of herself. Maybe it was a bit on the poor side. Was she the disappointment her mother always claimed she was? And was she really destined to end up like her aunt after all: fat, frigid, and all alone in the world?

'Okay, so we've talked briefly about our poor self image. Now let's think about the ways it may have been laid on us...'

Two male members of the camp staff, who were leaning against the railings and watching from the carpark, began to

233

shout and whistle at a couple of young women walking on the beach below them. Unperturbed, Kingsley continued. Meredith waved to catch their attention and they looked down at her. She put her finger to her lips, and mouthed, 'Be quiet!' No-one could have been more surprised than her when they obeyed. A few seconds later they turned and disappeared from view.

Kingsley was at the sketch board now and drawing fast. He stepped back to reveal a manger scene. 'I'm here today to tell you that there is Someone Who thinks the world of you, and His eyes are full of concern and love every time He looks at you; there's no hint of criticism or judgement in them. He longs for you to know His love and care. And that's why, one day, two thousand years ago, He did something about it. He left His home in Heaven, and came down to live amongst us. Now, I know it's not Christmas, but remember that Baby in the manger? In human terms, He couldn't get much lower: a tiny, innocent baby, born in a cattle shed, and becoming a refugee when his parents had to flee to Egypt.'

He flicked the sheet over and drew a large cross. 'But let's not linger at the manger, let's move on another thirty years, to when that baby had become a man. A man who allowed Himself to be nailed to a cross. If that doesn't grab your attention, then hopefully this will, and show you why He would allow such a thing to be done to Him - and how it relates to each and every one of us here. A group from my church are going to perform a short sketch now. I want you to imagine that you're in a court of law, and that the judge is just about to declare the verdict.'

Three members of Launchpad stood and performed the sketch, in which the criminal in the box was sentenced to death for his sins. The punishment was to be carried out immediately. However, the judge stood and stepped down from his bench - in this case, the third step - and declared that he would take the criminal's place. Everyone in the court - in this case, five other members of Launchpad who had remained seated - were amazed, and began to ask why. The judge patiently explained his reasons for wanting to pay the full and ultimate cost of the guilty man's punishment himself, stating that he was willing to be sacrificed on his behalf. In that way, the court's demand for justice would be satisfied. The debt would be paid, and the guilty man could go free. He would take all the man's sin upon himself, and, in return, he would give him His righteousness.

A guard removed the toy handcuffs that had been placed around the prisoner's wrists and began leading him away. Just before he left, the prisoner turned towards the judge, and asked, 'Why would you do such a thing for the likes of me? You know what I'm like; I'm not worth it.'

'Because I want to be your Heavenly Father,' replied the judge. 'I've always been here for you. I've always wanted to share your life, and I longed for you to know how much I have always loved you. Let me do this for you, my child. I will take your place on the gallows. I will take your punishment. Then your crimes will have been paid for, and justice will be satisfied.'

Kingsley then went on to give a short Gospel message, after which he invited everyone to pray. 'And now, I'd like us all to close our eyes and keep them tightly shut. If any of you have come to recognise that you've been going the wrong way in life, and want to turn around to receive God's forgiveness, then pray this prayer with me. It's also for those of who are suffering from a poor self image, and want Jesus to help you to be free from it - and have the image of yourself that He died for you to have. And it's even for those who have no problem in that area, but simply want to turn around and receive God's love, and to start living His way. If you recognise yourself in any of these ways, then I would invite you to put your hand up as I pray. We'll ask Jesus to forgive us for our sins, for dying on the Cross in our place, and for taking upon Himself the punishment we all deserve. Then we'll thank Him, and ask

Him to get down from that Cross - and come and live in our hearts. I'll pause after each bit, and you can repeat the prayer after me. Or, if you're shy, say it silently in your head. Do whatever you feel comfortable with, as long as you sincerely mean what you say. All eyes staying shut please. Let's pray...'

Meredith felt some movement coming from the gangly youth sitting next to her. She fought hard against the temptation to look to see if he had raised his hand, or if he had just shifted his position again.

The prayer ended, and another chorus was sung, then Kingsley asked those who had prayed to spend a few minutes with him before leaving. A blessing followed, after which Meredith went to have a chat with the group from Launchpad, frequently turning to look over in Kingsley's direction. To her delight, she saw the gangly youth amongst those who had gathered around him.

Walking away, she began to realise just how badly dented her own self image had become recently, and prayed quietly that God would forgive her for allowing herself to believe such harmful and incapacitating lies.

She decided to spend the rest of the evening designing and drawing another card. The poor self image theme played on her mind, and she came to the conclusion that the most self-effacing and humble animal she could think of was a donkey. Taking a plain white, A4 sized card, she folded it in half and drew a horizontal line across the front section. In the top part she drew a little figure of a donkey with droopy ears, its head cast down, as it lay forlornly in the dust. In the bottom part, she drew the same figure, but this time with his head held high, and his front paw raised as it appeared to be strutting proudly along a colourful path of cloaks and large green leaves. Astride it sat a man, dressed in a plain, cream tunic, and looking as she imagined Jesus would have on his triumphal entry into Jerusalem on Palm Sunday.

Laying the card aside, she felt inspired to write some words on the inside. It was to be another hour before she felt satisfied and sat back to look over her work. The thought occurred to her that the words she had just written could be used as the basis of a story. But it was getting late. She stretched and yawned. Feeling pleasantly tired, she decided to turn in for the night.

Her mattress seemed to have developed another lump, and she lay awake thinking about the card and the words she had written inside it. Then, unexpectedly, she began to imagine what life would be like in prison. At least she was used to old mattresses and basic accommodation. And maybe there would be some advantage to being forced to live such a confined and less busy life after all: she might have plenty of time to create a whole series of cards - and maybe even write a children's story! A story that Cherry would like!

Strangely comforted by the idea, she fell asleep.

CHAPTER 34

The last week of the season finally arrived; this was set aside specifically for the mentally handicapped, and most of the staff, comprising mainly of students, had already left to start the new academic year. Jacko had come to rely heavily on Murphy and was going around the place complaining and sounding as miserable as he looked.

Meredith went into the Dining Room. She was just about to make a start on her meal when her eye was caught by the rhythmic movement of a man, seated several tables away. Instead of eating, he appeared to be totally absorbed by a stack of bread, piled high on his plate in front of him. He rocked back and forth in his chair, stroking the sides of the stack tenderly, and whispering secret things to it. Obviously used to his strange behaviour, his companions, including the aids, ignored him, and carried on with their meal.

'Kingsley called in when you were at lunch. Left that for you,' said Tom, pointing at a folded note on her desk. 'Says he's had to go away.'

She read the note.

Dear Meredith,
Sorry to have missed you again and that we didn't have a chance to catch up after last night's Open Air. Someone from my past, who was very dear to me, has passed away and I shall be away for a few days - or possibly longer.
Doreen and Dave have asked me to tell you that they're here for you, as are all your friends in the fellowship. However, if you feel you need to talk to me, you can

reach me at my parents' house: Tel:0306-3524.
You know you are very much in my prayers.
Yours in Christ, Kingsley.

'How long's he gone for?' asked Tom.

'Just a few days, or maybe a bit longer. Someone close to him has died.'

'Is he doing the funeral then?'

'He doesn't say.'

'Well, he can come and do mine any time soon now. Hilda's driving me into an early grave with all her nagging. She actually expects me to give her a report on the progress we've made on *her* report! Thank God she's not a trustee!'

Meredith smiled, 'What a lot you've got to be grateful for!'

❖

She noticed the man perform the same ritual with the stack of bread at breakfast the next day, and again during lunch. As far as she could see, he only took the odd mouthful of food in between his obsessive whispering, stroking and patting. She began to feel some concern for him, and went over to speak to one of the aids.

'Don't you worry about Jamie. He won't go hungry,' she was told. However, she wasn't convinced, having seen the same aid giving him bars of chocolate and packets of crisps from the vending machine earlier that day.

The same pattern of events occurred the next day, and this time she went to have a word with Nick. She was relieved when he said he would arrange to have his meals put by for him, to be taken either before or immediately after the set meal times, '...as long as he comes in with an aid. I'll make sure there's no bread involved. Damn nuisance! But the man's got to get something substantial down his neck.' She checked back with Nick to see if the plan was working after the following evening meal. 'I've been keeping a good eye on him, especially with the mash. His plates come back half-eaten now. Takes a ruddy long time about it too!'

So, she thought, Nick did have a heart! Somehow, she had always suspected that he had. 'It's only for another four days, and thanks Nick.'

Kingsley was still away the following week. Two of the deacons had taken the Sunday services, and the rest of the diaconate were well able to keep the church routine going during his absence. Meredith's offer to help run Launchpad was eagerly accepted. She had led a discussion on the theme: 'How not to be the type of miserable Christian who only starts to truly live when they die!' - knowing that she was speaking as much to herself as she was to everyone else. There was still no sign of Fleur at the group, nor at church, although Julia frequently mentioned her name during conversation.

Fred Turnbull's niece had returned her call and invited her to go and view the static van. As a result, arrangements had been made for her to move in the following week. She had informed the solicitor of her impending change of address, and was frustrated when she was told that there was still no date set for the court case. Feelings of foreboding, even fear, would try to take her over, but she disciplined herself to keep busy and her mind occupied - and especially to pray more regularly.

At last, the final group of campers were leaving. The collective exhaust fumes from a fleet of assorted minivans revving up outside the building hung thick in the air. 'The Bread Man', the title she had privately given the bread-obsessed man, came to reception with another one of the aids. She tried to appear unconcerned as she watched him carefully lift a plate, stacked high with bread, on the counter in front of her. Muttering to himself, he began tenderly stroking the sides, before taking a sudden jump back, only to jump forward again and pat the top slice with a series of swift, excited movements.

'Jamie went around and collected all the leftovers. He'd like you to look after this for him,' explained the aid, giving her a knowing look, and hoping she would comply with the strange request.

She played along. 'How very kind! Thank you, Jamie.'

Jamie muttered something incoherent as he pointed at an area on his side of the stack. She looked to see what he was trying so hard to tell them, and noticed a layer of jam oozing out.

'You're highly honoured. He's never used jam before,' remarked the aid.

'Really? Well, that is an honour.'

Jamie stuck his neck forward and stared at her. She felt the back of her own neck prickle and hoped that he could not read her thoughts. He returned to the stroking motion, tenderly caressing the sides of the stack - up and down, up and down - the action almost hypnotic. Mystified, she watched. And then, a thought struck her - could it be - but that was *too* strange - but then again - *could* it be that he was trying to show her, to tell her, that this simple stack of bread was actually meant to represent something else? That, in his mind, it was something completely different? Was she being given, through this man's eccentric behaviour, a sort of sign, or even confirmation, that she was not alone, that The Lord was surrounding her - defending her? Like a tower - *A High Tower?* The Bible was full of stories of the unusual ways He communicated with people; why not through a stack of bread?

Quietly, almost timidly, she spoke his name, 'Jamie, Jamie.' He lifted his entranced gaze. 'It's a tower, isn't it? You've made me a tower, a very special tower?'

So loud were the excited, incoherent noises that began to emanate from his mouth, that Tom came smartly out of his office to see what all the commotion was about. The aid moaned and rolled his eyes, then, with some effort, but obviously using a technique he'd had to develop, succeeded in pulling and pushing his excited charge away from the counter.

'Thank you Jamie!' called Meredith, 'I understand, I really do. Thank you so, *so* much!'

The pair disappeared through the doors, but not before Jamie managed to turn and flash her a brilliant, toothless grin.

❖

Wendy kindly offered to drive her and her belongings to the static van the next morning. There was plenty of room in the car, and only one journey was needed.

'I'm curious to see what one of these really old ones are like,' Wendy said, stepping inside when they arrived.

'Long past its sell-by date, I'm afraid, but it'll do me,' replied Meredith. 'Anyway, make yourself at home. We'll have a cuppa in a minute.'

Wendy began her inspection in the kitchen as Meredith carried in the remaining bags. Cupboards and drawers were opened and closed. 'Bit cold isn't it? Looks like you've got everything you need, but that's a *huge* frying pan!'

'I'll get a smaller one. I'm looking forward to doing some cooking.'

'And you're sure she's not going to change her mind and suddenly start charging you rent when you're in?' Wendy was still having trouble accepting the terms of Meredith's occupancy, despite having had them spelled out to her several times already.

'No, Wendy. I wish you'd believe me. She won't charge me a penny - as long as I baby-sit for her on week nights so she can do her office cleaning job. I'll only have to pay towards the utilities, and that's all.'

Wendy peered inside the oven. 'Huh! Let's hope she sticks to it then. And you'll have to keep an eye on the gas; you don't want to run out half way through a roast. I'd be scared stiff having that big bottle right outside. What if it gets hit by lightning? And she didn't do a very good job of cleaning in here, did she?'

'I'll soon sort it. And sorry, I've only got dried milk. I'll get to the shops later.'

'It'll do.' Wendy opened the fridge. She took a large whiff of the interior, satisfied, she moved into the lounge and bent to study the gas fire. 'I don't like these things. I'm always scared they'll blow up. If I was you I'd get an electric one.' Standing, she looked around, and asked, 'Where's the telly?'

'There isn't one, but Dad's promised to get me a second hand one.'

'What's your mum got to say about that?'

'Well, you know my mother! It's to be an early Christmas present anyway.'

Pamela had been told about Meredith's move, and had declared herself to be 'totally horrified.' Meredith was not surprised when her father told her. Her disappointment towards her parents had faded during the past weeks, and she had already decided that they would be the first people she would invite over for a meal. She would show them both just how practical and cosy the place could be. Even so, she was fully expecting her mother to continue finding fault with her and her new accommodation, but she was determined to shrug all such negativity off. She had made the break, and there was only one way to go now, and that was forward - provided she didn't get sent to prison.

'Have Manpower got you fixed up yet?'

'I told them not to till next week. I feel like a bit of break.'

'You're going to miss having your dad's car.'

'Expect I'll manage, and the bus stop's not far away. I'll be okay, as long as they send me to places on the main routes.'

Wendy opened the first bedroom door. 'Hmm. Bunk beds, and it feels *really* cold in here.' She opened the next door. 'This one's bigger, but not much of a wardrobe. What about bedding?'

'I'll use my sleeping bag for now.'

'Why didn't you tell me? I've got plenty of spare you could have had. Neville's mother gave us all her stuff when she went into the home. To tell you the truth, I'll be relieved to get some room back in my airing cupboard. There's a big old eiderdown and loads of double sheets; flannelette, a bit faded, but plenty of life left in them.'

Meredith hesitated. She had planned on buying new, but then again - with the threat of spending the next few years in a prison cell. 'Well, if you're sure. That would be great.'

'I'll drop them off tomorrow on my way to the Co-op.'

She returned to the lounge and looked out of the back window. The garden had no fences, and, to her mind, looked a bit too exposed. 'That man doesn't know you're here, does he?'

Meredith knew she was referring to Conrad. 'I haven't told him, and I think he must still be away.'

'Good, let's hope he stays away. Your new landlady won't think much to having a drunk around the place!'

CHAPTER 35

She stopped by the public telephone box on the way back from church the next day and called her parents' house. She invited them for tea the following Saturday evening. By then she would have given the van a thorough clean and be ready for visitors. However, she was disappointed when her mother procrastinated, making one excuse after another. She walked back to the van slowly, trying to come to terms with the fact that it looked like there was going to be no family reconciliation at any time in the near future.

Her baby-sitting duties had begun, and, as Linda had predicted, baby Bernadette was easy to look after. As long as she'd had her bottle and was in a clean nappy, most of the two hour shift usually passed quietly and pleasantly enough.

Her card making was turning into quite a project, and she had made a good start on a short story, using some of the characters she had already created for her cards: *Alma: The Alarmed Llama; Katy: The Cantankerous Kangaroo; Christopher: The Crooked Crocodile; Kitty: The Cross Kiwi, and Olive : The Ostracised Ostrich.* So engrossed was she with this new challenge, that she jumped when someone knocked on her door late one afternoon. She recognised the visitor's shape through the opaque glass, and quickly went to open the door.

'Kingsley! You're back?' she exclaimed.

He stood there, smiling, as he thrust a large package, wrapped in clear cellophane, into her arms. 'Late last night. Heard you'd moved. Hope you've got room for these; apparently they're dead easy to look after.'

She backed into the small entrance area. 'Come in, it's good to see you. African Violets! They're lovely; thank you so much.'

He followed her, looking around, and remarking, 'This looks cosy.'

'Who told you I was here?'

'Doreen left a note at the manse. I passed the camp on the way; looks strange seeing the main gates shut and nothing going on behind them.'

'Yes, I always think that. Anyway, take a seat.' She pointed to the long seating in the lounge, 'Tea - coffee?'

'Coffee'd be good. So how are things? Any news?'

'No, I've heard nothing.'

'Still early days, I suppose. But you're looking well,' he replied, pausing to scan the card-strewn table before sitting down. 'This looks interesting. Can I take a look?'

'Yes, it's just a project I've been working on. A few ideas to keep my mind occupied...focused, you know.'

He picked up one of the completed cards and sat back, stretching one arm over the top of the seating. 'Ha! Cute. *Paddy, The Tap Dancing Platypus.* Nice brogues!' He opened it and laughed. Selecting another, he laughed even louder at the sight of the jewel-festooned bird: *Maggie, The Tinkling Magpie.* Hey! These are good. What are you going to do with them?'

She looked at him through the framework of kitchen shelves. 'I'm thinking of giving the zebra one to Tom and Sue as a christening card for Zoe. You'll see that I've left a blank space inside to write dedication, or christening - or baptism. Has he come back to you about that?' Having unwrapped and watered the violets, she took them through into the lounge and put them on a shelf near the front window, placing three of her four saucers beneath them.

He began searching through the small pile of cards. 'No. I think he's still having trouble with his mother-in-law. I've told

246

him I'd be happy to have a chat with her. We'll have to wait and see. Anyway, where'd you get your ideas from?'

'They just come.'

He found the zebra card. 'Hmm, *Dotty, The Mixed up Zebra.* Colourful!'

'That was the first one I made. One of the children who went on the zoo trip gave me a drawing of a zebra. It's up there.' She pointed at Cherry's picture, framed now and on a corner shelf. 'My original inspiration. After that, I just sort of carried on. Actually, I'm doing a story using some of the same characters. I keep getting all these ideas, and can't seem to get them down quick enough.' She put his drink down on the table and pulled up a stool, then sat down opposite him. 'Here,' she opened and handed him a tin of shortbread biscuits. 'Another housewarming gift.' Then, changing the subject, she said, 'I was sorry to hear about your friend. Had they been ill for some time?'

She noticed a frown pass quickly over his face as he turned to look out of the window at a passing lorry. Back here, the sound was slightly muffled.

'No. The news came out of the blue. I...knew her some time ago. She was...' he hesitated. On the drive home he had debated with himself about what he could, and should, say about Deborah, and to whom. In the end, he could think of no good enough reason to be secretive about that part of his life, feeling that it would be hypocritical of him to be so. After all, he was in the business of encouraging others to 'open up', and share their own deep-seated emotional wounds. Still, he would need to exercise wisdom about who he would share the knowledge with. And Meredith's name was on that very short list.

'I met her, her name was Deborah, during my first year at university. We were on the same course.'

'You knew her all that time, then?'

'Yes. She wasn't sure what she wanted to do with her degree, only that it would be something to do with the Church. But I knew it was always going to be the ministry for me.' He looked back into the room and down at the cards again.

Meredith waited, then, hoping to encourage him to say more, asked, 'And what did she decide on, in the end?'

'Well, I should say that we were inseparable, and got engaged during our final year. She seemed happy enough about becoming the archetypal manse wife, but, let's just say…things didn't turn out that way.' It was obvious that he was choosing his words carefully. 'She couldn't wait, and neither could I. We had it all planned, right down to the last detail. We'd be the perfect team; her gifts were more in the pastoral line, mine in preaching and teaching, as well as evangelism. And we seemed to be blessed; both getting honours. We agreed that it would be a good idea for her to get some practical experience before we got married, and we had our choice of churches, but for some reason she accepted an invitation to go to one nearly fifty miles away from the one I'd been called to.' He looked up and into Meredith's face. 'We thought we'd manage, seeing less of each other. I bought an old car, and her parents were well-heeled and bought her a new mini as a reward for getting her degree…but then…'

Meredith held her breath, trying to imagine what dreadful thing could have happened to prevent the couple - the 'blessed' couple - from ending up together.

He continued. 'It was a challenging time for both of us. We waited a year, and then I thought…the time was right. But then she wouldn't commit to a date, and kept saying she needed more time to think things over. It was Easter, always a busy time, and we didn't see each other for a while. And then she told me that she needed a break and was going over to Australia to visit her sister. I tried not to read too much into it; she was only going for a month, so I sat tight and waited.' He paused. She noticed a fleeting shadow of sadness, then resignation, pass over his face. 'She was different somehow when she came back. Detached. She seemed to have lost interest in everything and everybody, including me. I put it down to post-holiday blues, and convinced myself that she just needed more time, that we'd soon be back on an even keel. But then the excuses started again, she'd been making them for a while before she left. She couldn't meet me, someone was taken ill, someone had to be visited, someone needed taking somewhere...' He shrugged. 'We only met up a few times over the next six months, but still I refused to recognise what was really going on. I was still in denial. And then her letter came - with her engagement ring inside. She announced that she was going back to Australia. She wanted to live there; that was where her real life was.' He paused to take a sip of his coffee.

'And...and did she stay out there? Did she make a life for herself?'

'Hmm. Wouldn't you know it? Turned out that she'd met someone, and went back to marry him.'

Meredith gasped. 'And you had no idea?'

He nodded, his lips pressed in a tight line. 'The only one who must have known what was going on was her sister; even her parents didn't have a clue!'

'That must have been devastating. What did you do?'

He shrugged. 'What could I do? She'd made up her mind. I felt like getting on the next boat, but thought better of it when I heard from her mother that the wedding was only weeks away. I knew we'd probably end up rowing, and I'd come away with my tail between my legs; and my pride had already been hurt enough.' He took another sip of his drink.

'When did this all happen?' she asked.

'Over eight years ago. Took me a long time to get over it. Anyway, turned out she had a child four months later. His child. They were married by then. I didn't hear any more about her till last week, when her mother contacted me and told me that she'd come back for a visit...and died.'

'It was her...who died?' exclaimed Meredith, obviously shocked, and, for the moment, not knowing what else she could sensitively say, or ask.

'Hmm. Seems they'd gone on to have two more children. She'd just started taking the contraceptive pill. Apparently, she'd complained about having some pain at the back of one of her calves soon after she'd arrived.' He paused again, and sighed heavily. 'It developed into a blood clot...and went to her lungs.'

Meredith was aghast. 'That's dreadful!' She had heard of other women suffering a similar fate as a result of the taking the new 'wonder drug'.

Kingsley nodded. 'She should never have flown, and might still be alive today if she'd only had it checked out sooner. Anyway, I went because I felt that I needed to see her; she was in the Chapel of Rest. There were things I felt I had to say.' He fell silent. Remembering.

Meredith allowed the silence to continue for what she thought an appropriate length of time, then asked, 'And were you able to...say those things?'

He looked at her, his eyes heavy, tired. 'Yes. It wasn't too bad. I'd done all my forgiving, but it was good to clear the air, even though her spirit was long gone. I'd often wondered how I'd feel if I ever saw her again. But once I was there, standing by her, there was nothing, no feeling - only sadness - for her, and her husband, especially her children. And it wasn't just because she couldn't interact with me. She'd been a big part of my life for a long time, but she'd chosen to bring our relationship to an end. All I felt was...peace.'

She looked into his eyes and could find no sign of any lingering, tortuous angst or despair there. 'You look peaceful, Kingsley; tired, but peaceful.'

'Yes, that's how I'm feeling. That chapter is closed. And I don't know how she was with The Lord before she died, but she had loved Him before - when we were together. We must trust in His mercy, His faithfulness, not ours.'

They both remained silent, neither aware that the other one was silently praying.

At last, he said, picking up a few of the cards, 'You've got to do something with these.'

'Really?'

'I think so. Hey! Why don't you let me take a few to the next coffee morning? Here...' he picked two up, 'are these finished?'

'Yes, but...are you serious?'

'Of course! How much do you want to charge?'

'Charge! Nothing! Anyone can see they're handmade. I'd rather give them away.'

'Well, okay. Let's see how they go. But if you get asked for more, maybe you should think about asking for a token amount?'

She shook her head. 'Alright! But pence, and that would only be to cover the cost of the envelopes.'

'Fair enough. Anyway, let's focus on you now. You know I've been on the hotline about you,' he pointed Heavenwards, 'about your parents as well. And what are you doing jobwise now, and how's your RAF friend?'

And so, for the next forty minutes they discussed her situation, all thoughts of the tragic, dead ex-fiancée pushed well to the back of both their minds.

Turning to leave, he looked back at her, a thoughtful expression in his eyes. 'You know, Meredith, I've discovered that mountain top experiences are great, but fruit grows in the valley, and I know that's where you are right now. But you'll be up there again, one day. Keep trusting in Him. He'll get you through this. I know He will. Well, goodnight...'

CHAPTER 36

Despite the menacing cloud of the court case looming over her head, Meredith was able to establish some sort of reasonably satisfying routine over the next month. Her days were occupied with work, either with temping, or going into the camp office when the agency was unable to give her an assignment. Her evenings passed by just as swiftly, mainly due to her babysitting and writing projects. The two cards Kingsley had taken had been snapped up. She took two more to church the following Sunday and left them on the book table during coffee after the service, from where they quickly disappeared. As a result, Kingsley recommended again that she start charging a nominal amount, suggesting that she could donate some of the money to a charity of her choice if she felt uncomfortable about accepting any payment. The idea sat well with her, and she began to put the small amounts by for one of the church's charities: The Leprosy Mission.

She often thought back to the night when he had revealed such a private part of his life to her, and felt that she should not bring the subject up herself, but wait for him to mention it again - if he ever did. All this time she had known how much she really liked him, and now she was having some difficulty looking upon him as just her minister. Months ago she had decided not to do anything about such feelings; she would neither encourage, nor discourage him. Anyway, she mused, what minister of a church would be foolish enough to start a relationship with someone who was looking down the barrel of a two year prison sentence? Now, whenever she was in his company, she would watch carefully for any change in his attitude towards her, but he appeared to be as friendly and approachable as ever, and she decided that it was probably just out of habit that he nearly always came to sit next to her at the Launchpad and house group meetings.

Saturday nights were the only times she could invite friends over for a meal, feeling that it would be good, at last, to be able to return some of the hospitality she had been given over the years. Wendy and Neville were the first.

'Have you seen Julia around?' Wendy had asked, helping to clear away the dishes after the first course.

'No. Why, have you?'

'Bumped into her at the Jolly Tar last week. Told me she was staying overnight.'

'Really? I thought she was working in Norwich?'

'Didn't say. She was with some young girl; couldn't have been more than sixteen…seventeen. I reckon they'd got a room there.'

'Why'd you think that?' Neville asked.

Wendy shrugged. 'Just a feeling. Anyway, everyone knows what Julia's like.'

Neville smirked. 'What a waste! Couple of nice looking birds like that.'

'What was the girl like?' asked Meredith, hoping that Julia would have moved on from Fleur by now.

Wendy strained hard to remember, 'Um…'

'Long blonde hair, nice little figure, and quite pretty,' said Neville, who obviously had no trouble in remembering.

Meredith tried to hide her disappointment. 'I see.'

'Why? Do you know her then?' Wendy asked, starting to become curious.

'Not sure,' she replied, trying to sound uninterested. Then keen to divert the conversation, went on to ask, 'I'm wondering if she's going to come back next season. She did hint that she might not if she found a decent permanent job.'

Wendy bent to take the pavlova, their contribution towards the evening, out of the fridge. 'I've been wondering the same thing. Did you remember to get the cream?'

'In the Granville jug, on the top shelf.' Glad of the distraction, Meredith took three desert bowls out of the cupboard.

Thankfully, Wendy's mind was elsewhere by now. 'I hear Tom and Sue still haven't decided where to get Zoe done. I bet that mother of hers is still upsetting the applecart. I've already finished the cot blanket I'm giving them as a christening present.'

And so the evening wore on. A pleasant, relaxed time, and, Meredith hoped, the first of many.

The following Saturday she invited Doreen and Dave, Jennifer and her new husband, and Kingsley. Her intention being, that with four other people present, Kingsley wouldn't feel obliged to focus on her. She was delighted, although a bit nervous, when they all accepted.

The small lounge felt welcoming, and she was glad that she had taken Wendy's advice to make the curry the day before; it really did taste better reheated. Her guests were full of compliments, especially when they tasted her lemon sorbet.

Doreen and Dave left with Kingsley just before ten o'clock, but Jennifer and her husband stayed on until well past midnight, and it soon became obvious that they were keen to discuss her situation. They offered to pray for her and she gratefully accepted. By the time they left, she felt peaceful and more confident that she would overcome, no-matter what lay ahead. She had always known that The Lord had a plan for her life; her spirit and soul were secure in Him; He would never let her go - or let her down. He was her *High Tower*.

Later that week her father brought her a small portable television set.

'When are you and Mum coming for a meal?' she asked, watching him manoeuvring the indoor aerial in an attempt to pick up a signal.

'Don't ask me! She's still fretting over Allan not putting in an appearance before going back to university.'

Unable to see any connection, and feeble though the excuse had sounded, she chose to let the matter drop.

'Has Conrad called in to see you yet?' he asked.

'Conrad! He's back?' she replied, suddenly remembering him; how far he had been from her thoughts lately.

'Your mother bumped into him up town yesterday. Reckons he's doing okay now. Just uses a stick.'

'His therapy must have gone well then?'

'Expect so, and apparently he's moved into some accommodation above the garage.'

'Yes, he did say something about that before he left.'

'Anyhow, she says he asked after you.'

'And I suppose she told him where I was?' she asked, failing to disguise the note of irritation in her voice.

Simon turned towards her, 'What's the matter? Don't you want to see him?'

She hesitated. It had taken quite a few prayer times for her to be able to forgive Conrad for interfering in her own family, but she was still struggling to leave at The Cross the fact that he had refused to go to the police and confirm that the so-called 'drugs' she had in her possession that night were his painkillers. 'No, not really,' she replied.

'Well, he told her to tell you that he'd be calling in. Seems he's full of some scheme about starting a motorcycle business.'

'Yes, he told me about that too before he left. I don't think it's a good idea, especially after what's he's been through.'

'Don't see why not! He's had a bike for years. Seems to know his way around them, anyhow.'

'But things are a bit different now. And those things are so heavy.'

'I shouldn't worry about him. He's not like those yobbo's that drive like lunatics through the town at night.'

'I know. But he does like his drink.'

Simon rolled his eyes. 'You're not back on that tack again? You women! Your mother can't leave the subject alone; forever going on about it.'

Her hackles were up now, and she decided to fight her own corner. 'Is she still blaming me for that night around Wendy's? Why does she always take his side? He's never been able to put a foot wrong with her.'

Simon knew she was right. Just that morning he'd had to put up with another of Pamela's regular laments, 'That poor boy, being treated like that by our very own flesh and blood. It makes my blood boil…I'll never forgive her…*never!*'

Meredith quickly relented. She had been delighted to welcome her father into her new home, and was truly grateful for the television set. She shouldn't be trying to involve him in something that wasn't even his fault. 'I'm sorry Dad. Let's drop the subject. I take it then, that you and Mum won't be coming for a meal any time soon?'

'Er, don't bank on it love. Maybe Christmas. Let's see how things go.'

'Alright. I won't ask again, and she knows where I am. But I hope you'll still call in whenever you want to?'

At last, a clear picture flashed across the television screen. 'Bingo! I was beginning to think you were in a black spot. And just try and stop me! By the way, I'm thinking the outside could do with some brightening up. How about a few planters? Plover Nursery's got some nice autumn shrubs in.'

Having successfully tuned the set in, he began a thorough inspection of the van's interior, stopping to tighten up any loose screws with the small screwdriver he habitually kept in his jacket pocket, as well as noticing several other things that needed some maintenance. 'You've got some mould growing behind the bath, I'll bring some sealant next time, and that bit of edging in the kitchen needs fixing.'

All too soon the visit came to an end. She gave him a long, heartfelt hug before he drove off. It had been lovely to spend some time with him again; how she had missed him. He was always so kind and thoughtful. She turned and went back inside, determined to pray even more earnestly about his association with the Masons. At least that was one thing she could do for him.

CHAPTER 37

Pamela must have known and told Conrad about Meredith's babysitting routine, because he called around after eight the following Monday evening. She was tired, it had been a long day. Manpower had assigned her to the offices of a factory some distance away, and she was having to catch two buses. For the next two weeks she would have to leave an hour earlier than usual in order to arrive at the offices for the half past eight start. The weather had turned cold and damp, and the bus station had nowhere warm where she could wait the thirty minutes for the connecting buses. At least she had been able to negotiate a slightly earlier leaving time in order to be back in time for her babysitting duties.

Tonight she found Bernadette unusually fractious, her baby face was flushed and her body felt warmer than usual. No amount of gentle coaxing or rocking seemed to pacify her, and Meredith had resorted to praying over her tiny charge. The storm eventually passed, and Linda returned to find the house quiet, with the child sleeping peacefully in her cot and Meredith dozing in the rocking chair beside her.

She poked Meredith's arm. 'Hey, wake up sleepy head! How's she been? Did she finish her bottle?'

Meredith stirred, 'Sorry, must have dropped off. She only managed half, and her nappy was *awful!*'

Linda went over and touched the baby's head. 'She feels a bit cooler, but I think I'll get her to the doctor's tomorrow. By the way, there's some post for you in the porch, it's been there a few days.'

Meredith yawned as she shrugged her coat on. 'Okay, I'll fetch it now. Hope you both have a good night.'

❖

The van was cold and dark. She heard what sounded like the throaty rumble of a motor bike engine pulling up just outside as she hurried to light the gas fire in the lounge. With a sinking heart, she realised that it could only be one person, and someone she was in no mood to face right now.

The visitor knocked loudly on the glass door, and called out, 'Meri? Open up! Guess who?'

Reluctantly, she went to let him in.

'Hiya!' he said, brushing past her and depositing his helmet loudly on the kitchen worktop. 'Pleased to see me then?'

There was no sign of a stick, but she noticed that he had a marked limp as he went, uninvited, through into the lounge and sat down.

'Do come in!' she exclaimed, taking her coat off, before moving the helmet onto one of the long seats near him. 'Why don't you make yourself at home?'

'Don't mind if I do,' he replied, looking around. 'Bit pokey isn't it? And bloody cold too. How much is she charging you?'

Determined not to allow him to rile her, she replied, 'Nothing, but I'm surprised my mother didn't tell you!'

'Oh yes, so she did. Something about some babysitting. Father's not around then?'

Despite the fact that everyone knew that Linda was an unmarried mother, no one, apart from Wendy, had asked her the same question. She replied, coolly, 'I don't know. Anyway it's none of my business. And I suppose you want a drink? I don't keep any alcohol in; you'll have to make do with something hot.' She returned to the kitchen. 'And I haven't had my dinner yet…'

'Charming!' he exclaimed. 'Not even a, "How've you been?" or "How'd it go?" And don't put yourself out, will you? I've already eaten.'

'Just as well, I'm only having soup. Anyway, you're looking well. Come on then, tell me all about it while I get on in here.'

He didn't need telling twice, and lost no time in embarking upon a lengthy discourse of how painful the physiotherapy and subsequent remedial gym sessions had been. She brought him a coffee, and he consumed the remainder of her precious Scottish shortbread as he graphically described how much he had suffered in the process. A few minutes later, she carried her soup in, clearing a space at the table, which had been covered with her card making materials.

'Don't tell me you're still on that lark?' he asked, looking down at the cards.

'I am,' she replied.

'What are you going to do with them?'

'Well, usually I give them away.'

He looked scandalised. 'Give them away! You should charge for them.'

'That's not why I do them.'

'More fool you then!' He reached over and picked one up. *'Kitty: The Cross Kiwi.'* Humph! Can't see the attraction myself.' He tossed the card aside carelessly.

'I enjoy doing it, and some people seem to appreciate them. I've even been asked to make some for special occasions.'

'Such as?'

'Church, the Sunday School, and...'

'Still letting yourself be brainwashed by that lot then?'

Momentarily stunned at his comment, she stared at him. No matter how much they had disagreed about things in the past, he had never criticised her faith or churchgoing before.

'I still go, if that's what you mean.'

He drained his cup. 'Another coffee wouldn't go amiss, and have you ever thought that you could be wrong - and that there's no such thing as God after all? You're in for a big suck in when you find yourself landing in oblivion with the rest of us when you pop your clogs.'

Oh no! She thought, here we go again. Julia Mark II!

'You'll have to wait a minute. And the thought does cross my mind now and again, it's only natural to have doubts. But that's where faith comes in. And it's all a matter of freewill anyway. I chose to believe in Jesus years ago; it seemed the most sensible and reasonable thing to do. Still does.'

'Sounds like a lot of wishful thinking to me.'

'Then you might think differently if you were really interested and took the time to find out for yourself.'

'And how would I do that?'

'Join us one Sunday.'

'No fear! Got more important things to do. Anyway, can't understand why you still bother with it all, especially now.'

'Why?

'Well, what's it done for you? Your mother tells me you might get banged up for a couple of years! Doesn't look like God's done much for you lately.'

There was so much she could have said, especially how some of her troubles had only started when he came back. However, she managed to keep things on a less personal level, as she replied, 'He's not a good luck charm. I don't believe in Him just so that I can get things out of Him. Anyway, Jesus didn't promise us a bed of roses. Everyone would believe in Him if they thought He'd give them a great, problem-free life. But what kind of faith would that be? There'd be no real affection, no genuine love involved. He certainly didn't live a charmed life, so why should those who believe in Him expect to?'

'Yeah, but...come on Meri, after what happened to you...and now prison for Christ's sake! When are you going to see the light, and do some growing up?'

She paused, praying silently and asking for wisdom. 'Whatever happens, I know I'll be alright. I trust Him, and

He's never let me down yet; He's been with me through thick and thin, and I know He always will be. I may not understand things at the time, but I often see some purpose in them afterwards, and I know it'll be the same this time. I've decided to always trust Him, whatever the future holds.'

'Then you really are mad, woman! And it all sounds a bit risky to me, especially because you're barking up the wrong tree.'

'How do you know that? Can you prove it?'

'Don't see why I should.'

'Anyway, even if I am wrong, at least I've have had a far happier and more worthwhile life than if I hadn't believed in Him. My life's been...richer, more meaningful because of my faith. It would take me ages to write a list of all the good, positive things I've experienced because of it. Other people try counting sheep when they can't sleep, I count my blessing. Never got to the end yet!'

He rolled his eyes, then decided to go on the attack. '"Blessings"? Rubbish! That's just good luck, and the world's full of it...' Now he thought he could be clever, and use some of her own words against her, '"For anyone who's interested and takes the time to find out for themselves," - and got the courage to get out there and grab some of it. The trouble with you, Meredith Sanderson, is that you're too bloody narrow minded. You should do some travelling, then you'd soon find out what a load of rubbish your...religion is. Causes nothing but trouble anyway.'

'Well, who's to say that I won't do some travelling? And it sounds to me like you're just regurgitating things you've heard others say. And, actually, I agree with you about religion, but someone who's had a real encounter with Jesus - that's a *real* Christian - and has a living relationship with Him, is usually a peacemaker - and not a troublemaker.'

'Encounter...what the bloody hell? Go on then, tell me all about this "encounter!" Prove to me that you're not as naïve as you sound!'

At any other time or place, and with any other person, she would have jumped at the chance to give her testimony. But somehow, to him, here and now, she knew that he was not prepared to give her a reasonable or fair hearing; she would just be shadow boxing.

'You're quick enough to call me narrow-minded,' she said, 'But it sounds to me like you're being narrow-minded about anything to do with faith, or God. Tell you what, why don't we start being fair here? It's okay for you to ask me to explain why I believe, but what about you? Why don't you explain your *lack* of belief, and what it is that you believe in - if anything?'

Obviously choosing to ignore her challenge, he retorted, 'Explain? Don't be daft! I've got nothing to explain.'

Coward, she thought. 'You know Conrad, you've done nothing but belittle me and criticise my faith since you arrived. All I've heard from you is other people's opinions. At least I can back my own beliefs up with personal knowledge based on my own experience. Can you say the same?'

'Huh! Can't be bothered.' He looked dismissively at her cards, 'Especially to someone who's still daft enough to believe in Noah's bloody Ark, for God's sake! Give me good old science any day!'

Without realising it, he had hit on one of Meredith's favourite subjects: Creationism versus Evolution. 'Science! Oh, I see! And you're not being...naïve then? Swallowing, hook line and sinker the manmade religion of evolution? Even though it's actually just a theory! I'm the stupid one to believe that we were created, but you're the wise one to believe that we evolved after crawling out of some primeval swamp?'

He looked askance at her. 'Er, yeah!' He held his hands up, palms uppermost, and then moved them up and down, as though weighing some invisible forces. 'Darwin, your stupid old Bible - Darwin, your stupid old Bible. Hmm! Quite a choice!' He lowered one hand with a jerk, 'Oh, look at that! Darwin, every time!'

'You know that they've still not found any evidence to back up his theory, don't you? It's all a load of hypotheses and speculations, and it's all built on chance anyway.'

'Come off it! Everyone knows it's based on fact.'

'Er, I think you'll find that it isn't! So why are they still hunting around for that "missing link" then? And every time they dig up an old bit of bone, out they come with some big announcement - and then scurry off back into their labs to try to make it fit their theories!'

'My God! You're worse than I thought? Alright Miss Know-it-all, you tell me how come the world's so old? What about cave men? How'd you explain them away?'

She knew she was wasting her time, but still she persisted. 'I'm not denying that there were Neanderthals around thousands of years ago, but *thousands* of years, not billions! It's a shame that science doesn't stick to its own rules when it comes to evolution. *Real* science demands rigorous, objective testing and *real* evidence. But people prefer to put their faith in anything but God, and my guess is it's because they know they'd have to do some changing if they did. In the meantime, they accuse us of being the ones in the wrong and being delusional!'

He shook his head slowly at her, and said, condescendingly, 'Glad I didn't go to your school if they taught rubbish like that! You're totally deluded. Wacko!'

She shook her head slowly back. 'That's strange! That's just what I was thinking about you! And what's so delusional about refusing to believe *everything* science says? And tell me what's fair about teaching that everyone has a choice about whether to believe in God or not - that's it's a personal choice - but then expecting them to believe in the *theory* of evolution?

No choice there! And did you know that Darwin actually wrote in his personal correspondence that he had, "awful misgivings", and that he felt he had - and I quote - "deluded and devoted myself to a fantasy"? He even confessed that he had been "determined to escape from a personal God at all costs." What have you got to say to that?'

He stood, and as much as he was able to without losing his balance, bowed down to her, as he said, sarcastically, 'Pardon me! I didn't realise I was in the presence of a mind greater than Einstein or Darwin!'

Not to be put off, she replied, 'And if you'd care to take the time to read about Darwin, you'd find out that he was supposed to have been agnostic; he was never an atheist. Even he never denied the existence of God!'

'Oh, just shut up!' He picked up her latest card, *Charlie, The Cheerful Chip,* and tossed it down. 'All this babbling. You're starting to sound like one of your stupid monkeys!'

'Really? Well then, can you explain - can science prove and explain - why there are still plenty of them around the place? Why haven't they all "evolved" too? Surely to goodness they've had enough time - like the rest of us "monkeys"! Science can't create one single original thing; all it can do is copy and reproduce. How do you explain the spark of life in a seed? Who put it there? At least I've taken the time to find things out for myself, and make up my own mind up. I haven't just blindly gone along with whatever the fashion of the day is…'

He had heard more than enough. Banging his hand down hard on the table, he shouted, 'For God's sake, shut up! Just shut up! All this bloody nagging. I didn't come here to be lectured.'

'And I didn't ask to be cross-examined about my beliefs.'

They stared hard at each other, the air between them almost crackling with tension. At last, she asked, 'So why did you come here anyway?'

265

'Hell's bells! Do I need a reason to see my girlfriend…'

'*Girlfriend!* Pardon me! Since when?'

He looked genuinely shocked. 'What…what do you mean?'

'Well, for a start, what kind of boyfriend's nowhere to be seen when his *girlfriend* needs some support? What kind of boyfriend doesn't speak up for his *girlfriend* when her own mother blames her for things that aren't her fault - and then allows her to go on believing the worst? What kind of boyfriend is too scared to go to the police, and tell them that she was only looking after his painkillers? That doesn't sound much like a boyfriend to me!'

He stared at her, understanding beginning to dawn. 'So-o, that's what all this bloody nonsense is about? You couldn't give a damn about what I've been going through. It's all about you, you, you!'

'That's not true! Of course I want to know…'

'And I could accuse you of not being there for me too! You haven't even bothered to find out how I've been getting on. You didn't even let me know you'd moved!'

She closed her eyes, how tired she felt. How she wished he would go. It was time to put an end to this. She spoke, quieter, calmer, willing him to understand every word. 'Conrad. I didn't want to call your house; I know what your parents think of me. And I am *not* your girlfriend. I know we wrote to each other for years, and that we went out whenever you came home. But you've got to admit, we've never really been that close; not in a boyfriend-girlfriend kind of way.'

He averted his eyes and looked down.

She continued, 'I've never had any of those kind of feelings for you, and I'm sure you haven't for me. I've just been convenient…useful for you; someone available for you to spend a bit of time with when it suited you.'

He remained as he was, his head lowered, silent, his mouth working. He needed time to think.

She went on. 'Look, from now on, let's just agree to be friends, and nothing else. I know you've been through an awful ordeal, and that you've had to rethink where you're going in life, but you seem to be coming out of it okay. At least you've got a plan, a way ahead, and you've got your parents' support. You've got a lot going for you. I hope you'll meet someone one day who'll think like you, and will want to share your life, but…well, I'm afraid it's not going to be me.'

At last he looked up. 'Alright, now let me say something. You've let me down badly, Meri. Really let me down. I expected more of you, some support…"

'Then I suppose we're even, aren't we?'

He knew she meant every word she said. He knew he had lost. And without another word, he picked up his helmet and stalked out, his limp more pronounced than ever. He slammed the glass door so forcefully behind him that she hurried to check that it hadn't been damaged.

She watched him drive off, and it was only when she couldn't hear the bike's engine any more, that she turned and went back inside, shivering and praying: 'Please keep him safe on that bike, Lord. Please bless him - whatever he does in life.'

Her soup was cold. She looked at it, then poured it back in the pan to reheat, thinking that this was turning out to be a year for cold soup. Her mail was still on the worktop. One envelope looked more official than the rest. Slitting it open quickly, she skimmed through the document, her mouth becoming suddenly dry when she realised what it was. So, here it was - at last: the court summons, informing her that she was required to attend the magistrates' court in Brunston. And in just two weeks' time.

CHAPTER 38

The rest of the week passed quickly for Meredith. She tried to organise herself as best as she could in between informing various people about the court case.

Her father was still convinced that she had only been called so that she could describe what had happened, and that she would be, 'in and out in a jiffy.'

Wendy went uncharacteristically quiet and promised to come and visit her if she was given a custodial sentence. 'I wonder where they'll send you? What if it's miles away? That one in Norwich is just for men,' - making Meredith realise that this was something she should have found out already.

'What's old man Bartrum's got to say about it?' asked Tom.

'Nothing. I telephoned and spoke to his secretary. All she said was that they'd already been informed.'

He looked surprised. 'And he doesn't want to see you again?'

'No. but I wish he would. I think I could do with some pointers about what to expect, you know, courtroom procedure and all that.'

'Well, if it was me, I'd ask to see him; make an appointment.'

'I've already tried, but he's off sick. He's had an operation and isn't expected back till next week.'

'That's a shame. But I shouldn't worry. The old boy knows what he's doing. And what about Manpower? What've you told them?'

'Nothing much, only that I shan't be available that week, and maybe the week after.'

There was nothing more she could do now. Everyone who needed to know had been told. She had already agreed with Linda that, should the worst happen, her father would come and collect her belongings from the van. 'I shouldn't fret; with good behaviour you'll be out before you know it,' was all her landlady could say. Even though the doctor had only diagnosed the onset of teething, the young mother appeared to be more concerned about Bernadette's hot cheeks and continued 'bad' nappies than the possibility of losing her baby-sitter.

Her friends at church assured her of their continued prayers, and Jessica promised that she would fast on the first day of the case, and maybe even longer, should the need arise. Kingsley reassured her, once again, that he would always be there for her, and rearranged his whole diary for the rest of that particular week. He then surprised and delighted her by saying, 'By the way, there's some authors coming to the library for a mini-literary festival next week, including a children's one. It might be useful for you to go and get some tips, and I wouldn't mind going along myself.'

She readily agreed. The court case would be just forty eight hours away; at least it would take her mind of things, if nothing else. And a whole day in his company, as well as the chance to meet some real writers - and a children's one at that - sounded too good to be true. He even suggested that she take some of her own work along, 'In case there's an opportunity to get an expert opinion'.

Although not confident about showing her work to anyone outside of her own circle, she considered the idea, and then spent the next few nights working hard on tidying up her latest story on her portable typewriter.

He picked her up the following Saturday morning. They arrived ten minutes late due to heavy traffic. As already agreed, she hurried away to attend the romantic fiction novelist's talk, whilst Kingsley went to hear what the biographer had to say.

They met up for the mid-morning break, and then went together to hear the crime novelist.

'Have you noticed that they've all been to university, and they're either teachers or doing something in the literary field?' she asked Kingsley as they walked to the nearest café for lunch. She was feeling more insecure about her work now than ever. 'I don't think I'll bother that children's author.'

But Kingsley wouldn't hear of it. 'That'll be a shame; you're only after some advice. And when are you going to get another chance to get a professional to look over something you've done for free?'

'But I bet there's loads of stories like mine out there. You saw the shelves in the Children's section.'

'If you use that argument, then no one would ever write another book! And I honestly believe you've got talent, a God-given talent. Look, if you really can't bring yourself to do it, then give me what you've brought, and I'll take it up and show it to her for you.'

She felt her bag resting against her leg under the table. 'But what if…what if I do go to prison?'

He frowned. 'Is that what's holding you back? You don't think the world would want to know you if you've got a bit of a history?'

'Well, yes. It doesn't…sound right, especially because everything I write is for young children.'

He considered. 'Let's not dwell on the worst case scenario; let's focus on the here and now. And I still believe you'll walk away from that court with your head held high. And then you'll kick yourself for missing out on this opportunity.'

She could see the sense in his argument. 'Alright then. But only if she's got time after her workshop.'

❖

They split up again after lunch, this time to attend the workshops of the same authors they had heard during the first part of the morning.

'How'd your romantic session go?' he asked, joining her for the mid-afternoon break.

'Interesting, but not for me. It's too serious.'

'Serious?'

'I think I'd get depressed. All that angst and moping around. I like a bit of fun, you know, action and colour. What about you? Have you been inspired to write your biography, or anyone else's?'

'No fear! I think I'd get depressed with all that angst and moping around as well! I'm like you; I like a bit of fun and action too.'

She laughed. 'That's a shame! I wouldn't mind reading some life stories of some crazy vicars!'

'Crazy, eh? Is that what you think of us?'

'Er, well, you can't deny that you've had some strange experiences on the camp.'

He nodded, agreeing. 'Tell you what, I'll tell you all about some of my other strange experiences one day, and you can use them in those animal stories of yours.'

'You're on!' she replied, definitely liking the sound of that.

The children's novelist workshop was next. Meredith soon found herself engrossed and made copious notes during the teaching session. The short writing exercises they were set afterwards proved to be no problem for her, in fact, her only difficulty was in trying to limit herself to the required number of words.

Several people stayed behind to speak to the author when the session was over. Kingsley urged her to join them, but by now she was convinced that she would be told what she already suspected - that there were already too many hopefuls like her out there.

The group began to disperse. He took her hand and tried to pull her up and out of her seat. 'Go on! It's now or never. What've you got to lose?'

The writer had obviously heard, and looked over in their direction. 'Yes? What have you got?'

Meredith wasn't quite sure what the accepted procedure for such a meeting was. Nevertheless, she went over and put her work on the table, explaining, 'I've made some cards, for children - and some stories. They all have a Christian theme.'

Well used to being presented with similar efforts, the author began to sift quickly through the cards. 'Age group?'

'Four to seven, or eight. I'm not sure.'

The author picked up the first few pages of one of the stories and began to read, frowning heavily. Meredith watched her closely, trying to detect any sign of approval or indifference. She was feeling more nervous by the second now. Standing immediately behind her, Kingsley took hold of one of her hands and squeezed it.

At last, the author looked up. 'You've got an engaging way of expressing yourself. Look, this isn't my age range, but if I was you, I'd think about sending some submissions off to a few literary agents.'

Meredith looked stunned. 'Really! You think I should?'

The author nodded. 'You're a bit rough around the edges, but there may be some promise here. As to the cards, again, not my field.' She tidied them together and handed the small pile back. 'They're cute though. Here...' she wrote something on the back of a business card and handed it to Meredith, 'my agent's details. Send her a submission and a few cards and tell her a bit about yourself. She may be able to point you in the right direction. And good luck!'

'Told you. How'd you feel now?' asked an obviously delighted Kingsley as they returned to their seats.

'Fantastic! I can't believe it! I never expected anything like that. But I've got no idea what a submission is.'

'Well, you're in the right place to find out. They've probably got something about them in the reference library. We'll take a look after the next workshop.'

272

'That's the poet, isn't it?'

'Mmm,' he replied, not sounding too keen.

'Do you want to hear him?'

'Not really, I'm not into poetry.'

'Good! Then let's do the reference library now.'

She invited him in for something to eat when they returned to the van. He accepted, even offering to come and help her in the kitchen, 'Got any eggs? I make a mean omelette.'

'There's not enough room for two cooks in here. You go and sit down, and make yourself at home.'

He walked into the lounge and noticed several boxes stacked against the far wall. 'Packing?'

'Linda's asked me to get my stuff together…in case…'

'And how do you feel about that?'

'Can't blame her. I see her position.'

She cracked open and began beating the eggs. 'Cheese and tomato okay? Tea or coffee?'

'Fine, and tea please.' He settled back in the same spot he had sat in before and remained silent as she busied herself preparing the meal. At last he spoke, 'Remember me telling you about my…Deborah…when I was here last?'

'Yes. How are you feeling…about that now?'

'Okay. I had another letter from her mother. Apparently she'd taken dual nationality, and she's been flown back to Australia to be buried.'

Meredith thought carefully before replying, 'Really? That must be hard, for her family here, I mean.'

'Hmm. I know they were hoping that she'd be laid to rest over here.'

'Maybe they'll go for visits, especially as they've got grandchildren over there.'

'Probably. They're not short of a bob or two.' He reached over and picked up the card she was currently working on. 'What type of bird's this? It looks very odd!'

273

'It's a cassowary. They live in tropical forests, and I believe there's even some in Australia.'

'But...a blue face? And what on earth's that wedge shaped thing on its head?'

'It's a sort of peak that keeps growing; they're not sure why, it could be something to do with its acoustics. And I read in one article that their heads and necks can change colour, according to their mood.'

He looked askance at her. 'You're joking! I've never heard of them.'

'Take a look at its feet. Just three toes, and the middle one's enormous! They've been known to attack and kill other animals, even humans. They like to swim, and can make sounds that are heard up to three miles away. The females can grow to over six feet!'

'Wow! Can they fly?'

'No, but they're good jumpers.'

She carried the mugs of tea over to the table. 'Here, take a look at this,' she opened her 'Resources' folder. Recently she had started to collect articles and illustrations of any animal, bird or fish that caught her eye; these, along with her notes on ideas for future stories, had grown into a considerable collection. She found the relevant article, and placed the folder in front of him. 'Read all about it.'

He stared at the picture, nodding in disbelief. 'I wouldn't want to come across one of those on a dark night!'

'You'd be okay if you left it alone, apparently they're very shy.'

Fascinated, he proceeded to read the article as she returned to the kitchen, wondering at the fact that the strange bird had taken his mind so completely off the subject of his dead ex-fiancée.

The omelette turned out well. They chatted amiably about everyday things, occasionally mentioning her impending court ordeal. He had already told her that he would be there for the duration of the case, no matter how long it took. Then, and despite her protestations, he insisted upon helping her with the dishes, making her laugh out loud as he attempted to create what he imagined were the sounds of a cassowary. She knew he had a good sense of humour, but now he was surpassing himself.

He appeared to be in no hurry to leave, so she offered him another drink, which he accepted. They had already spoken about her family situation, and the fact that her father was still attending the Masons. 'And what about your RAF friend?' he went on to ask. 'I've seen him around. He seems to be walking better.'

She made short work of glossing over Conrad and his plans. She was far more interested in him, and began asking him questions about his past. And so she learned that his parents had divorced when he was fourteen, after which he had been sent to live with his maternal grandparents; his two younger sisters had stayed with his mother. His father moved to France and had since remarried. At the age of eighteen he left school, then went to university, and then onto theological college. When things didn't work out between him and Deborah, he joined the VSO and worked as a volunteer for a year in New Guinea. Returning home, he did a six month stint in a hardware shop, then another in the stores of a large engineering works. Afterwards, he worked as an aid in a council-run old folks' home, then for two years at a Dr. Bernardo's children's home. He needed to do a year's refresher course at theological college before being selected to enter the ministry proper, after which he joined the ministry team of a large church in Leeds. Two years later he felt able and confident enough to put himself forward for selection for a church of his own.

'Phew! We knew you'd done other types of work, but I had no idea you'd done so much. And is that when you came to us?' she asked.

'Yes. And I suppose I should thank my failed relationship with Deborah for that. My tutors were all for us getting some secular work experience before we started pastoring a church. Going straight from theological college into the pulpit doesn't really equip anyone for shepherding a church full of people living and working out there, "in the world."'

'And were they right?'

He looked over at the gas fire, his mind trying to see beyond the low flame. 'I'd like to think so. I felt lost for a while, but we go forward in faith, don't we? Even if we can't see or feel the stepping stones beneath our feet. If we're walking with Jesus, we need to keep trusting that He knows where we're going - that He's guiding our steps.'

Now it was her turn to reflect quietly. Was prison going to be her next 'stepping stone'?

He broke into her reverie, and surprised her by asking if she would read her Cassowary bird story to him. Far too shy to do any such thing, she declined, so he picked up the manuscript and began to read it aloud himself. This turned out to be helpful, because she began to detect the awkward phrases and places that needed more work. Every so often, he would stop and make a suggestion. She was flattered that he seemed to be taking her writing so seriously, and they spent the remainder of the evening going through her 'Resources' folder, and thinking up ideas for other stories. At times, this proved almost impossible, as he frequently broke out with strange animal impressions. She could not remember when she had laughed so much. Neither could he.

Towards ten o'clock he said that he should be going, and offered to pray for her. She agreed, pleased that she now had a whole raft of new writing ideas to keep her mind occupied. But as for her heart - well, that was a different matter.

CHAPTER 39

Kingsley stopped at Fenton's garage for petrol on his way to the court, and was surprised to see Conrad behind the till when he went in to pay. 'You're not going to the court then?' he asked.

'Someone's got to hold the fort.' Conrad recognised the stranger from his photograph on the events board at the camp. He handed him his change, wondering what business it was of his whether he went to the court or not.

'But won't Meredith be expecting you?'

Conrad shrugged, 'She'll cope.' He turned to go into a room behind him. He'd had enough grief from his mother that morning. Both she and his father had left for the court well before they needed to, and he wasn't going to waste his time on something that was nothing to do with him anyway. He had his own life to get back on track; Meredith Sanderson would just have to roll with the punches.

Kingsley found himself becoming offended on Meredith's behalf. How could the man be so unfeeling? Hadn't they known each other for years, and, no doubt, been romantically involved for some of them, and maybe still were? It sounded as though he really couldn't care less about her. It was only natural that she would want him there. Unable to stop himself, he called out, 'Does she know you're not going? Did you tell her?'

Conrad ignored him and began poking the end of his stick viciously against the metal wracking. Why didn't the man mind his own business, and let him get on with his?

But Kingsley was not to be ignored. He walked around the counter and went to stand in the doorway. 'I should have thought you'd have gone to support her. There must be someone who could have covered here?'

'Well you thought wrong then, didn't you. And what's it got to do with you anyway?'

Kingsley stood still, trying to think. Although he had never met the man, he knew of his recent difficulties, and had had some sympathy for him. But now all he felt was dislike. 'I like to think that I'm her friend,' he replied.

'Bully for you! But we can't all drop everything and go running every time the girl's stupid enough to get herself into trouble, can we?'

Kingsley was aghast. 'I think you've got your facts wrong. As far as I'm aware, this is the first time Meredith's ever been in trouble, and none of it of her own making!'

Conrad was feeling very uncomfortable by now. He wanted the man gone. He pushed his way past Kingsley and went back into the shop, saying, 'You'll have to go, I'm closing, and I'm sure you don't want to be late and miss all the fun now, do you?'

Kingsley would have preferred to have stayed and challenged him more, instead he bit his lip, and turned to leave. He heard the door slam shut and being locked behind him. All he felt now was disgust, but at least he had learned something important about Conrad Fenton - although how and when he could, or would, use the knowledge, he wasn't sure.

He arrived fifteen minutes before the case was due to start. He spotted Meredith's father, sitting alone in one of the corners of the dreary waiting room. Jessica and several others from the fellowship were there already, and he acknowledged them with a wave as he made his way through the crowded room.

'Hello Simon.'

Simon attempted to smile. 'Kingsley! You're here too? That's good of you.'

'Where's Pamela?'

'Gone to her sisters.'

Kingsley sat down next to him. 'How was Meredith when you picked her up?'

So full of his own feelings, Simon found that he needed time to think before answering. 'Calm. Quiet, but calm. She doesn't deserve this. I had a few words with her solicitor when we arrived. It's so bloody unfair. I used to admire our police, but...' he lowered his head and clenched his hands tightly, trying hard not to give way to his pent up anger.

'Don't give up Simon. We must keep hoping and praying.'

'Yes, but that's hard to do, especially since he told us that it'll probably be an open and shut case, at least as far as the youths go. Except for one of them, they've pleaded guilty already. It's just a...a matter of...' he faltered. 'But Meri's different. She pleaded innocent, and now she'll have to go through it. *Really* go through it.'

'I see.' Kingsley sat back on the bench. 'Well, that might actually work in her favour. The court will hear her side of the story firsthand when she takes the stand.'

'But she isn't! He told her she won't need to. Nor the other one.'

Kingsley was shocked. 'What? Are you sure?'

'That's what he said. But I...I don't know. I don't trust these legal types anymore. Not after this. Once they've got their claws into you...' he sighed heavily and held his hands up, letting them fall again in a gesture of hopelessness.

'Don't leave The Lord out of the picture, Simon. We must keep putting our trust in Him, not in man. He's the greatest Judge of all, and I believe He'll see her through. The truth will come out. You know I believe in miracles, and I've been praying that we'll witness one today.'

Simon looked into Kingsley's determined expression. Yes, if God and this man had anything to do with it, then everyone would know that Meredith was innocent, and she would be walking out of here soon - just like he had kept telling her she would over the past four months.

'I hope you're right, Kingsley. I just want her home.'

Kingsley would have liked to have prayed with him, and would have offered, had not the noise level around them suddenly increased as more people arrived. Attempting to give the distressed father something else to think about, he said, 'I stopped off at the garage on the way and was a bit surprised to see her RAF friend there. I should have thought he'd be here for her.'

Simon jerked his head towards the far corner where a middle aged couple was sitting with an older man. Kingsley recognised the nervous looking garage attendant and the garage owner, and assumed that the woman, sitting bolt upright and looking disapprovingly at everyone around her, was his wife.

'His parents. And that chap with them's the garage attendant, you know, the one that was there that night,' explained Simon.

'Thought I recognised him. But why isn't the son here? Conrad isn't it?'

'They fell out ages ago. And to tell you truth, I'm glad. I never could take to him. There's something not quite kosher about the lad. Bit fly if you ask me.'

Kingsley tried to sound less interested in this piece of information than he actually felt. 'So they're not seeing each other anymore?'

'Not since that night - although maybe before, come to think of it. And I don't think she was ever serious about him anyhow. They only knocked around with each other when he came home on leave.'

'Hello!' Wendy's voice broke in. 'Well, this is a do, isn't it? Poor Meri. I'll bet she's frightened stiff. I think it's disgusting that it's come to this. Talk about the law being an ass...'

'I keep telling you woman, she'll be fine,' interrupted Tom, who had given her a lift in and was fed up of hearing her complaints.

'Why'd you keep saying that?' she retorted, impatiently. 'How do you know? It's not done a very good job if it's let things go this far, has it?'

Obviously exasperated, Tom responded, 'These magistrates weren't born yesterday; they know the score.'

'Well, I only hope you're right.' Her voice reached a pitch as she turned her head towards the nearest group of youths. 'When I think of all the *real* criminals out there, getting away with blue murder, and then they go and drag someone like Meri through the mud, it makes my blood boil...'

Much to Tom's relief, her tirade was cut short when an attendant appeared, and proceeded to lead all those interested in the case into the courtroom.

Meredith was sitting in the front row of the dock. Alongside her were the white youths; the Asian youths were in the row behind. She recognised the youth she had tried to protect that night. He looked over at her and nodded, she nodded back.

She studied each face as people were led in and guided into the public gallery. Doreen and Dave saw her and smiled; Dave gave her a thumbs-up signal. Jessica followed, she put her hands together and mouthed, 'Praying for you.' Her father came next, and her heart went out to him when she saw how drawn he looked. Kingsley was behind him; he saw her and smiled. She smiled back. Wendy looked anxious; she gave a small wave before turning her attention to the youths, who she glared fiercely at. Tom winked, then jerked his head in Wendy's direction, rolling his eyes. There was some disturbance when Conrad's parents voiced their objection at having to sit near the back. The usher was obliged to have a few words with them, and they eventually took their seats with bad grace. She had not expected Conrad to have the courage to come as well, and so was not disappointed, although part of her wished he had. Somehow it seemed so unfair; yet again, he was keeping himself well clear of the whole unpleasant business.

With everyone in position, the court was told to stand. Three magistrates entered and took their seats on the bench. Two of them, a man and a woman, looked to be in their early forties, the other, another man, looked older.

Meredith became aware that her heart was beginning to pound as the trio took their time arranging their belongings in front of them: notepads, pens, spectacles. She decided that the law could do with the streamlining services of an efficiency expert; surely it would be more cost-effective, and less stressful for people in a similar situation to her, to be given the opportunity to speak to them somewhere privately. Then people like her father and friends would not have to be subjected to all this uncomfortable embarrassment. Noticing the jug of water on the bench, her mouth felt dry, and she wondered if she would be allowed to suck one of the mints she had in her pocket. No, she had better keep them for later. Who knows how long this would go on for?

And then, like the well-rehearsed drama that it was, the proceedings got under way. The main players appeared to know their roles fluently. Like everyone else unused to being in such a rarefied atmosphere, Meredith sat spellbound, trying to grasp hold of anything and everything that made some sort of sense. Soon, all the preliminary procedures were completed, and the court heard that all but two of the defendants: Mr Iftikhar Ahmed, and Miss Meredith Sanderson, had already pleaded guilty.

The first witness was called. The garage attendant entered the witness box and looked around nervously as he swore the oath. Then, with frequent promptings, the prosecuting lawyer allowed him to describe what he had seen and heard on the night in question. Satisfied, the lawyer sat, and Arthur Bertram was invited to begin his cross-examination.

When asked if he had seen the young woman do or say anything to cause or inflame the situation, the witness answered, 'No. Looked to me like she was only trying to help.'

'"Only trying to help", I see. Now, Mr Watkins, we have heard how you remained in the booth throughout the incident, only emerging when the ambulance crew arrived. Even so, did you see, or get the impression, that the young woman raised her voice at any police officer at any time during, or after, the incident?'

'No. I never saw anything like that.' He then went on to confirm that Meredith had stayed at the injured youth's side until the ambulance arrived, after which, '...she just stood around - all quiet like.'

A buff folder of photographs was produced. The woman magistrate reached across the bench and began looking through the set they had already been issued with. The witness was then asked to look through the folder and confirm that these were the same ones he had taken during the incident.

'Yeah, there're the ones alright.'

'And can you tell the court your reason for taking them?'

'I only do nights and like to keep a camera handy, just in case, and I began clicking as soon as things started kicking off.'

'And why did you take so many of the group in the centre of the forecourt?'

'Well, that one...' he replied, pointing at the youth in the dock who had taken the beating, 'was having it rough, and then the girl...' again, he pointed, this time at Meredith, 'went over to him. "Flippin' heck," I thought, "she'd better watch out." She had it rough too, but fair play to the lass, she stuck by the lad.'

'You described in your statement that Mr Ahmed had been operating one of the petrol pumps, and how relieved you were when you saw another Asian youth replace the nozzle. However, a considerable amount of fuel had already been spilled. Can you tell the court where Mr Ahmed and Miss Sanderson were in relation to the spillage?'

'Right in it! That's why I kept taking the photos, in case…you know…'

'In case of what, Mr Watkins?'

There was a slight pause, then the witness said, 'Some of them had fags in their mouths.'

A few gasps came from the public gallery. He continued, 'Drop one of them - and they'd all go up in flames. That's why I kept snapping, you know, if they needed to be…identified.'

'I see. That was very thoughtful of you, Mr Watkins, and would certainly have proved extremely useful should that unfortunate event had happened. Now, in your opinion, was Miss Sanderson aware of the danger she was in?'

'She must have been. The smell…it being wet and all. She was kneeling in it.'

Every eye in the public gallery fixed itself on Meredith now. Embarrassed, she focused her attention on the witness.

'And yet she remained beside Mr Ahmed - who, with the court's permission, I shall refer to as the injured youth from now on - her concern only for him, and thereby choosing to ignore her own safety?' asked Arthur Bartrum.

'Yeah! I thought, "That's some plucky lass!"'

More murmurs sounded from the public gallery.

'And at what point did you see the police officer, who we can clearly see in some of the photographs, approach Miss Sanderson?'

'Just before the ambulance arrived.'

'That would explain why he only appears in the last three photographs?'

'Reckon so.'

'When did you stop taking the photos?'

'When I ran out of flash cubes.'

'And what was happening by then?'

'They'd been separated, the gangs,' he pointed at the Asian youth again, 'and he'd been put in the ambulance.'

'Now, can you tell the court, Mr Watkins, if you saw the same policeman who had approached Miss Sanderson at any time attempt to assist the injured youth in any way?'

'No.'

'And did you see him attempt to do anything to protect Miss Sanderson, or assist her in any way, or even try to remove her from the area, and, therefore, out of imminent danger?'

He shook his head.

'We need to hear your answer, Mr Watkins,' instructed the female magistrate.

'No, I never saw him do nothing like that.'

'Now, I've asked you this question already, but I would like to ask it again, just so that we can be clear about the issue. At any time throughout the incident, did you hear, or notice, or was in any way aware of Miss Sanderson subject any police officer to any foul language?'

'No.'

'Or attempt to knock any of their helmets off?'

'"Knock their helmets off"?' the witness repeated, obviously surprised by the question.

'That's right. Did you see her do any such a thing?'

'No. I did not!' he replied, emphatically.

'But how could you be so certain? After all, weren't you in the booth all the time, and behind the glass partition?'

'Well, yes, but she was bent down...right up until they took him away. She never stood up. But I could see her alright. She kept talking to the lad and ignoring everything else. She only shoved the copper's...policeman's hand off when he went and nabbed her.'

'"She only shoved the policeman's hand off,"' repeated the solicitor. 'And this is the same policeman we can see in these photographs, the one standing by her and the injured youth?'

'Yeah, that one.'

'And, apart from shoving that policeman's hand off, did you notice if she reacted towards him in any other way?'

He paused . 'No, I mean, she looked up at him...I could see her face...she was all kind of shocked.'

'"She looked up at him." And what position was she in at that time?'

'On her knees.'

'"On her knees," and you didn't see her attempt to get up?'

'No.'

'What happened then, Mr Watkins?'

'He just walked off and left them.'

'Who did?'

'The copper.'

'And what position was the young woman in when the policeman "just walked off and left them?"'

'Still down on her knees, in the petrol.'

'"Still down on her knees, in the petrol." And still in imminent danger?'

'Yeah, that's right.'

'When did you see her get to her feet?'

'When the ambulance came. They went straight to them.'

'And where was the policeman at that time?'

'I don't know...nabbing someone else.'

'Now, let's backtrack slightly, about that particular policeman's helmet. Are you able to tell the court where it was throughout the time he was standing over Miss Sanderson, and afterwards, when he walked off and left her and the injured youth, both still in the petrol and in very real danger?'

Somewhat surprised at the question, the witness looked around him. He had been expecting a trick question and wondered if this was it.

'I...er...'

Arthur Bartrum repeated the question, reassuring him that this was indeed an important factor in the case.

'Well, on his head, I suppose!' he replied, at last.

'And if it wasn't, do you think you might have noticed?'

'Maybe. There were a lot of helmets around. They all had them.'

Arthur Bartrum turned to address the panel of magistrates, requesting that they refer to their set of photographs. 'As can be seen from the last three photographs, the officer's helmet remained on his head throughout the entire time he was standing by the injured youth and Miss Sanderson, and that it was still in same position when he left them.' Turning back to the witness, he asked, 'And afterwards, when everything had calmed down. Did you see her at any time approach, or be anywhere near the same vicinity as that same policeman?'

'Well, can't say I did. The gangs were split up and she was put with the white lot. I don't know where he was.'

'So you never saw if she approached the same policeman, or attempt to speak to him in an offensive manner?'

'No, I've told you, I never saw anything like that.'

'And, just to be clear, did you, at *any* time, see the young woman attempt to knock his helmet off his head, or any other policeman's helmet off?'

He laughed, 'No, but I wish she had of!'

Someone called 'Hear, hear!' from the public gallery.

Arthur Bartrum gave the witness a wide smile. 'Thank you, Mr Watkins. You've been extremely helpful; that was most illuminating.' He then turned and informed the bench that he had no further questions for the witness.

'In that case, you may step down Mr Watkins,' instructed the lady magistrate.

Meredith realised that Arthur Bartrum's "Bloodhound" nickname was very well deserved.

CHAPTER 40

The next witness to be called was the policewoman who had questioned Meredith at the police station after the incident. Meredith looked straight into the woman's face as she approached the witness box, however, the young officer averted her gaze to give the nearest male magistrate the benefit of her very blue eyes. After being sworn in, the prosecuting lawyer asked her to describe her involvement on the night in question. She began, speaking in a clear, confident tone as she told the court how she had conducted the interview with the defendant, Miss Meredith Sanderson, before obtaining a written statement.

It was noticeable that she had been allowed to make her speech without any interruptions. She was then asked several questions, each one cleverly formulated to make Meredith appear in a bad light. Meredith found herself becoming frustrated, and began to regret agreeing to Arthur Bartrum's decisions not to call any character witnesses on her behalf, nor to let her take the stand.

At last the prosecuting lawyer announced that he had no further questions and returned to take his seat. Then it was Arthur Bartrum's turn. The elderly lawyer stood and began his cross examination by querying the fact that no other police officer had been present during Meredith's interview at the station. He then insisted upon knowing the reason why the interview had not been taped. The officer was obviously prepared for such questions, and gave quick, off-pat replies, stating that, with so many people to process, time had been of the essence. Arthur Bartrum asked if she was aware that she had committed several serious breaches of police procedure, to which she replied that she was not. He feigned astonishment, then, approaching the bench, recommended that this was something that needed to be looked into, but requested that this could be done at a later date, because he felt that the case should be allowed to proceed without any further delay. The magistrates turned to discuss the issue quietly between themselves. Long seconds passed before the senior member announced that they would need to take the matter under advisement, and that the case could proceed.

Satisfied, Arthur Bartrum returned to his questioning. The officer now looked less poised, especially when he enquired how she had come to the conclusion that the so-called 'Suspicious Class B substance', that had been found in Meredith's handbag, were of an illegal substance.

The officer shrugged the question off, by answering, 'They looked peculiar, so I passed them over to a colleague, and I had nothing more to do with that side of things.'

Murmurs could be heard coming from the public gallery when Arthur Bartrum stated that, upon examination by the doctor on duty that night, they were declared to be nothing more dangerous than a high dose of aspirin, and were, in fact, a well-known brand of anti-inflammatory. 'Were you aware of that fact, Officer Poole?'

'No! Why should I be? I told you, I had nothing more to do with them. Anyway, the paperwork had already gone through.'

'Oh, you were interested enough to find out about the paperwork then? But not interested enough to admit that a gross miscarriage of justice had been done towards Miss Sanderson? Not interested enough to find out if a false accusation had been made against a totally innocent person?'

She stared hard at him. 'Well...there was no need. I knew it would come out...sooner or later.'

'"No need," Hmm! What a pity then, that it did not come out sooner, and save a lot of people a lot of time - and unnecessary worry.' The younger male magistrate cleared his throat loudly. Arthur Bartrum appeared not to notice, as, well into his stride now, he turned to his notes, and asked, 'Now then, are you aware that you left the door slightly ajar when you left the interview room? And that, sometime later, as you consulted with a colleague, Miss Sanderson - who you may be interested to know has excellent hearing - was able to clearly overhear the short conversation you had with that same colleague?'

The officer's eyes widened as her face began to turn pink.

Still referring to his notes, Arthur Bartrum went on, 'The court will be interested to hear part of that conversation. The colleague to whom you spoke, a male officer, suggested, and I quote, how you "...could pep things up and make it a bit more interesting to make it look good for them by getting the numbers up," and "...that he could easily get her for assault."' More gasps sounded from the public gallery. 'Whereupon, Miss Sanderson heard you laugh and suggest that you could, "have her done for possession." Now then, Officer Poole, I'm sure the court would like to know who it was that you and your colleague were conspiring against, and exactly how you then proceeded to "pep things up" in order to get "the numbers up," as well as to whom he was referring when he went on to suggest that he, "...could easily get her for assault."?'

The witness appeared to physically squirm as she attempted to strenuously deny any knowledge of, or ever having taken part in, any such conversation.

However, when asked why she had turned down Miss Sanderson's repeated requests for a solicitor, she found herself totally unable to offer an explanation, even after being pressed by the lady magistrate.

At last, Arthur Bartrum announced that he had no further questions. The officer kept her head low as she stepped down from the witness box - and exited the courtroom as fast as her legs would carry her. Gone was the self-assured young woman who had entered just minutes before.

❖

The next witness to be called was the officer who had arrested Meredith - and the person who had made the false accusations against her of using obscene language and committing an assault. Unaware that his colleague's previous testimony had just been so effectively undermined, he stepped confidently into the witness box, a proud, well turned out figure. When asked to describe the events of the night in question, he produced a small notebook from his top uniform pocket, and began flicking through the pages with a flourish. He spoke clearly as he described how he and other officers had been called to the garage, and how they had quickly managed to gain control of the situation, graphically describing how, 'The girl had subjected him to a barrage of foul language and assaulted him as he cautioned her.'

This was followed by a short time of questioning by the prosecution lawyer, which, once again, only served to show Meredith in a bad light.

When Arthur Bartrum stood and began by asking him, 'To describe exactly the nature of the supposed assault,' he replied, in a noticeably less confident tone of voice, 'She dislodged my helmet,' whereupon some laughter sounded from the public gallery.

'What with?' Arthur Bartrum asked.

'What do you mean?'

'What did she use to dislodge your helmet?'

'Well...her hand!'

More laughter came from the back, after which the senior magistrate instructed the public to remain silent.

Arthur Bartrum continued his cross-examination, repeating the same series of questions he had asked the policewoman. Once again, the witness denied all knowledge of ever having heard, or been part of, any conversation about, '...how things could be pepped up to increase the numbers,' and forcefully denied ever having said how he, '...could easily get her for assault.' He also stated that he had no knowledge that Miss Sanderson had requested a solicitor to be present during her questioning. However, he did confirm that he had been the officer that had been handed the pills to give to the duty doctor for examination, thereby unwittingly identifying himself as the mysterious conspiring colleague.

'Were you aware that those pills were later revealed to have contained nothing more innocuous than a high dose of aspirin? That, in fact, they are a brand of commonly prescribed anti-inflammatory?'

'Really?'

'I take it then, that you never bothered to find out? That you weren't interested enough to discover that fact for yourself?'

'No. I had job to do, and I got on with it.'

'And later, when all the paperwork was done, and the charges listed, you still weren't - interested? You never made it your business to find out what was in the so-called "Suspicious Class B substance?"'

'Of course not! Anyone would have been fooled. If you'd have seen them, enormous, pink…highly suspicious looking.'

'In that case, Officer Bingley, I hope you never have cause to look in my medicine cabinet!'

There were a few titters of laughter from the public gallery.

Referring to his notes again, Arthur Bartrum asked the policeman how he could explain the garage attendant's written statement that, in his opinion, '…the lass had only been trying to help the injured youth and ignored the policeman and did nothing when he went and grabbed her shoulder and nabbed her,' also that, 'He hadn't seen her go for any policeman throughout the whole thing.'

Everyone waited for his reply, but were to be disappointed, when he said, 'I can't answer for how other people *imagined* they saw things.'

Arthur Bartrum now turned and picked up the folder of photographs, and asked the magistrates to refer to photograph number four. He handed the photograph to the officer. 'I assume you have already seen this? It was printed in the local newspaper, The Bugle, four days after the event. Or is it just the camera *imagining* the scene?'

The officer glanced briefly at the photograph but made no comment. He was then handed another, and the magistrates were requested to refer to photograph number five. The officer's expression remained blank, almost bored, as he did the same.

Meredith felt that this was very unfair; why couldn't she be shown the photographs too? After all, it was her life that was on the line here.

Arthur Bartrum said, 'I would like to call your attention to the tall figure to the right of the photograph. Do you recognise him, Office Bingley?'

'Yes.'

'Would you care to tell the court who it is?'

'It's me.'

'And where is your helmet?'

There was a long pause before he replied, almost inaudibly, 'On my head.'

'Exactly so. And would I be correct in saying that this photograph was taken almost as soon as you and your colleagues had arrived on the scene?'

There was another long pause as the witness began to move his tongue around his closed mouth.

'Well, Constable Bingley? The court is waiting.'

'I...I expect so,' came the begrudging reply.

'As can be clearly seen, your worships, Officer Bingley's helmet is on his head. Now, Officer Bingley, please tell the court who the two figures in the centre of the photograph are, and what they are doing?'

'One's lying down,'

'Which one?'

'The Asian.'

'I assume you're referring to the *injured* youth?'

'Yes.'

'And the other?'

'The girl.'

'Miss Sanderson?'

Yes, alright!'

'And in relation to the injured youth, what position is Miss Sanderson in?'

'She's...kneeling by him.'

'And are they both very close to the petrol pump? In fact, just a few feet away from it?'

'Yes.'

'Thank you. Now, turning to the next photograph, number six, please describe who the three figures just off centre are, and what they are doing.'

'It's the Asian, he's still lying down, and the girl. I'm a few feet away.'

'And, again, where is Miss Sanderson, "the girl", in relation to the "Asian", the injured youth?'

'Still kneeling by him.'

'And are they still by the petrol pump?'

'Yes.'

'So Miss Sanderson is still kneeling by the injured youth. And where exactly is your helmet now?'

'Er, on my head.'

'Indeed. Now I would like you to take a look this photograph, number seven.'

There was some shuffling and sliding noises on the bench as the photograph was passed between the magistrates.

'We see the same group of three people just by the petrol pump. The injured youth, Miss Sanderson - who is still in a kneeling position by him, and both still in a pool of petrol - and yourself. You appear to have your right hand on her left shoulder. You've stated that this was the moment you cautioned her. Now, tell me, Office Bingley, again looking at this same photograph, where is your helmet?'

The witness's mouth came under some control as he pursed his lips tightly together. Then, with a note of what sounded like defiance in his voice, he said, 'On my head.'

'Exactly so. And now please describe what the three people we can see in photographs eight and nine are doing, and where they are situated.' He handed him more photographs.

Again, there were more shuffling and sliding noises from the bench.

Aware that the trap was closing, the witness quickly glanced at the photographs, then glared back at his persistent questioner. With a sharp edge to his voice, he replied, 'It's me, and the Asian, he's still lying down, and the girl's still beside him. *Satisfied?*'

'Not quite, Officer Bingley. Can you tell the court if the injured youth and Miss Sanderson are still by the petrol pump?'

'Yes! I've already told you!'

'And where is your right hand now?'

The witness emitted a long, exasperated sigh. 'Still on her shoulder.'

'And your helmet?'

'…on my head.'

'And now the tenth photograph?'

The officer glanced quickly at the incriminating document. 'The same, nothing different.'

'And in what position is Miss Sanderson, and where exactly is your helmet now, Officer Bingley?'

'Well, she's still kneeling, of course!'

'And what about your helmet?'

He rolled his eyes in exasperation. 'It's *still* on my head.'

'I see. Now, forgive me if I'm wrong, but at any time during this particular part in the proceedings, of which we have photographic evidence, and during the exact timeframe you have told already told the court that you had cautioned her, can we see Miss Sanderson stand, or attempt to reach out towards your helmet?'

'Well, no, but…'

'In fact, isn't it true to say that, at no time throughout the incident, we can see you that you were bareheaded?'

'But…she knocked it off…later!'

'Ah, I see! You wish to change your testimony? Your statement is incorrect? But how so, Officer Bingley? Why should the court believe you? After all, here we have photographic evidence, as well as two eye witness accounts, that Miss Sanderson did not say, nor do, any of the things you accused her of! You are a good six foot in height, are you not, and she remained beside the injured youth, in a kneeling position, and by the petrol pump, throughout the time you stated you cautioned her? She must have extraordinarily long arms indeed to have been able to have reached up and knock something off your head!'

The public were unable to stifle their laughter. This time the magistrates chose to ignore the outburst.

'It sounds to me, Officer Bingley, that you expect the court to believe that Miss Sanderson, who, you will be interested to know, the court has already heard from another witness, managed to maintain a calm and orderly demeanour throughout the incident, and is known to be a decent, hard-working, law abiding member of the public, *and* one who selflessly, and with no thought to her own safety, I might add, put herself in harm's way to protect an injured stranger - why this same young woman should suddenly turn into a disrespectful, foul-mouthed and violent trouble maker? And, before you answer that, may I remind you, that, apart from this photographic evidence, we also have the injured youth's own statement confirming that she remained calm and controlled throughout the incident, as well as the garage attendant's statement that at no time did he see Miss Sanderson subject you to any foul language, or strike out at you in any fashion. Taking these two completely formerly unknown, independent witness statements into account, both of which only serve to confirm one another, I put it to you, Officer Bingley, that you might possibly have made a very grave mistake by making such false accusations? And, may I remind you, you are under oath!'

Meredith closed her eyes and exhaled the breath she was unaware she had been holding.

'The court is waiting,' persisted Arthur Bartrum. 'Now here's an idea, I suggest, Officer Bingley, that in your blind ambition to climb the career ladder, you could well have made the mistake of attempting to blacken the good name of this innocent young woman...' he turned and pointed in Meredith's direction, 'to "...get the numbers up," and collect another arrest in order to impress the next promotion board? Or, to put it another way, it is my belief that you were prepared to sacrifice a completely innocent young woman's whole future on the altar on your own selfish ambition...'

'Mr Bartrum!' interrupted the younger of the two male magistrates. 'Please keep your questions to the matter in hand. We are not here to discuss anyone's career goals.'

'Indeed,' agreed the lady magistrate. 'However, we are here to learn the truth, and await your reply with interest, Officer Bingley.'

By now, the officer had managed to regain a measure of composure, and answered, 'The truth...the truth is that the Asian was confused. He'd been badly beaten and wasn't aware of what was happening around him. As for the girl, well, anyone would take the side of a pretty face. And I'd like to ask if we're seeing all the photographs? How do we know that there aren't some missing?'

The elderly magistrate spoke up now. 'You are here to answer the questions, Officer Bingley, not ask them.'

Arthur Bartrum began to walk slowly in front of the bench, his hands folded behind him. 'Yes, it is true that the youth had been badly beaten, and was probably suffering from shock. But I can tell the court that, when questioned soon after the event, and again the next day, he stated, emphatically, that, if it had not been for the calm courage of Miss Sanderson, he had no doubt that he would have suffered a far worse fate.' Stopping by the dock, he turned to look back at the witness box, and giving a long, slow smile, continued, 'Of course, we could ask the young man in question. Would you like us to do that, Officer Bingley?'

This was high drama indeed. Many in the public gallery began to scan the group of faces in the dock, trying to detect the identity of the once injured youth, having already forgotten the one the garage attendant had previously pointed out.

'Or we could recall the garage attendant, who remembers the night very well, and has already told the court that Miss Sanderson was still kneeling beside the injured youth when you walked away and left them in such a perilous position, and that he had not noticed her anywhere near you thereafter. Of course, he could simply have been mistaken, or just lying; although I fail to see what he could possibly hope to gain by doing so, after all, he wasn't there that night "to get the numbers up!"'

The officer remained quiet, staring hard at his persecutor.

'Or maybe you would prefer that the court calls the photographic expert who examined the film, and who would tell us that the photographs have not been tampered with in anyway, and are indeed in sequential order?'

The once erect shoulders of the officer were much lower now. At last, he attempted to reply, 'Er, well...'

'Well, Officer Bingley? What would you prefer the court to hear? The injured young man's account, the garage attendant's, or the photographic expert?'

The constable looked around, uncertainty written all over his face. The air was charged. Meredith felt like shouting, 'Yes, yes! Let's hear them all! PLEASE!'

Arthur Bartrum knew he had the officer on the run now, and lost no time in pressing home his advantage. 'There is one more thing I am curious about. Can you explain to the court why you did nothing to assist the injured youth, and attempt to remove both he and Miss Sanderson from imminent danger? Why, instead of doing your *real* duty as a police officer, a sworn defender of the public, you chose instead to make her situation even more unpleasant by actually cautioning her as she knelt in a pool of petrol? The photographs show, and you must have been aware, that several of the youths had lit cigarettes dangling from their mouths, and were perilously close to the area?'

Fighting for his good name and career now, the officer threw caution to the wind, and went on the attack. Flinging an arm in Meredith's direction, he said, 'I assumed *she* was the cause of it all!'

'The cause? What can you mean?'

'The girlfriend...of the Asian. She was all over him!'

'Oh! I'm not quite sure I understand you, Officer Bingley. Maybe you can explain that to the court a bit more?'

'She's white, and he's Asian...you know. It looked like a racial thing, and that's what started it all...caused all the trouble.'

'Ah! I see! And that's why you cautioned her? And went on to arrest her later? Thinking that she was, what, the catalyst?'

'Yes, that's right. It was my duty.'

'And when it became clear afterwards, at the station, that she was *not* the girlfriend, that she was, in fact, nothing more than an innocent member of the public who just happened to get caught up in the unfortunate incident, what do you think your duty was then?'

'Er, I don't follow you.'

'What I mean, Officer Bingley, is that as soon as you realised that you had made a mistake, why you didn't do everything you possibly could to correct it? However, we have learned that you did no such thing, in fact, we now know that you went on to compound matters even more, by, amongst other things, agreeing to collaborate with another colleague in concocting a cock and bull story about the illegal possession of drugs!'

'NO!' shouted the officer, allowing his temper to overtake his increasing panic.

'Why not admit that you made a mistake, and that Miss Sanderson is, in fact, completely innocent of the two charges you personally brought against her? Why not make a clean breast of it, and tell the court that she did not, at any time, subject you to any offensive language, nor did she, at any time, attempt to knock your helmet off your head?'

Every eye in the room stared hard, and unblinking, at the now extremely uncomfortable looking witness.

'No. Why…why would I do that?' he asked, almost defiantly.

'Because of the reliable statements and evidence of the witnesses I have already mentioned; people who have no axe to grind, and no reason to lie. But, more importantly, because it's the truth! Come, come now Officer Bingley! Bearing all that in mind, are you ready to admit that you might well have made a - what shall we call it - a slight error of judgement?'

At a complete loss now, and knowing that he had been well and truly found out, the witness remained silent, obviously struggling to admit to any such thing. The seconds passed by agonisingly slowly. After what seemed an eternity to Meredith, the lady magistrate broke the highly charged atmosphere, by asking, 'Please answer the question, Officer Bingley.'

At last, and almost indiscernibly, the reply came. 'May…be…'

Meredith blinked quickly. She had been staring so long that her eyes felt strained and dry.

Arthur Bartrum pressed home his advantage. His tone hard and authoritative, 'Are you admitting to the court that you falsely accused Miss Sanderson of the two of the charges you brought against her - that of using offensive language, and of assault? A yes or no answer will do.'

Meredith decided not to breathe. She needed to concentrate all her life-force on hearing the next words that came out of her accuser's mouth.

'Er...well...maybe...'

'Is that a yes?'

For Meredith, his previous halting responses had been hard to bear, but this one was proving almost impossible. And then, at last, it came. His whole upper body seemed to sag, as he said, quietly, 'Yes.'

'What was that?'

'Alright, YES!' he repeated, his shame now making way for anger.

'And as to the false charge of illegal possession of the so-called "Suspicious Class B substance?"'

'OKAY! OKAY!'

'Is that another yes?'

'YES! he shouted, desperate now to put an end to the whole excruciating affair.

Deciding that the officer had been subjected to enough torment, the senior magistrate intervened. 'Mr Bartrum, I think the court has heard enough. Do you have any further questions for the witness?'

Arthur Bartrum declared that he had no further questions. He had made his case, and he was satisfied.

'Then, in that case, you may step down Officer Bingley,' instructed the magistrate.

The witness left the courtroom. Not so proud and tall anymore.

Movements and subdued comments could be heard coming from the public gallery, and Meredith began to breathe easy again, knowing that her life had just been handed back to her.

CHAPTER 41

The first thing Meredith did upon returning to the van was to fall on her knees and pour her heart out to Jesus. After a while, she opened her Bible and reread the Scripture that had given her the courage to go forward earlier that morning:

> **I will stand silently before the Lord, waiting for him to rescue me. For salvation comes from him alone. Yes, he alone is my Rock, my rescuer, defence and fortress. Why then should I be tense with fear when troubles come?** *(Psalm 62: 1-2).*

Her tears flowed freely as, over and over again, she thanked Him for her deliverance. Apart from a few short minutes when she had been tempted to give in to some unhelpful emotions, from the very start of the fateful day she had been aware of a calmness within her spirit; a softly glowing confidence that had helped her to face the ordeal. Spiritual eyes would have seen her standing perfectly still, watching and trusting, surrounded by the walls of a strong, defensive fortress: her *High Tower.*

Her father had asked her to spend the night at home, but she had refused, explaining that she needed some time to be alone. She also turned down Wendy's invitation to go back to hers for a 'bit of something really fancy for lunch to celebrate', as well as Kingsley's offer of company on a walk along the beach. She just wanted to shut the world out and be alone with her Very Best Friend.

Linda was giving Bernadette her mid-day feed when she noticed Meredith being dropped off outside. Ten minutes later, she hurried across the yard and knocked on the van door.

'Meri, hello, it's me.'

Disappointed, Meredith stood to let her in, quickly wiping away all evidence that she had been crying.

Linda saw the tear-stained face, and asked, 'That bad, was it?'

'In a way, but it's all over now.'

'Great! So you'll be okay for tonight?'

'Er, yes, alright.'

'Oh, nearly forgot, I shan't need you on Friday, nor next Monday; I've got a friend coming for a long weekend and she's baby-crazy. Go on then, tell me all about it.' She went to sit in the lounge. 'Can't stay long; Berni's alone. Can you keep the door open so I can listen out for her?'

Meredith opened the door wide, then went to join her. She began to describe the morning's events.

'But that's crazy!' exclaimed Linda, after hearing that everyone in the dock had been bound over to keep the peace for two years, as well as being ordered to pay court translation costs.

'It was something to do with the Race Relations Act. They did explain it. And the trouble was that most of the white youths were already on probation, and, by rights, they should have been given a custodial sentence - but then the rest of us would have been sent to prison too, even the Asians. The one that got hurt and me were the only ones who pleaded innocent.'

Linda looked scandalised. 'But it was them who caused all the trouble! Do you mean to say that they'd have gone to prison if you hadn't been there? I've never heard anything so daft! Couldn't they have let you off, and let the others take what was coming to them? Fancy letting them go scot free!'

'They haven't got away with it completely; they'll have to watch themselves for the next couple of years, or they'll go straight to prison if they cause any more trouble.'

'Huh! Big deal! I hope they do. But aren't you going to fight it? Can't you appeal or something? I wouldn't be too happy being lumbered with a…a what was it again?'

'Bound over to keep the peace, and I've been advised not to.'

'Well it wouldn't do for me. I'd play merry hell about it. In my book, you're either innocent, or you're not. And why'd you have to pay translation costs anyway?'

'Some of the Asians couldn't speak English very well and needed someone with them, although I never noticed anyone helping them. And it only came to a couple of pounds each anyway.'

'Talk about adding insult to injury! I'd have refused. Bloomin' cheek! Coming over here, causing trouble…'

'But *they* were the ones being attacked…'

A wail came from the house. Linda heaved a heavy sigh, and stood. 'Looks like she'll be cutting another tooth any day now. Poor little mite, her cheeks are still burning. See you tonight then.' She hurried out, her indignation over Meredith's ordeal quickly forgotten.

She was walking on the beach the next morning when Kingsley called at the van. Disappointed, he slipped a note under her door asking her to phone him. It was a wet, cold day, but she was enjoying the sensation of wind and rain on her face, knowing that she could have been incarcerated behind cement walls and iron bars now, instead of out here, free, and experiencing all the sights and sounds of a restless sea and sky. For the first time in days she felt hungry; soon she would go back and have a big bowl of soup, and then make a quick visit to the local shop to re-stock her empty cupboards.

She was aware that there had been a journalist in the court, but she had been hoping that his report would be brief, and insignificant enough to be hidden inside any newspaper. And so her heart sank when she saw, on the stand outside the shop an hour later, emblazoned right across the front page of that week's Bugle, a large, clear photograph of her on the court steps. Her father and Kingsley could be seen coming down the steps behind her. Above the picture was the headline:-

COURT ORDERS LOCAL HEROINE
TO KEEP THE PEACE FOR TWO YEARS

The tone of the report was critical of the police force and justice system, making much of the fact that the two officers -

...had deserved more than the stiff reprimand they had received in court. A spokesman for the Force had announced that there was to be an internal enquiry, which, no doubt, will result in ranks being closed and the two officers involved being treated with kid gloves, whereas every right thinking person knows that they deserve nothing less than a dishonourable discharge.

It went on to ask, amongst other things -

...why an innocent young woman, who had done nothing but try to help and protect a total stranger, should be tarred with the same brush as the obviously guilty youths? Why should she have to suffer the indignity and threat of having a totally unjust two year order to keep the peace hanging over her head - like the sword of Damocles? The law is an ass and needs changing. From now on, any gang - of whatever nationality - that wants to stir up trouble will know that they only have to wait until some unsuspecting member of the public wanders into their midst in order to protect themselves from feeling the full force of the law.

Finishing with a flourish, it added -

...that anyone who is unfortunate enough to find themselves anywhere near such a gathering, would be well advised to flee from the scene, or they too could suffer the same fate as our local Florence Nightingale.

Wendy was delighted with the article, and waved the paper around excitedly when she turned up at the van later that day.

'They've done you proud! It's about time someone spoke up. And what a smashing photo of you. And look at Kingsley's face! You're not telling me he hasn't got a thing for you...'

Meredith allowed her to continue lavishing high praises on the report and speculate on Kingsley's feelings until she could stand it no longer, and interrupted the flow by asking if there was another reason for her visit.

'Oh, yes! Nearly forgot. Now I know you said you wanted some peace and quiet, but we've got to do *something* to celebrate, and I've got just the thing. I've been given two tickets for Saturday's matinee of *The Sound of Music* at the Palace, but Neville can't get off work. It's only the local amateurs, but they're okay. And you'll be back in time for your babysitting, so you've got no excuse. Come on, Meri, be a sport, and say you'll come with me.'

Meredith knew that she would never hear the end of it she refused; at least Brunston was twelve miles away and had its own local newspaper.

'Alright. Thanks Wendy, and I'm not babysitting tomorrow night anyway, but I don't want to back too late.'

'Fan-tas-tic! We'll go for a Chinese afterwards - my treat!'

'Okay, but let's make it a takeaway.'

Somehow she just couldn't face the house group that evening, and telephoned Jessica to make her excuses. 'But please, *please* say a huge thank you to everyone for all their prayers. They'll never know how much it means to me. I've asked The Lord to bless them all a hundred times over.'

'You'd have done the same for any of us, but Kingsley'll be disappointed; it's his week with us, and I know he's been waiting to hear from you.'

'He's always out when I phone the manse, and he wasn't there when I tried just now. I'll try him again tomorrow morning. I'll make it early. Can you tell him?'

'Will do. And will we see you on Sunday? It's the first week of Advent. We thought we'd try and get Launchpad to do something with the Sunday school, maybe do a variation of the nativity this year.'

'I'm…not sure yet. But I'll definitely be there next week.'

Wendy bumped into Julia in Plover the next morning, and learned that the toy section of the store where she was working had some very old stock they wanted to get rid of. She had expressed an interest on behalf of the camp, and it had been agreed that she could take it off their hands for a knock-down price. She had taken a series of photographs, but rather than post them to Tom, she asked if she and Meredith would have time to call in after the show to collect them. Curious to see where she was living, Wendy agreed, and arrangements were made.

They enjoyed the show, which was unremarkable, but a pleasant enough way to spend a cold autumn afternoon. Afterwards, they bought a takeaway and made their way to Julia's address, which turned out to be a small terraced house in the middle of a long row on the outskirts of the town.

Julia opened the door. She was scantily clad in a very short housecoat.

'Just out of the bath then?' asked Wendy.

Julia stood aside to let them in. 'And hello to you too! Show any good?'

'Not bad. You should go,' replied Meredith, stepping straight into the small sitting room.'

'Nah! Not my scene hun.'

'We can't be long. We've got a Chinese takeaway in the car,' Wendy said, noticing the used glasses and empty bottles of wine on the coffee table. 'Got company?'

'That's right.' Julia turned towards the door in the corner of the room. 'Now you're here, there's something I need to show you Meri, upstairs. You wait here Wendy, this won't take long.'

Wendy looked at Meredith, shrugged her shoulders, and sat down on the small two-seater settee. 'Alright, I'll make myself at home then.'

Julia ignored her as she opened the door leading to the stairs. 'This way,' she said to Meredith, 'and try not to make a noise.' Mystified, Meredith followed behind. Neither spoke until they reached another door at the end of the corridor. Julia turned and whispered, 'Just remember, I'm doing this for your own good, hun.' She opened the door slowly and stepped aside, giving Meredith a clear view of the scene in front of her.

A man and woman lay in a double bed, the top half of their naked bodies exposed. The man's face was clearly visible, his eyes were closed and his hair tousled. The woman's face lay across him, her features semi-hidden by her long, straight blonde hair. Meredith gasped. The man opened his eyes and gazed at her for a few seconds. Then, recognising her, swore as he struggled to sit up, jerking the woman's head violently off him as he did so.

'What...the hell...bloody hell! What are *you* doing here?'

'Hey! Watch it!' exclaimed the woman. 'You nearly broke my neck!' She turned and looked over at the doorway, pulling the curtain of hair away from her eyes. 'Oh! It's you!'

Julia grabbed Meredith's arm, effectively holding her in position. 'There! You needed to see. I knew you wouldn't believe me. Did you know he's into threesomes? And has been for some time?'

Shocked and disgusted, and without a word, Meredith shook her hand off, turned, and marched back along the corridor.

Julia hurried after her. 'Meri! Stop! Listen...'

Behind them, they heard the high pitched, almost hysterical sound of the young girl, giggling.

'Belt up, you silly little bitch!' shouted the man.

Meredith ran down the stairs.

'You stay up there!' shouted Julia to the couple in the room behind her, running after Meredith. Once down, she jammed the top of a hard backed chair against the handle of the door leading to the stairs.

Wendy thought she had recognised the man's voice, and was on her feet now. She stared at Julia. 'Is that...don't tell me? It's him, isn't it? And here, *with you!* Oh my Lord...'

The door handle was tried as a male voice called, 'What! You bloody maniac! Have you locked this? Open it, damn you, open it!'

'Shut up!' shouted Julia, 'I'll let you out when I'm good and ready. There's some things she needs to know.'

The handle was tried again, more violently this time. Curses sounded behind the door. '...I'm here, I can hear you. You'll be sorry...you mad cow...'

Julia was unmoved. 'The sooner you belt up, the sooner this'll be over. *So shut the hell up!*'

'JULIA!' called the man's voice. 'I'll bloody have you for this! Just you wait!'

Julia gave the door one of her lopsided smiles, and called back, 'You've got a short memory. You already have! Why don't you go and "have" her again? You could do with more practice.'

Meredith stared hard at Julia. 'What's going on, Julia? What's all this about?'

'Oh, you'd be surprised! I've got a lot to tell you, so be a good girl and sit down.' Julia looked fiercely at Wendy, 'You too!' Turning back to Meredith, she commanded, 'Sit!' as she went to sit on the nearby armchair.

Without a word, Wendy and Meredith sat on the settee.

'Don't you see? I've done you a big favour. I've stopped you from carrying on, and making a fool of yourself - and making the biggest mistake of your life!'

'BITCH!' A fist slammed hard against the door. All eyes focused on the wooden panel to see if it had splintered. The door was tried again and more bangs followed, but, much to everyone's relief, the barrier remained intact. Exasperated, low growls were heard, then uneven steps pounded up the stairs, accompanied by a stream of foul language.

Julia tutted and sat back, pulling her housecoat lower over her bare thighs. She was pleased, everything had gone to plan. 'Now you've seen for yourself. I wanted you to know what he's been up to. He's been at it for months - even before he went away. It's surprising how agile someone can be, even in plaster!'

'It is him, then? What a creep,' said Wendy, her eyes enormous as she looked from one to the other. 'Who's he with, I could hear a woman...'

'But why?' Meredith interrupted. 'And what's all this about making a fool of myself, and making a big mistake?'

'Just hear me out, and you'll understand. Now look, Meri, I know we've had our differences, but you've always been straight with me, and I've always known exactly where I stand with you.' She gave Wendy a withering look, 'Not like some other people. And it got up my nose to see the way he was cheating on you behind your back. And you, poor love, didn't have a clue now, did you?'

The heavy creaking of a mattress could be heard coming from the room directly above them.

Wendy looked up, and asked, 'So he's been...at it...with you and...who's that woman?'

Ignoring her, Julia reached down to pick up a newspaper from beside the chair. She held the front page up. 'I made up my mind when I saw this. I couldn't believe how you'd been shafted; you deserve better. Better than the likes of *him.*' She jerked her thumb towards the ceiling. 'And then I realised that there was one thing I could do for you.'

Meredith was incredulous. 'What, by letting me see...*that?*'

Julia nodded. 'Worked, didn't it? The spell's broken? Now you've seen him for what he is?'

Understanding began to dawn on Meredith; she sat back, hardly able to believe what she was thinking. 'So...so you deliberately...arranged this, and got me over here just so that I could see...find you, and him...and...' she faltered, not wanting to mention the name of the third person involved. The creaking above them came to an abrupt stop. All three looked at each other.

'Got it in one,' replied Julia. 'There's no way you'll end up with the swine now.'

Wendy looked at Meredith with obvious alarm, 'End up? With him? Oh good Lord! Tell me you weren't going to marry the man! Not that creep? You can't Meri. *You can't!*'

Meredith took a deep breath before responding. 'No. Of course I'm not! Where on earth did you get that idea from, Julia?'

Now it was Julia's turn to be mystified. 'Him! He told me. I've known it's been on the cards since the summer. He said he was only waiting for the right time to ask you.'

Meredith did a hasty stock check of all the conversations she and Conrad had had, searching for any clues that he had even hinted at marriage.

'Are you saying that he hadn't got around to it yet?' asked Julia, looking increasingly concerned.

'No! He only suggested that we get a place together, but that's as far as it went. There was never any mention of *marriage!*'

Julia stared at her. Then, closing her eyes, she asked, 'And you aren't even *engaged?*'

'*NO!*' Meredith replied, emphatically. 'Anyway, all we seemed to do was row, and then we had a serious falling out some time ago.'

Julia opened her eyes and looked towards the ceiling. 'And this...all this...I didn't need to...'

'No. Definitely not!'

Julia covered her face with her hands. 'Oh, Gawd! What a mess! I'm sorry.'

'I should jolly well think so too!' exclaimed Wendy. 'What a carry on! Honestly Julia, I don't know what you were thinking. Hasn't she been through enough lately, and then to put her through this - on top of everything - it's just too bad of you!'

Now that she had a clear picture of Julia's motives, Meredith began to feel some sympathy for her. 'It's alright, Wendy. I think she only did it to help. You weren't to know that there's nothing between us, Julia. But I can't think why he let you think there was?'

Julia uncovered her face, revealing a deeply troubled expression. 'Well...maybe he was hoping you'd come around? He's always talking about you.'

'Huh! He'll be talking a lot more about her from now on!' Wendy retorted. 'And I hope you'll make it your business to put him straight!'

Recovering quickly, Julia responded with a firm, 'Too right I will! Then I'm kicking his backside out of the door!'

Now Meredith found herself becoming disturbed by something Julia had said earlier. As far as she was concerned, Conrad's behaviour towards her was of no real consequence. However, if he had been picking up young girls - like Fleur, and maybe even younger - on the camp, then that was a different matter, and she would have to have a word with Tom about him. And Fleur, the once supposedly innocent young girl, still in that bed upstairs. The same young girl that Julia had taken up with not so long ago. Not so innocent now.

'And I'll be kicking him from here to kingdom come if he dares to set foot on camp again!' Wendy exclaimed. 'But what a way to do things, Julia! Why couldn't you have just told her?'

Julia gave Meredith a troubled, pensive look. 'Someone had to stand up for you, Meri . You've always been straight with me, never judged me,...and I've always loved you for that. And then, trying to tell me...about things...with Kingsley...'

Meredith nodded, recalling the discussions they'd had, and how all she had ever wanted to do was to tell her about the other kind of love - God's kind.

Julia continued, 'Maybe your God's really been looking out for you - if you'd already finished with the jerk - and now the truth's out about that night at the garage, I guess...it's...it's like you said...you are helped.'

Overcome with a sudden affection for her, Meredith went to stand in front of her. 'I wish you hadn't involved other people. You know, I would have believed you if you'd have just told me.' And then, and despite knowing what she had been doing maybe just minutes before - and with whom - she stooped and put her arms around her. 'And God's looking out for you too, Julia. He wants to help you too.'

Obviously close to tears now, Julia inhaled deeply, then hugged Meredith back tightly. 'Oh hun! I'm so sorry!'

'It's alright Julia. It's alright.' After a few seconds, Meredith stood again, 'But now I think it's time we were leaving. We've got a take-away getting cold in the car.'

'Hang on, the info...on the stock,' Julia said, wiping her face with the back of her hand as she stood and went over to a sideboard. She opened a draw and handed Meredith a large envelope. 'There's a lot of toys and stationery items; Tom should go for them. I'll be able to get him a good deal.'

Wendy was already standing by the open door. Meredith followed, then turning back, said, 'Give him a ring next week. And don't dwell on this, Julia. I won't.'

'Oh hun!'

'It's alright Julia. Really, it is.'

She paused at the car door and called back, 'Will we be seeing you in April?'

'I...don't know. I like where I am now. Maybe it's time that I put some proper roots down.'

'I think that sounds like a very good idea. God bless you Julia. And remember, He loves you.'

Wendy turned on the car's ignition, wondering if she should start looking for a different magazine; the astrologer in her usual one was starting to get one too many things wrong. There had been no mention of anything even remotely similar happening in her forecast for that week.

Meredith fought against the temptation to look up at the bedroom window as they pulled out. It was inevitable that she would bump into Conrad again, but some time and space was needed before that happened - and even more prayer.

CHAPTER 42

Kingsley turned up the car's heater. Meredith had left a message on his answerphone to say that she would be out all afternoon, but he was hoping to be able to have a few minutes with her before she left for her babysitting duties. A car slowed and parked just behind him. Looking through the mirror, he saw two figures in the front, Meredith, and the outline of another woman. He stepped out and waited.

Wendy was the first to notice him. 'Well, look who it isn't! Fancy meeting you in a place like this!'

'Hello Wendy. How's tricks?' he asked.

'Not bad, thanks. Long time no see,' she replied, 'And how's yourself?'

'Truly blessed. Hello Meredith, thanks for your message. You're a hard person to track down these days. How are you doing?'

Although pleased to see him again, Meredith wasn't sure how sociable she could be. The deeply embarrassing scene at Julia's seemed to have sapped the last of her energy. She gave him a tired, slow smile, and replied, 'A bit tired, but come on in.'

'Huh! I'm not surprised, I'm feeling shattered myself after that little fiasco!' exclaimed Wendy.

Meredith's heart sank. All the way back Wendy had talked of nothing else, and now that there was someone else to tell, she knew that there would be no stopping her. Trying to change the subject, she asked, 'Fancy some Chinese, Kingsley? We've got more than enough here.'

'Well, if you're sure. That's very kind of you, but I can't stay long. I've got a deacon's meeting later. But what about your babysitting?'

'She's been let off tonight,' replied Wendy. 'Put the oven on Meri; it's gone stone cold, thanks to all that carry-on around Julia's.'

Kingsley looked questioningly at the pair.

'Take a seat, Kingsley. Coffee?' asked Meredith.

'Great. What's that about Julia? You've seen her? Is she alright?'

A knock came on the door. Both women turned to look at each other. 'Don't tell me that's him! He's followed us!' exclaimed Wendy, a note of panic in her voice.

'Who? Who's followed you?' asked Kingsley.

'That swine! Just you let me get my hands on him!'

Meredith hurried to answer it, and was relieved to find Linda standing there.

'Your Dad phoned. He says your Mum's back and wants to see you, and can you phone him.'

'Thanks, I'll do it later. Sorry you've been troubled.' This was the first time her father had used Linda's number; she had told him not to unless it was really important, or an emergency. Now she realised that she would have to trek over to the phone-box when her guests had gone. It looked like it was going to be a late night after all.

Wendy left soon after the meal. In vain, Meredith had tried to prevent her from revealing all the finer details about what had happened around Julia's, but eventually gave up, and decided to let the chips fall where they may. At least she had not been able to reveal the identity of the other woman involved.

And now, at last, Kingsley had Meredith all to himself, which was something he had been asking The Lord to arrange since they had spent the day together at the library. He had watched Meredith closely as Wendy had graphically described the events around Julia's, looking for any clue that she was in any way disappointed or upset about being confronted with Conrad's behaviour, but all he could see was a quiet

317

resignation in her expression. He took heart. Her father had told him that there had never been anything between them, but now he was needing to hear it from her own lips.

'I couldn't help noticing that you didn't seem particularly disappointed when Wendy was talking. Did you know that he was behaving like that?'

She was surprised that he had returned to the subject, and in such a direct way. 'Er, well, no, not really.'

'And you really aren't upset?'

She speculated that he was wearing his minister's hat, and only asking out of purely pastoral concern. What other reason could there be? 'No, not at all.'

'So there's...nothing between you?'

She gave a small laugh. 'No!'

'And there never has been? You were nothing but friends - whenever he came back on leave?'

She looked at him, puzzled. This was starting to sound very unpastoral. 'That's right. More like pen friends who met up occasionally. It was all the rage some years ago; I had one in Canada and another in Holland, but I lost touch with them after a few years. If he hadn't have lived locally, I expect we'd have lost touch as well.'

'Pen friends! Yes, of course.' He recalled how his sisters had been caught up in the craze when they were younger.

'Why do you ask?' she asked.

'Just curious.'

He seemed to be preoccupied, as though his thoughts were far away, and she began to wonder if he had heard more news about his ex-fiancée - although what that had to do with her and Conrad, she had no idea.

At last he spoke. 'I'll have to be going soon, but I don't suppose I could trouble you for another coffee?'

'Alright.' She walked into the kitchen and started to mix the drinks. Now she felt sure he was going to confide in her again. Maybe she should do some confiding herself - about

Fleur. It would be good to get the thing over and done with. She said, 'By the way, Wendy doesn't know who the other woman was, the one he was in bed with.'

'She didn't see her?'

'Thankfully, no.'

'Was it someone you knew?

'I'm afraid so. And I'm sorry to tell you this, Kingsley, but it was Fleur.'

'Fleur!' he looked stunned. 'Are you sure?'

'I saw them...together.'

He stood, put his hands deep in his pockets, and walked quickly across the lounge, then, just as quickly back again. 'That's a blow! Poor, silly, mixed up little Fleur! And complicates things too - with her parents. They were devastated when she took up with Julia and stopped coming to church. I've been talking with them; trying to persuade them not to shut her out.'

In her mind's eye, Meredith could see again the young girl's face as she peered at her across the bed; horror was the word that came to mind. But the giggling afterwards? Maybe she was 'mixed up' after all. 'If only Julia hadn't have gone after her, and I'm sure she did, Fleur might not have...gone that way.'

'Possibly. The trouble is that there are no boundaries anymore; they're being eroded, bit by bit.' He sounded sad, almost defeated. 'She's got to know that she'll always be welcome to come back. But the damage she's doing to her soul...' he faltered.

'What, even though she's involved with things like that?' The kettle boiled and she poured the drinks.

'Of course! We need to pray that she'll come to realise how much she needs the Lord. We must be ready to encourage and help her. It's important that she knows that the door will always be open to her.'

Meredith stirred the coffee thoughtfully. 'I don't know how I'm going to be around Julia next season. Something in me hopes she doesn't come back; she mentioned something about wanting to put down roots. I think I'll always be on the lookout, you know, watching out for any signs that she's after another young girl.' She took the drinks through.

'Thanks. But you were alright with her when you left? Wendy said you even hugged her!'

'Yes, I felt I wanted to after she'd explained her reasons for setting the thing up, misguided though they were.'

'Hmm. Maybe that's how she felt about our efforts to sort her out; that we were misguided too. And it does sound as though she really values your friendship, and doesn't want to lose it.'

'But she volunteered to go for counselling! Don't you remember? No-one forced her into it. I was surprised when she told me that she'd arranged to see you.'

'That's true. And I've a feeling she wouldn't have wanted to come within a mile of me if she was genuinely satisfied with her life. I sensed there was no real peace in her. Still, you never know what impact we've made. Later on in life she might look back and wonder if things could have been different. The Lord will always be there for her - if and when she's ready to meet Him.'

'I hope she will, Kingsley. I really hope so. But what about Fleur's parents? How are you going to tell them?'

He considered for a moment. 'There's no point in letting them know. After all, she's supposed to be an adult, and it's her business.'

They remained silent for a while. Then he surprised her again by returning to the subject of her association with Conrad. 'And so nothing ever developed between you and Conrad? He was always happy to keep your friendship purely on a casual level?'

She shrugged. 'Yes, although recently he'd started to become a bit more demanding. Especially since his accident. And I did feel sorry for him.'

'And that's why you were spending more time with him?'

'Yes. Ferrying him around, hospital appointments, going out for the meals. He needed cheering up.'

'But he's back on his feet again now, isn't he?'

'Just. The trouble is he likes his drink. And he'll have to watch himself, or he'll end up having another accident, only this time on that bike of his.'

'And if he does, how would you feel about that?'

'What do you mean?'

'Well, would you want to be there for him again?'

She paused, wondering where on earth this conversation could be heading 'No. He'll need to find someone else to get him around.'

'You're certain about that? There's no hidden strings he can still pull?'

'Why are you asking me these things, Kingsley? Do you think that I've got some sort of weakness, and can't help myself when it comes to him?'

'Weakness? No. I think you've got more common sense in your little finger than it sounds like he's got in his whole body! It's just that, well, I need to be sure...' And now he knew he would tell her what he had been wanting to tell her these many months; the time had come to reveal his interest in her - and not just as her minister or as a friend. He looked into her face, which, despite her obvious tiredness, still had the healthy, appealing openness that he always found so attractive. 'Meredith. There's something I've been meaning to say to you for some time, and now that I know you're a free agent - do you remember that night - when I told you about Deborah?'

She nodded, feeling disappointed that this was something to do with his dead ex-fiancée after all.

'I always believed that she was the love of my life, and when I lost her, I thought I'd never be able to feel that way again, about anybody. And then I met you, and straight away I recognised there was something…an attraction, but something more…a warmth…a peaceful kind of warmth. I've always felt comfortable and relaxed with you. There's definitely something special between us, isn't there? You feel it too, don't you?'

Her eyes had opened wide as he spoke. She was struggling to come to terms with what she was hearing. Of course she could feel it! She always had. She must tell him, but he had taken her surprise; in fact, she was…what was she? Oh, if only she could feel more like herself; this tiredness was dulling her senses. 'Well, yes, I have - I mean, I do!'

He smiled. 'I know you've been through hell and back, especially during this past week. Maybe I'm not being fair, springing it on you like this. But I'd like us to start seeing each other, and really get to know each other.'

Now she felt stunned that this man, the very man she had admired so much since he'd arrived, was sitting just inches away from her, and asking her to be his…his…what? If only she could think straight.

'But, if I'm wrong, if I've embarrassed you, and you'd rather things stay as they are between us, then I'd appreciate it if you'd tell me, and soon. The last thing I want is to make you feel uncomfortable in any way.'

At last, she found her voice. 'I'm sorry, Kingsley. It's just that…you've taken me by surprise, that's all. I…I really do like you, but so much has happened…and keeps happening…like today…'

'It's alright,' he interrupted. 'You don't have to explain.' He gave her a long look, then drained his cup. He stood, and smiled down at her. 'I'm being unfair, I can see you're exhausted.'

'No, no! You're not. And I'd like to talk about it…'

'Then we will, but not tonight. Let's take a rain check, and talk about it again in a few days' time.'

'I...thank you. But I...I'd like to get to know you better too, really. It's just that I feel I need some time to...get myself back on an even keel.'

By now he had reached the door. He turned to look at her again. 'Of course. It's no wonder after what you've been through. And don't forget, we're all here for you if you need to talk and pray with someone. Well, goodnight, and bless you, bless you sweet Meredith. Bless you for being you. Get some rest and sleep now. And take all the time you need. We'll talk again, if, and when, you feel ready.' And with that, he left.

She sat perfectly still, her drink going cold; the only sound the hiss of the gas fire. At last, she said a prayer, but already she knew what she must do. Gathering some loose change, she put her coat on and went out to the telephone box.

The first call she made was to the retreat, the second to her parents' house. Her mother replied, her manner was defensive, but at least she listened to what Meredith had to say without interrupting her. Then her father came on the line, and arrangements were made for her to have Sunday dinner with them the following week. Then she walked back to the van and locked the door firmly behind her.

CHAPTER 43

The train pulled into the small, picturesque town of Brantington-on-Sea, a much loved destination for the more discerning holiday maker wanting to enjoy a less commercialised coastal break. She was grateful to have had the compartment to herself; the last thing she had felt like doing was trying to make polite conversation with other passengers.

She took a taxi to Dove House and was shown to her small but comfortable room by Sheila Curzon, who, along with her husband and two other staff, ran the modestly sized Christian retreat often used by the fellowship for quiet days and weeks away.

It was a relief to be away from everyone and everything, although there was one Person she never wanted to distance herself from. She wanted these next four days to be a special time of fellowship with Him - and Him alone. Jesus knew her; He knew her better than she knew herself; He knew what she had been through, and He knew how she was feeling now. And He knew what tomorrow would hold for her. After all these months of not knowing what lay ahead - prison or freedom - she wanted to concentrate on realigning her thoughts, and her life, to His will. She would spend the time reading His Word, going for long walks, and talking to Him. But what she really wanted to do was to listen to Him - and she had no doubt that she would hear Him. This was no mere wishful thinking on her part; she had years of experience behind her. There was so much she needed to ask Him. Although not one to indulge in long periods of introspection, she felt the need to spend at least a few days concentrating on her own life - now that she had been given it back. And she needed to know what He wanted her to do with it.

She passed another guest in the corridor, a slight, elderly woman. They acknowledged each other and went their separate ways. She unpacked and lay on her bed, then picked up the only book she had brought with her, her Bible. She had been tempted to bring her writing, but had decided to leave it behind, knowing that it would only be a distraction. This was one of the things she would be seeking The Lord's guidance over: should it remain as part of her life? And, if so, what should her next step be?

Then there was her working life. She had found this season more difficult than usual. Did The Lord want her to return to the camp, or should she start looking for another job somewhere else? And if she was to stay in the area, should she return home to live? - although, now she had made the break, she hoped she would not be guided that way. She had been able to forgive her mother for her lack of love and loyalty, but there was no doubt that their relationship needed some serious work before a true restoration could be achieved, and she was willing to do her part. Although things were fine between her and her father, she was still burdened about the fact that he was a Mason, and felt the need to repeat all the cutting off of the unhelpful, spiritual chords that could still be affecting and hindering her as a result of his involvement with the organisation.

Conrad was another issue she needed clarification over. He had become a real thorn in her flesh, and part of the reason why she had wanted to get right away for these few days. She thought she had forgiven him for his disloyalty, even cowardice, but now she was wondering if she really had.

Julia and Fleur were two more people she wanted guidance over. Kingsley had sounded to be clear in his own thinking about how he would be with them both, and she wanted to feel the same way.

Then there were the two police officers who had lied about her and caused her so much trouble. If she was still holding on to some unforgiveness over them, then that would need laying down too.

And then there was Kingsley. Kingsley. She remembered how she had felt when he had first come to Plover. How easy it would have been to have said 'Yes' to his offer of a relationship then! But so much had happened over the past eight months - maybe too much. She knew she had feelings for him, strong feelings, but would that be enough for whatever lay ahead? Any relationship they may embark upon would inevitably become serious; it usually did with people of their age. He had told her how he had loved and lost so deeply in the past, and despite what he had said last night, she questioned if he really was capable of entering into another relationship, especially so soon after the death of his last one. How did she know that she wouldn't just be a rebound case, someone to latch onto out of his own need, or unresolved feelings; someone who would end up having to live the rest of her life knowing that she was - and would always be - nothing but second best?

It was with these issues, and her confusion over them, that she had packed her metaphorical suitcase, as well as her physical one, and come away. Each one would have to be brought out into the open and exposed to God's refining and purifying light. Then she would know what to do.

'Hello dear. My word it's cold, isn't it?' said the elderly guest, clutching a shawl tightly around her shoulders when they passed each other again in the corridor later that day.

'Nice and warm in here though,' Meredith replied, noticing how painfully slow the thin figure descended the stairs.

Tiredness seemed to overwhelm her now. She would have liked to have gone out for a walk, but it was all she could do to focus on her Bible; her eyes would keep closing. By early evening, she gave in and undressed and prepared for bed. She switched her light off, and sleep came just minutes later.

❖

She awoke early the next morning and lay perfectly still, trying to hear any sound around her. But there was no baby crying, no voices of people walking along the pavement, no car, wagon or bus rumbling past on the road, no telephones constantly ringing in between loud and frequent tannoy announcements - and especially no crowds of excited, half-drunk campers walking past her door: the sounds of her life so far. All she could hear was the muffled sound of the sea; not even the occasional cry of a passing gull. Such peace. She lay and luxuriated in the undemanding stillness. Then she began to imagine a cup of tea.

She made her way to the small area at the end of the corridor where a kettle, small fridge and a selection of hot drinks were kept. The tea made, she returned to her room, and stood looking out at the view, appreciating the fact that there was nothing for her to get up for. Nobody was expecting her: no court case and prison sentence awaiting her, no dissatisfied mother, constantly criticising and judging her, no queue of campers asking questions and making demands, no persistent telephone calls requiring prompt attention, no 'needy' man wanting to be ferried around, no buses to hurry for, no office managers unreasonably expecting her to competently fill a permanent typist's shoes, and no crying baby needing her nappy changed: the pressures and demands of her life so far. She was completely free. If she chose, she could stay in her room all day: resting, reading, and praying. She didn't even need to get dressed and appear at meal times, having decided that she would spend the next few days feeding only on the Word of God: hot drinks only had always been her preferred method of fasting.

She sat in the comfortable armchair and picked up her Bible. What did The Lord want her read? She closed her eyes and waited, then turned to **Psalms** a few seconds later. Like many people, **Psalm 23** was very special to her, and she read it now, quietly, speaking the words out slowly, meditatively, pausing to drink in every picture they created in her mind:-

Because the Lord is my Shepherd, I have everything I need! He lets me rest in the meadow grass and leads me beside the quiet streams. He restores my failing health. He helps me do what honours him the most.

Even when walking through the dark valley of death I will not be afraid, for you are close beside me, guarding, guiding all the way.

You provide delicious food for me in the presence of my enemies. You have welcomed me as your guest; blessings overflow!

Your goodness and unfailing kindness shall be with me all of my life, and afterwards I will live with you forever in your home.

So calming were the words that she began to doze. She woke up, stiff and thirsty, a few hours later. Coffee this time. She washed and changed, and then feeling in need of some fresh air, decided to go for a walk.

It was raining lightly, but at least the wind wasn't too strong when she stepped outside. Undeterred, she set off and headed for the cliff path. Fifteen minutes later she reached the bench by the viewing spot. It was wet, but she was prepared. She took a small sheet of plastic out of her bag, spread it out, and sat down.

'Well, Jesus, here we are. Thank You for getting me here, and thank You so much for a good night's sleep, and for all this peace...' And so for the next hour, all she could do was thank Him; that was all she felt like doing. To anyone else, she would have looked like a rather sad, solitary figure, sitting or walking alone in the rain. But nothing could have been further for the truth, for she certainly wasn't feeling sad, nor did she feel alone.

For the rest of the day she focused her prayers on her working life. She wasn't a prude, but things were definitely changing at the camp, and, in her opinion, not for the better. Thanks to Jacko's influence, things that would have been thought of as unsuitable, or even coarse, just a few years ago, were now considered modern and entertaining. She remembered how she had found herself agreeing with nearly all the comments and suggestions Hilda had made in her report, and had been disappointed that Tom had implemented only a few.

However, the work side of things was not her only misgiving; she was not coping as well as she used to with the accommodation side of things. Living in the staff corridor, or in a chalet, had been fine when she was younger, but this last season had highlighted her need for a quieter place to spend her off duty. Neither was the end of season move back to her parents' home something to look forward to any more. The van was no real answer; she would probably still be required to babysit for years to come, but the arrangement was proving very restricting as far as she was concerned. Linda had obviously coped before, and she hadn't sounded all that bothered when she thought that her babysitter could end up in prison! If she did move out, maybe Linda could revert to her former arrangement - whatever that was.

Taking all of this into account, she asked The Lord if she should continue working in such an environment. Did He want her to stay there? Or was it time that she left, and find a job that she could do for twelve months of the year?

By the time she climbed into bed that night, she knew the answer, having felt the she had received very clear guidance from His word; she would not be returning to the camp for the new season. And she would be looking for a more suitable and settled form of accommodation.

The question of Kingsley frequently interrupted her thoughts, but she stoically pushed them away, having already decided that she would focus on him after dealing with everything else on her list. She wanted her decision-making to be free of any impact he may - or may not - have on her life.

CHAPTER 44

She attended the short informal service held in the guest lounge the next day, then she set out on her first serious walk. There was a fine view of the church across the water, but today it was shrouded in a sea mist. And it was bitterly cold. This was the morning she had set aside to seek The Lord's will over her writing. She knew what she wanted His answer to be, and was really hoping that her will would prove to be in line with His.

She walked carefully, trying to avoid the puddles and wet grass that drooped over the narrow cliff path. Still some distance away, she could just make out the outline of a solitary figure on the bench, and was surprised to find the elderly woman from her corridor sitting there. Not wanting to intrude, she said, 'Good morning' as she passed by.

'Did you...do you want to sit down?' came the faint reply as the woman attempted to stand, only to fall back hard. 'I'm just going. I just needed a few minutes...it's so cold...'

'No, it's alright, thank you,' replied Meredith, looking back, and noticing how pinched and very pale the woman's face looked.

The woman tried, but failed, to raise herself again. 'Oh dear, oh dear! I've been sitting too long.'

Meredith turned around and took a few steps back. 'Are you alright? Do you need a hand?'

'Are you...you're the young lady from the retreat aren't you?'

'Yes. Are you sure you're alright?'

'No, not really. I wonder…can you just wait till I…I need to…I'm so very cold. My legs…the mist came down so quickly…' the thin frame shuddered.

'Can't you stand?' asked Meredith, feeling some concern now.

'No…I…' the old lady tried to push herself up, only to fall back hard yet again.

'Here, let me help you,' said Meredith, going to stand in front of her, and reaching down to put one of her arms under hers. 'Maybe if I hold on to you.'

'I…I don't know.' Once more the woman tried to get to her feet; once more she fell back, and now she looked close to tears.

Meredith decided that she really needed to intervene. 'Would you let me try to lift you up?'

The woman nodded.

'Okay. Let's give it a try. I'll try not to hurt you,' She put both her arms under the woman's armpits and clasped them around the small frame. 'Come on, let's get out of this cold.'

'Oh, oh dear! Don't…don't hurt yourself…'

She began to lift her carefully as the woman grasped the side of the bench at the same time and tried to push herself up. Although awkward, Meredith found her surprisingly light, and soon she was able to get the woman standing.

'My sticks, can you give me my sticks…'

Still supporting her with one arm, Meredith handed her the two walking sticks that had been hooked onto the back of the bench. At last, the woman was able to steady herself. 'Can you…would you…'

'Of course; I'm not going to leave you. Try and take a few steps. I'll keep hold of you.'

Slowly the woman shuffled forward. One small step, then another, and another.

'By the way, I'm Meredith Sanderson. I'm in room 4, just along the corridor from you.'

'Catherine…Katy…' was all the struggling figure could reply.

Soon, they managed to achieve a rhythm, and this time Meredith was unable to avoid stepping into the puddles.

It took them over half an hour to reach the house. Sheila spotted them through one of the front windows and rushed out to help. It took several minutes to get Katy, now completely exhausted, up the stairs and back into her room. Then, safely tucked up in bed, and crying with mortification and relief, once again the old lady tried to apologise, 'I'm sorry. I wanted to get…you know - my poustinia. The mist, it blew in so fast…all this fuss.'

Sheila gently brushed away some hair from the ashen face with her hand. 'Hush now, Katy. Just you rest back, and we'll fetch you a nice hot cup of cocoa.' She signalled Meredith to leave the room with her, thanked her, and asked her to make the cocoa and a few hot water bottles, then hurried away to telephone the local doctor.

The external mist lasted most of the day, however, her internal mist over what The Lord's will was regarding her writing cleared by early afternoon. She had been prepared to lay it down, but the more she prayed, the more convinced she felt in her spirit that He wanted her to continue. In fact, she was unable to stop several new characters and story lines from pouring into her mind. She still hadn't contacted the Literary Agent that the children's writer at the library had given her the details of, but now knew she would, as soon as she got back.

It was in this excited frame of mind, and needing another drink, that she came across Sheila coming out of Katy's room later that afternoon.

'How is she,' she enquired, 'Has she recovered okay?'

'She'll live. Poor love, she got herself bone cold. The doctor said she's got a moderate case of hypothermia and that we'll have to keep a close eye on her. And bless you, dear.

What a good job you came across her when you did. I dread to think what could have happened if you hadn't. Are you popping in? She's awake, and I know she's keen to see you again.'

'Okay, I'll just go and take my things off.'

'And she'd like another cup of tea; can you take her one? I'm needed downstairs. White and two sugars, and a few more biscuits. But anyway, how are you, Meredith? I'm pleased to see you've got a bit more colour in your cheeks now than when you arrived.'

'I'm doing great. It's doing me the world of good being here. I'm starting to think straight again.'

'Praise The Lord! We have been praying for you.'

'Yes, I know. And thank you.'

'And there's nothing you need to talk to any of us about?'

'No, but I'll let you know if there is.'

A few minutes later, Meredith knocked on Katy's door and went in. The old lady looked warm and comfortable in bed, although her face was still dreadfully pale.

'Hello, it's Meredith. Remember? I was here a few hours ago? I've brought you a cup of tea. How are you feeling now?'

'Oh, how lovely! I've been asking The Good Lord to send you.' she struggled to sit up. Meredith went over and helped her.

'Are those ginger?'

'Yes, and a few Marie.'

'My favourites. Now come and sit down, dear, I need to tell you what the Good Lord has been saying to me about you. You're here to meet with Him in a special way, aren't you?'

Meredith smiled, knowing that this was no great revelation; everyone who came to this place was hoping for such a meeting. She went to sit beside the bed.

'And you're a single girl, aren't you, dear?'

Meredith looked down at her ringless fingers, and nodded.

'Now listen to me, dear. The Good Lord doesn't want you to be as foolish as me. I'm alone, you know, all alone. I never married.'

Taken aback, Meredith asked, 'Oh, and what...what do you think The Lord wants to say to me...about that?'

'He wants me to tell you to be brave.'

'Be brave! Why? What about?' Now she was beginning to feel some alarm. Surely there weren't even more unpleasant things coming her way!

'I wasn't. I was too proud, you know. There was a young man, and I...I could have been devoted to him, but I was such a headstrong young woman. You see, I was serving the Good Lord and preparing to go on the mission field - to China. And marriage...I felt it would be such a hindrance. Men can be so helpless, can't they?'

Puzzled at the way the conversation was going, but thinking that the old lady must be just a bit confused, Meredith decided to play along, and asked, 'And the man, he didn't want to go with you?'

'No dear, he hadn't been called, you see.'

For some reason, Kingsley came into Meredith's mind, but she could see no connection. She was hardly bound for the mission field - at least, not that she was aware of!

'I was proud, you know. And off I went. But he was still there whenever I came home.' She paused, then said with an unmistakable tone of sadness in her voice, 'Still waiting. Always waiting.' There was another pause, longer this time. At last, she continued, a slightly harder edge to her voice now, 'But I was determined, my work wasn't finished, I was going to serve The Good Lord, and no husband was going to stand in *my* way!' She dunked a biscuit. Staring into the cup, she kept the biscuit where it was, it broke, but this didn't seem to bother her. She ate the dry half. 'Foolish...foolish! I kept him waiting too long, you see.'

'So you never married him?' Meredith asked, feeling herself being drawn into the story now.

'No.' It was just one word, but it was full of sadness.

'What did you do - in China?'

'Teach. English. Oh, they were such happy days! All those dear children. My dear, dear little children! I missed them so much when I had to come back. No more children to care for, no more dear little ones to love. But children are given to women who are braver than me. A woman has to be brave to get married - and promise to honour and obey her husband, doesn't she?'

'Well, it's a bit different nowadays; the obeying bit isn't so - compulsory. It's more like an equal partnership. And if it's the right man...'

'Oh yes, dear, and that's what The Good Lord wants me to tell you.'

Meredith held her breath, realising that this really was something to do with marriage - and her!

'You mustn't be scared, dear. Yes, that's it! The Good Lord has a plan for your life and, if you stay close to Him, you'll know the man He's chosen for you. I was proud, you know. I was proud of my faith. Spiritual pride is such a deadly thing, don't you think? But now...I can see...looking back, I didn't do what I should have. I ignored the one true love He sent me. I was too proud. And scared.' She dunked another biscuit, and this time, managed to eat both halves successfully.

'What happened to the man?'

A heavy sigh followed. A faraway look in her eyes. 'He waited for me for over twenty years...*over twenty years!* But I kept closing my eyes...and my heart. And then if he didn't up and marry someone else! A Catholic! And she gave him six children! Six! Four boys and two girls. And grandchildren, eleven.' She shook her head slowly, and now, almost overcome with the memory, began to fumble beneath one of her pillows. She drew out a lace edged handkerchief and began to wipe her eyes. 'All those children. My only regret. And now The Good Lord is calling me home.' Her story told, she lay back, her face slowly relaxing as she closed her eyes.

And then Meredith understood: this old lady was dying; that explained the thin body and the waxen pallor. 'Oh, I'm…so sorry!'

Opening her eyes again, Katy looked at her and smiled. 'Don't be, dear. I'm not! I can't wait to see Him…and my dear Mama and Papa…and friends…and my dear, dear little children…to be with them again. So many of them died. Too young, too young. I've waited so long. I've been alone you see, all these years, all alone. That's why I come here. Sheila and Richard are the closest I've got to family; they've always been so very kind to me. And now…now they're letting me stay here…'

There was nothing Meredith could say, as close to tears herself now, she reached over to hold the thin, frail hand.

Katy gave her a long look. 'I had long brown hair like you, with a nice curl. And I was pretty too. There is a young man, isn't there dear?'

'Er…well, I don't know.'

Katy gave her shrewd look. 'Be brave dear.'

'Well, there is someone. But he's just a good friend. Only…only, just before I came away, he told me that he'd like to get to know me more. And I do like him. But…but he loved someone else, and I'm not sure if he still doesn't, despite what he says.'

A stern, disapproving look crossed Katy's face. 'That will never do! Very bad of the man! Young men these days have no sense of honour.'

Feeling that she had misrepresented Kingsley, Meredith went on to quickly explain, 'No, it's a bit different. You see, he was engaged to another woman, someone he'd known for years. But she broke it off and married someone else. This was all eight years ago. Anyway, he found out that she'd died recently, and I can't help feeling that he never really got over her. He says he has, but...I don't know.'

Katy lay still, thinking, then said slowly, 'If this is the man The Good Lord has chosen for you, then time will tell. And maybe he'll be the man you must be brave over. Do you care deeply for him, dear?'

Meredith stared into the shrunken eyes. Did she care deeply for Kingsley? Yes, she knew she did. But to 'care deeply' wasn't the same as loving someone - or was it? She had never been in love. How did she know? How could anyone know? 'I...I don't know. I really like him, and he's so kind and thoughtful. He's always been there for me, especially recently, and I know I'm grateful to him.'

Katy closed her eyes again. 'Safe, you feel safe with him, don't you dear?' Her voice became a whisper, 'Your protector...' She looked exhausted.

Meredith knew she should leave her to rest. 'Yes, I suppose I do. But go to sleep now, Katy. I'll come and see you again later.'

She closed the door quietly behind her. Kingsley - yes, he had been a sort of protector: a true friend to her; always encouraging and supportive, and always there - apart from when he had gone away because of his ex-fiancée! But no, she must stick to her plan; the rest of the day was for concentrating on other issues, like a way forward with her parents, and how she would be with Conrad, Julia and Fleur. She wasn't ready to think about Kingsley just yet.

CHAPTER 45

It was a struggle, but the spiritual mist eventually cleared as she came to terms with what she felt The Lord's will was with regard to her problematic relationships. However, this desirable state only happened after she had done a lot more forgiving and letting go. And then, at last, she actually began to look forward to seeing her mother again. She prayed that she would have the ability to let her habitual criticisms simply bounce off her, and that she would only respond in positive and confident ways.

Although still disappointed that her father had not heeded her warnings about the Freemasons, and after more spiritual chord-cutting, she knew that all she had to do was to keep trusting him to The Lord. He loved him far, far more than she ever could.

Her mother and her father: two people who had a great respect for The Lord, but that wasn't the same as knowing and loving Him. Yes, she must trust them both to Him. After all, He was the One who had died for them.

Julia and Fleur were easier to pray about. Kingsley had helped her to realise that they were both trying so hard to fill the gaping hole inside them that only The One Who truly loved them could fill. They were looking in the wrong direction, and substituting any kind of human affection to satisfy and feed their spiritual hunger. No doubt, they believed themselves to be open-minded 'free-thinkers', when, in fact, she felt that they were the exact opposite when it came to the needs of their own souls - here their minds were closed and prejudiced against the One, Perfect Love. So, yes, she would try and stay in touch with them, and keep pointing them towards His Cross.

Then there was Tom and Wendy: two more people she would try and stay in touch with, no matter what the future had in store for them all. Dear Wendy, so kind and curious; but another soul that was looking in the wrong direction.

Conrad was another matter, and she had to spend a considerable amount of time on him. She had to steel herself to forgive him, but she did. One of the instructions that Jesus gave to His disciples just before He sent them out to minister spoke clearly to her now:-

I am sending you out as sheep among wolves.
Be as wary as serpents and harmless as doves.
(Matthew 10:16).

Yes, she must remember. He was a truly needy soul - if only he knew it, weakened in his mind as well as his body. If only he would even *begin* to think about Jesus, and be prepared to listen and hear about His love for him. How she pitied him. But that didn't mean that she would allow him to involve her in his life anymore. She would be polite and respectful towards him, and always keep pointing him towards The Cross - but that was all.

These matters resolved, she slept well again that night.

Tomorrow, she would concentrate on Kingsley.

It snowed earlier the next morning, but by nine o'clock the clouds separated and allowed the sun to break through and shine in patches of clear, blue sky. She had called in on Katy before setting out on her walk, and found the old lady settled and comfortable in bed. A plate of some unwanted bacon and scrambled eggs lay on a breakfast tray beside her.

'Where are you going today, dear?'

'To the village, but along the cliff path. I'll come back the beach way if the tide's out.'

'I would so love it if you could bring me back a shell, you know, one of those big flat cream ones with little grooves. I try and find one every time I come.'

The smell of bacon was tempting. This was her third day of fasting, and although her stomach was complaining, she didn't feel uncomfortable, weak or even hungry. Her mind felt sharper than ever. 'Okay. I'll look around when I'm down there.'

❖

There were patches of snow along the cliff path, but today there was a clear view across the bay to the church. She sat on the bench, Katy's 'poustinia', and asked her questions.

'What shall I say to Kingsley, Lord? I don't know how I truly feel about him. You know I like him. I've always liked him, and You know that I would have jumped at the chance of getting closer to him before other things got in the way. Or did I let them get in the way? But, anyway, maybe he wasn't ready then, and only ready now, or thinks he's ready. I think I'd like to…to go ahead, but to take things really slowly. Is that what You're saying? That it's up to me? You're expecting me to use my sanctified freewill and common sense? But what about Katy - and what she said to me? Have you really been speaking to me through her? I need to be sure, Lord. Please, *please* tell me what to do, just like you've given me guidance and peace over all the other things I've brought to you. Please guide me over Kingsley as well.'

She closed her eyes and concentrated for all she was worth on listening with her inner ear, trying to discern what her spirit, deep within her, was saying. But all she could feel was a calmness; there felt to be no struggle there, just a quiet reassurance that all would be well.

The minutes passed. Noticing that the tide was going out, she stood and walked on, sorry now that she had left her camera back in Plover; it was such a beautiful day - full of colour. She looked across the bay to the church. How many times had she looked at the same scene: the old, Anglican church with its tower. What would she have done without the comfort and protection of Jesus, her own *High Tower,* over these past months? His presence had been so very real to her. There had been times when she had nearly given way to despair, but then, through the kindness and friendship of others, He had always found a way of reminding her of His constant care; of His constant love. She smiled when she remembered Jamie's sticky tower of bread. And Kingsley, she had always known that he believed in her. What a wonderful support he had been.

No-one else was around. She had the sun, the sky and sea all to herself. Just her and Jesus. Maybe that was going to be the way of it for her. Maybe she was destined to be like Freda - and Katy, alone and single. Until one day - would she look back and regret taking such a solitary path as well?

Her eye was caught by the sight of someone else walking on the beach ahead of her. A man, and he was walking towards her. There was something familiar about his outline. She stopped, unsure, surprised. But...how? Her father must have told him! He was the only one who knew where she was.

'Meredith!'

Kingsley! He had come. Kingsley!

She waved, staring at him - and the church tower - now clearly visible, and directly behind him.

A Tower.

A High Tower.

Above Kingsley.

Above Kingsley!

He opened his arms and called her name again.

'Meredith!'

And now she understood.

Now she knew.

Jesus was his **High Tower** too!

A Tower she could walk into.

A Tower where they could be together.

A Tower where they could love and serve **Him** together.

With him, and in **Him**, she would be safe.

'Yes Jesus, I'll be brave!'

She started to walk towards him - and then she ran. All thoughts of taking a step at a time and going slowly now forgotten.

They reached each other.

He looked into her face, then put his arms around her.

'Found you!'

She put her own arms around him.

'Yes. Yes, you have.'

What a Friend We Have in Jesus

What a Friend we have in Jesus, all our sins and griefs to bear!
What a privilege to carry everything to God in prayer!
O what peace we often forfeit, O what needless pain we bear,
All because we do not carry everything to God in prayer.

Have we trials and temptations? Is there trouble anywhere?
We should never be discouraged; take it to the Lord in prayer.
Can we find a friend so faithful who will all our sorrows share?
Jesus knows our every weakness; take it to the Lord in prayer.

Are we weak and heavy laden, cumbered with a load of care?
Precious Saviour, still our refuge, take it to the Lord in prayer.
Do your friends despise, forsake you?
Take it to the Lord in prayer!
In His arms He'll take and shield you;
you will find a solace there.

Blessed Saviour, Thou hast promised
Thou wilt all our burdens bear
May we ever, Lord, be bringing all to Thee in earnest prayer.
Soon in glory bright unclouded there will be no need for prayer
Rapture, praise and endless worship
will be our sweet portion there.

(Joseph M. Scriven).

The End

❖

By the Same Author:

THE HIDDEN PATH

It is the spring of 1970. Yvonne Williams is walking along a quiet Highland road when she encounters a man sitting alone in the heather. He is Alexander Grant, a Christian, who has stopped to rest and pray. Unnerved, she rushes back to the safety of the Inn.

Yvonne is a troubled young woman who is haunted by a painful past. For ten years she has moved from one seasonal job to another. Now, at the age of 27, she has made a decision which she hopes will give her some peace. Could the remote Tananeach Inn be the place where she can find it? To discover the answer, she must first overcome some unexpected challenges, the greatest of which is the unsettling presence of the enigmatic *Man in the Heather.*

Time and curiosity lead her to begin reading the *super-natural* book she has been given. The thaw sets in and a tragedy is discovered. Many tears are shed - and then she starts to think the unthinkable...

Two people; both burdened with secrets.
One knows the way ahead.
Can the other trust their footsteps to be guided along -
The Hidden Path?

ISBN-10: 1517012767   e-ISBN-13:978-1517012762

Made in the USA
Charleston, SC
29 September 2016